Zéspedes in East Florida, 1784–1790

Zéspedes in East Florida, 1784–1790

Helen Hornbeck Tanner

Publication sponsored by the
St. Augustine Historical Society

University of North Florida Press / Jacksonville

The University of North Florida Press is a member of University Presses of Florida, the scholarly publishing agency of the State University System of Florida. Books are selected for publication by faculty editorial committees at each of Florida's nine public universities: Florida A&M University (Tallahassee), Florida Atlantic University (Boca Raton), Florida International University (Miami), Florida State University (Tallahassee), University of Central Florida (Orlando), University of Florida (Gainesville), University of North Florida (Jacksonville), University of South Florida (Tampa), University of West Florida (Pensacola).

Orders for books published by all member presses of University Presses of Florida should be addressed to University Presses of Florida, 15 NW 15th Street, Gainesville FL 32603.

Library of Congress Cataloging-in-Publication Data

Tanner, Helen Hornbeck.
    Zéspedes in east Flordia, 1784–1790 / Helen Hornbeck Tanner.
       p.   cm.
    Bibliography: p.
    Includes index.
    ISBN 0–8130–0958–8 (alk. paper)
    1. Zéspedes, Vicente Manuel de.   2. Florida—History—Spanish
colony, 1784–1821.   3. East Florida—History.   4. Florida—
Governors—Biography   I. Title.
    F314.Z47T36   1989
    975.9'03'092—dc20
    [B]   89–33715
                                                                          CIP

This book is dedicated

to

Irving A. Leonard

and

Don Worcester

Contents

Illustrations follow page 150.

Acknowledgments

In carrying out this research project, many people have given greatly appreciated assistance, beginning with Mr. Julien C. Yonge who guided historians interested in Florida for many years. He continually encouraged interest in Spanish Florida as head of the P. K. Yonge Library of Florida History. Miss Margaret Chapman of the same library located important supplementary information. Special records used in this dissertation were provided by Dr. Howard Cline of the Hispanic Society, Mr. Harley Freeman of Ormond Beach, Florida, Mr. W. S. Murphy of New York City, and Mrs. Doris Wiles of the St. Augustine Historical Society. Dr. Herbert S. Wolfe, Department of Horticulture, University of Florida, identified the plant life and explained the natural scenery of colonial Florida. Dr. Guillermo Lohmann-Villena of the Peruvian Embassy in Madrid secured the copy of Zéspedes' service record, the basis for reconstructing the governor's early life and military career.

A fellowship from the American Association of University Women made possible periods of research at the Library of Congress and P. K. Yonge Library of Florida History. For their persevering aid in the completion of this manuscript, I am grateful to the following members of the faculty of the University of Michigan: Dr. Irving A. Leonard, Dr. William S. Hanna, Dr. Howard H. Peckham and Dr. Ross N. Pearson. My family has shown exceptional patience throughout the long period of manuscript writing and revision. For an excellent job of final typing, I am indebted to Anne Clarke.

Map production was carried out with the aid of Elna Lahti MacMullan, head of the Graphic Arts Department of the Audio-Visual Education Center at the University of Michigan.

The use of the line drawings of St. Augustine's eighteenth century houses, which appear as chapter heading, was most kindly permitted by the St. Augustine Historical Restorations and Preservation Commission.

Preface to 1963 Edition

The Florida peninsula, from accidents of geology and geography, was destined to become a source of international friction from the sixteenth century until its inclusion within the boundaries of the United States in 1821. If the earth's crust had cooled and settled with greater symmetry, this sandy extension of the North American continent should have sunk below the surface of the ocean without ever occupying its rather disproportionate role in European and American affairs. But once this extrusion of dry land was claimed by Spain, it became an area of new-world rivalry, of interest alike to France and England. Florida never was a source of wealth to Spain, but possessed great strategic value because of its location along the Gulf Stream, the shipping lane for treasure-laden ships returning from Mexico. Spain also retained Florida in order to exclude other nations from the shores of the Caribbean, and prevent the establishment of foreign bases which might lead to attacks on her more valuable possessions, Cuba and Mexico.

Although Florida remained of questionable intrinsic value, Spain tenaciously held the territory for over three centuries following its discovery in 1513, with the exception of a twenty year interval from 1763 to 1783 when Florida was a British possession. This latter period has been the subject of comprehensive research, but no narrative history exists for Florida in the years following its return to Spain in 1783. This Second Spanish Period, from 1784 to 1821, is a small but well-defined gap in the later colonial history of the Spanish empire as well as the background history of American territory.

The following chapters present the career of Vicente Manuel de Zéspedes y Velasco, first governor of East Florida during the Second Spanish Period, who served at St. Augustine from July 14, 1784 to July 7, 1790. His régime coincides with a particular interval in eighteenth century history. In general, these years might be characterized as a period of readjustment following the American Revolution and preceding the general holocaust touched off by the French Revolution. The period naturally begins with the signing of the second Treaty of Paris in September, 1783, by which Florida was returned to Spain and the thirteen British colonies gained their independence. A series of events occurring in 1789, during Zéspedes' governorship, presaged a change in the

European-American scene. Critical events of the year were: The inaugu-
ration of George Washington under the new American constitution in
April; the fall of the French monarchy and imprisonment of the royal
family in July; and the ascent to the Spanish throne of a weaker king,
Charles IV, in September. The period between the American and
French Revolutions was far from static, however. In governing the border province of East Florida, Zéspedes had to take into account changing currents within and between the nations engaging in the recent
American war.

Zéspedes came to St. Augustine from Havana in June, 1784 with an
occupation force of five hundred soldiers and several hundred other
government employees. The retiring British governor and the last fifteen hundred of a total ten thousand British evacuees did not leave the
province until September, 1785. During Zéspedes' régime, East
Florida's population was reduced to about three thousand people. Most
of the civilians, remnants of British-sponsored colonial expeditions,
came from Greece, Italy and Minorca. The population also included
British Loyalists who fled from northern colonies during the American Revolution, and a few Cubans, Spaniards and Canary Islanders.
Zéspedes' province was small in size as well as population. While reas-
serting Spanish authority, he recognized the boundaries established by
the English who in 1765 signed an Indian treaty restricting European
settlements to a small corner of northeast Florida.

Vigorously combatting aggressive American interest in Spanish Florida and Indian hunting lands, Zéspedes reported many American
schemes to court officials and provided guns and ammunition enabling
the Creeks to restrain Georgia frontiersmen. Within East Florida, Zéspedes governed with rare human understanding and devotion to the
royal service. He supported the parish priest in establishing a public
school for European Negro boys, and enthusiastically sponsored the
program to convert Anglo-Saxon Protestants living in the province. His
efforts to develop East Florida economically were hampered chiefly by
a perpetual shortage of funds, by Spain's mercantilistic commercial
policy, and by the demise of sympathetic higher officials.

Zéspedes' principal task was the re-establishment of Spanish rule in
the province of East Florida following the twenty year period of British
occupation. Aside from matters of military defense and provincial administration, documents concerning his régime reveal a surprising
amount of information about social life and customs, religion and
morals of this Spanish colonial town in the late eighteenth century.
Zéspedes' single term as governor of East Florida was his only political

office, coming at the conclusion of a long army career in Cuba. After returning to Havana in 1790, he was promoted to the rank of *mariscal del campo*, and later named governor of Yucatán although he was unable to serve the king in this latter capacity. His death occurred in 1794, and he was buried in the convent of San Francisco in Havana.

A word should be added about the spelling of the governor's name. Although modern spelling is "Céspedes," it seems too great a liberty to make this alteration after reading hundreds of contemporary letters, signed in a precise yet flourishing hand, "Vicente Manuel de Zéspedes."

Preface to the 1989 Edition

In the years since I was immersed in research concerning Vicente Manuel de Zéspedes' life in St. Augustine during the years 1784 to 1790, little information has come to light concerning the old governor himself. One rare item did turn up shortly after the publication of my book. In the fall of 1963, the Clements Library in Ann Arbor, Michigan, acquired a collection of private correspondence that included General Nathaniel Greene's long personal letter to his wife written after visiting St. Augustine in March 1785. Greene, owner of land on Cumberland Island adjoining the Florida border, made the trip from Charleston in an awning-covered canoe accompanied by Benjamin Hawkins, who was appointed that year as American commissioner to treat with the southern Indians (60–61). Greene's account of dinner with the Zéspedes family gives an intimate picture of the governor's household eight months after coming to East Florida:

> We were introduced to his Lady and daughters and compliments flew from side to side like a shuttle cock in the hands of good players. You know I am not very excellent at fine speeches. My stock was soon exhausted; but what I lacked in conversation I made up in bowing.
>
> The Governnante is about fifty five, as chearful as a Girl of sixteen, and enters with spirit and pleasure into all the amusements of the young people. She is sister to the Vice Roy of Mexico and highly respected both from her family and pleasing manners. The daughters are not hansome, their complexion is rather tawny but they have got sweet languishing Eyes. They look as if they could love with great violence. They sang and played upon the Harpsichord and did every thing to please if not to inspire softer emotions. Hawkins professed himself smitten. The old Lady unluckaly asked me if I was married and in so unexpected a manner that I had no chance to evade the enquiry. This limitted my gallantry or perhaps I might have got in love too.
>
> The Governor who is rather corpulent has a good share of natural benevolence and is more remarkable for politeness

than understanding, gave us an entertainment. It was the first
he had given since his arrival. . . . The dinner was truly elegant
and I believe in my soul there was from one hundred and fifty
to two hundred dishes of different kinds servd up in seven
courses. French cookery prevails with the Spannish. I was
posted by the Governnante and Mr. Hawkins by the Young Ladies. Dinner lasted five hours and as I was obliged to taste most
of the dishes from the attention of the Governnante, I was not
unlike a stuffed pig and almost in the condition of the Country
tennant who said he had rather fight than eat any more. We
had a variety of Spannish, and some good French Wines. We
spent the Evening at Cards and retird about ten at night.

   Next Morning the Governnante sent us a large basket of
cakes and fruit curiously ornamented with flowers and cut
paper. And among other things there was a large box of guava
Jelly. This I left to be forwarded to you. (Tanner 1964, 14–16)

It seems likely that on this occasion, the governor was deliberately ob-
tuse, since he did not want a representative of the new American republic to learn anything about the military weakness of Spanish Florida.

   My view of the Zéspedes era remains unchanged, but there are some
corrections and comments that should be made. I now know that the
Creek leader called Cowkeeper (83) was not the same person as
Secoffee. I know also that the talented diplomat among the Upper Creek
Indians, Alexander McGillivray, did not hold a position of hereditary
authority within the allied Indian towns (86), yet he exerted a forceful
personal influence in many Creek towns and served as their spokesman
in dealing with British, Spanish, and American outsiders.

   Many of the people who appeared so briefly in East Florida obviously
had stories of their own, usually impossible to pursue through the im-
personal documentary records. I tried unsuccessfully to untangle the
evidence surrounding the death of Lieutenant William Delaney (72) in
"The Delaney Murder Case" (Tanner 1965). The solution to the crime
was subsequently discovered by Bruce Chappell, P.K. Yonge Library,
University of Florida: He reports that a soldier who was never a suspect
at the time of the murder made a deathbed confession in Louisiana
in 1802.

   Some life stories continued even farther away from St. Augustine.
Thomas Powell, who revealed a sinister web of American frontier plots
to Zéspedes in 1787 (154), disappeared from the regional records after
returning to Charleston. I kept his name in mind, since he had declared

his intention to settle in the Spanish provinces. Although it may be a long shot, I did find a Thomas Powell who had previously been in New Orleans among the early settlers of Stephen Austin's Texas colony in 1827 (Powell 1924, 1701).

As part of these retrospective observations, I should explain that I have come to appreciate the value of the preresearch experience of living in Florida for three years, 1945–48, in a virtually unpopulated strip of land between the Atlantic Ocean and the Indian River, now Melbourne Beach. In 1944, my husband was transferred to the Banana River Naval Air Station near Cape Canaveral, a military site recently removed from the wartime list of places considered "overseas" duty. The potential for dangerous incidents in the offshore Gulf Stream shipping lane was still apparent in the final months of World War II. Our home was equipped with blackout curtains to conceal the location of the tiny community fifteen miles south of the base.

From a vantage point two blocks from the beach, we observed the predictable pattern of Florida's seasonal changes, the tides and shifting winds, the variety of blossoms and foliage. We survived the heat of summer and the sudden "northers" in winter and fled to the mainland during a severe fall hurricane. Neighbors brought turtle eggs that looked like dented ping-pong balls and stocked the refrigerator with fillets when the bluefish were running. The shorebirds and porpoises became seaside companions, and there were repeated warnings about snakes and panthers, for beyond the fenced backyard the unbroken scrub extended thirteen miles south to Sebastian Inlet. Boats foundered on the reefs as they had in earlier centuries.

These experiences, and a subsequent year in the pine and savanna land around Gainesville, removed the barrier of time when I began to read the books and and documents for this account. Life was discernible in all the old letters, transcripts, photostatic copies, and yellowed originals—some full of wormholes and covered with transparent silk cloth for preservation. After I had lived in both coastal and interior sections, with trips to St. Augustine, northeast Florida seemed like familiar territory. As a consequence, I undertook writing about the Zéspedes era with a warm feeling for the land that had provided the stage setting for so much human drama in the late eighteenth century.

Helen Hornbeck Tanner

Introduction

by *Patricia C. Griffin*

First published a quarter of a century ago, Helen Hornbeck Tanner's *Zéspedes in East Florida: 1784–1790* almost overnight became the standard work on the Second Spanish Period in East Florida. It still serves this function, although it covers only the first six years of that thirty-seven-year period. One ventures the thought that no scholar of Florida history is unaware of this work, and, in fact, "Have you looked in Tanner?" has become a standard question among those dealing with the years of Spain's second dominion in the Floridas.

After two centuries of Spanish occupation, Florida was in Britain's possession for a short twenty years under the terms of the first Treaty of Paris in 1763. Afterward, the Floridas, by then divided into the provinces of East and West Florida, were retroceded to Spain in the second Treaty of Paris in 1783, part of a general readjustment of European affairs. Vicente Manuel de Zéspedes y Velasco came to East Florida as the first governor in the new regime with high hopes that the colony would be a credit to the Spanish empire, recently revitalized under the enlightened rule of Charles III.

The original volume of the work reprinted here is essentially the author's doctoral dissertation (Tanner 1961). It was a rarity: a thesis written with a deft literary hand yet grounded in unimpeachable scholarship. Amazingly enough, Tanner had not used any other doctoral dissertation as a guide but had developed her own concept of such a work. To his credit, Irving A. Leonard, chairman of the Romance Languages Department at Michigan and chairman of Tanner's doctoral committee, himself an accomplished writer, encouraged her approach, even, she only recently discovered, defending the style of writing, which drew some criticism from committee members who had envisioned a more pedantic presentation.

Indeed, throughout her scholarly career, Tanner has found her own way, although she was set on course early by historian Donald E. Worcester, under whom she completed her master's thesis (Tanner 1949). He urged her to find a research topic in a collection acquired by the P.K. Yonge Library of Florida History from Joseph B. Lockey, who had assembled documents relating to the Second Spanish Period in East Florida. After the delays of a move with husband and daughters, the births of two sons, the restructuring of her doctoral committee at the University of Michigan, and the receipt of a fellowship from the American Association of University Women, she finally completed the research for her dissertation on Zéspedes.

The reviews of the published book were positive. John TePaske (1965) was captivated "with the enthusiasm and ingenuousness of her style." Robert Gold (1965), concluding that it was "a very successful case-study of the East Florida governorship in the first six years of Spain's return to the peninsular province," summed up the general opinion. Rembert Patrick (1964), commenting that "whenever a comprehensive history of the Second Spanish Period is written, her work will be an indispensable source for information and interpretation," indicates that none foresaw that the book would serve for some years as the main work for this era of East Florida's history.

There are several reasons for the general neglect by historians of the Hispanic influence on the national heritage, one even more pronounced where the Floridas are concerned. Many scholars are troubled by the double difficulty of working in the Spanish language and of deciphering the difficult calligraphy. More serious is the ambivalence toward Spaniards and things Spanish that is part of the history of history writing in the United States. The bias toward the Anglo and Celtic cultural streams as the foundation of the commonwealth is well known. Early historians, mostly northeasterners, overemphasized the frontier push from east to west, neglecting the push from north to south. They paid lip service to early Spanish explorations but ignored Spain's early claim to all of North America and gave only minor attention to the undulating Hispanic hegemony ebbing and flowing around the southern and western fringes of the continent from the seventeenth century into the nineteenth.

Not a little of this neglect has been due to the persistence of the so-called Black Legend, a concept of the Spaniards as bloodthirsty, evil, barely civilized, cruel to native peoples, lazy, and given to the worship of "popish" idols. Unfortunately, historians themselves dignified these distortions either through their writings or through benign disregard of North America's Spanish heritage. Almost singlehandedly, historian Herbert Eugene Bolton, at the beginning of the 1920s, worked to correct this deficiency by turning his attention and that of his students (including Donald Worchester and Irving Leonard, Tanner's mentors) to the much neglected "Spanish Borderlands" (Bolton 1921).

On the other side of the ambivalence, and equally misconceived, was the notion of the "romantic Spaniard," fostered in the early days of California tourism and spread by the incipient movie industry. The Spaniard in this guise is seen as a noble explorer of the wilderness, brave, fearless, governed by an honor code and chivalric ideals—a dashing, romantic figure. Any bloodshed occasioned by the conquistador was diluted by the image of the kindly mission padre with an unquenchable love for the Indians and a laudable desire to bring Christianity to the New World.

The conjunction of such conflicting images meant that the real Spanish colonial story was never told with any objectivity. In telling the story of the Spanish Floridas, early historians concentrated on tales of the conquistadors and the missions; the Second Spanish Period, which many thought not to be very Spanish at all, was largely disregarded.

Furthermore, Florida was at the eastern tail of the Spanish dominions in the late eighteenth and early nineteenth centuries. Nor was it the tail that was wagging the Spanish dog. Even Bolton in his first definitive work, *The Spanish Borderlands*, covered the second Spanish era in the Floridas in one paragraph. In the 1950s two book-length monographs appeared that were written from the American (that is, U.S.) point of view: Richard K. Murdock's *The Georgia-Florida Frontier, 1793–1796* (1951) and Rembert W. Patrick's *Florida Fiasco: Rampant Rebels on the Georgia-Florida Border, 1810–1815* (1954).

Tanner stepped into this void with the publication of her story of Zéspedes, written from the Spanish point of view and based on Spanish documentary research. The book did not start a trend, but three other governors in the Second Spanish Period eventually received attention. Rogers C. Harlan (1971) wrote a military history of the governorship of Enrique White, L. David Norris (1981) produced a dissertation on José Coppinger, the last Spanish governor of East Florida, and Janice Borton Miller (1981) published her dissertation on Juan Nepomuceno de Quesada, the governor who succeeded Zéspedes.

There has been a steady trickle of articles on Spain's second occupation, a flow facilitated by the calendaring and increased availability of the East Florida Papers, the primary documentary source material for the era (McWatters, Chappell, and Getzler-Easton, 1978). The first full-length treatment of the period was by Ramón Romero Cabot (1983), whose dissertation written in Spanish at the University of Seville is not readily available to U.S. scholars. A symposium sponsored by the St. Augustine Historical Society with financial support from the Florida Endowment for the Humanities led to the publication of *Clash between*

Cultures (Fretwell and Parker 1988), encompassing the Second Spanish Period. Helen Hornbeck Tanner's participation in that symposium stirred new interest in making her book on Zéspedes more available to the public, an interest that has led to this reprint.

Tanner distills the essence of her subject matter in one terse sentence when she concludes that "during his governorship, Zéspedes struggled valiantly to make a flourishing colony out of the most expendable province in the Spanish empire" (148). Painting a picture of the times with the narrow brush of Zéspedes' part in them, Tanner illuminates the clash of Indian, American, British, and Spanish cultures in this remote outpost of the New World, setting it against the backdrop of an Old World embroiled in a turbulent transition from ancien régime to modern world.

Zéspedes was a gentleman of that ancien régime, yet he had the strength and wisdom to attempt stabilization of the regained colony in a new colonial mold. He was born into a Castillian family of the lesser nobility in the district of La Mancha and, in a time-honored tradition, chose a military career as an acceptable avenue for advancement. After serving in the occupation forces in Algiers, he was sent to the Caribbean and so distinguished himself in the War of Jenkins's Ear that he was chosen to be secretary to the governor of Cuba, where he married into a well-placed Creole family. After a seven-month period as an officer in the force sent to subdue the Creek Indians attacking Pensacola, he played such a creditable part in the defense of Havana against British attack in the Seven Years' War that he received a citation from the king. Subsequent to participation in a number of crises, including the role he played in Alejandro O'Reilly's successful but bloody attempt to quell the insurrection of the French in Spain's new possession, Louisiana, he received several promotions and was made interim governor of Santiago de Cuba.

At last, after much personal lobbying and through the patronage of his superiors, Zéspedes was awarded the governorship of Florida. Since he was sixty-four years old, it was to be the capstone of his career. His Castilian birth, noble lineage, distinguished military career, fortunate marriage, administrative experience, and personal qualities all fitted him for the post. Tanner concluded that the man and the place were suited to each other: "The ancient European rivalries that molded Zéspedes' attitudes and the eighteenth-century wars that controlled his personal career also determined the fate of the land called Florida" (18).

The new governor encountered a host of problems. The British lin-

gered in East Florida for over a year, creating a dual regime with attendant difficulties. Banditti lurked in the hinterland, taking advantage
of the transfer of government for their own ends. Each government
tried to cope with the lawless element in a different manner, and tempers flared. Ownership of slaves also became a sore point, and disposition of this matter was compounded when slaves were stolen along
with other portable property by roving bands of outlaws. Even after
the British evacuation there were civic problems of deteriorating buildings, the poverty attendant on the unpredictable arrival of the *situado*
with pay for the province, and moral problems such as the practice
of prostitution and homosexuality. The lack of a legal officer made the
solution of these and other disputes difficult.

Internal problems, while exasperating, were to be expected, but on
the colony's frontiers problems were not so easily solved as in the capital city of St. Augustine. Zéspedes himself in his final report to his superiors named his two main areas of concern: "The two questions that
have historically constituted the most important tasks before this government of East Florida have undoubtedly been the weak defense of
the St. Marys River and the maintenance of good relations with the Indians" (quoted in Lewis 1984, 189).

During British rule of the Floridas, the frontier had changed drasti-
cally. No longer protected by a hinterland buffer sparsely populated by
Indians, East Florida had been subjected first to a stream of Loyalists
during the American Revolution and behind them a continuing surge
of American frontiersmen whose quest for lands and adventure inured
them to hardships. So aware was Zéspedes of the latter group that he
classified them into three kinds of "crackers," an interesting early use
of this designation. He compared the first, and worst, group to nomadic
Arabs and declared them "distinguished from savages only in their
color, language and the superiority of their depraved cunning and un-
trustworthiness" (Lewis 1984, 191).

The St. Marys River, the boundary between East Florida and Georgia,
appeared to be a natural division but was not traditionally so used.
From prehistoric times the chain of offshore islands along the southern
Atlantic coast had been considered an economic unit for purposes of
subsistence. In the eighteenth century traffic still flowed continually between Cumberland Island to the north of the river and Amelia Island,
the next island south, regardless of political borders. The boundary became an issue because the entrance of the St. Marys River offered a
much better harbor than did St. Augustine. While Zéspedes' superiors
would not allow use of the entrance to the St. Marys as an official port

of embarkation, it was used by necessity during stormy weather, and the Spaniards who used it found there vessels from the United States, England, France, and other countries as well as the illicit craft of privateers and pirates. The harbor became virtually a free port, while its banks provided a staging area for American depredations (quasi-official as well as unofficial) against the weakly defended Spanish.

American frontiersmen were also moving west and south, encroaching on Indian as well as Spanish territory. Over the centuries the Indians had gained a degree of sophistication in dealing with the Europeans. Tanner writes skillfully of the Indians' way of life as they had adapted to European contact and been modified by it. In this she foreshadows her keen interest in Indian treaty rights.

Zéspedes recognized that the British had evolved an effective system of trade with the Indians by giving a monopoly to Panton, Leslie, and Company, a British trading firm. He finally persuaded the higher Spanish authorities to continue the English company in this function in both the Floridas. This decision was not entirely a novel one: the Spanish had found, once they acquired Louisiana, that the only feasible way of dealing with the Indians was through the French trade network already in place (Bolton 1964; Whitaker 1970).

Good Indian relations were not only for purposes of keeping the Indians quiet but also to engage them as allies in a first zone of defense against the encroachment of other nations, a practice generally followed by those wrestling for control of frontier lands. It is Tanner's contribution to this subject that she takes us easily through the labyrinthine ways in which Zéspedes won the Indians' loyalty. Among other things he championed the leadership of Alexander McGillivray, who, he believed, best represented the interests of the Creek nation, against the claims of the adventurer William Augustus Bowles, who had also set himself up as the leader of the Creeks.

Emerging from Tanner's discussion is the recognition that Zéspedes was a good judge of people, adroit at picking good subordinates and using them effectively. He was especially fortunate in his secretary, Carlos Howard, who, before Zéspedes arrived, had been able to establish and maintain an effective and reliable intelligence network. Tanner believes that this network and Zespedes' own understanding of Indian problems were helpful to him in the 1788 crisis in Creek-Spanish trade relations. In contrast, Governor Estevan Miró in Louisiana, and especially Arturo O'Neill, governor of West Florida, relied on misinformation in decision-making at that time (194).

It is curious that O'Neill subsequently received more honors than did

Zéspedes. While all of the factors are not known—and O'Neill's longer tenure in the Floridas could have been significant—it is still possible to speculate that Zéspedes' lesser recognition prior to retirement might have resulted from his running afoul of the intendancy system. The fall of Havana to the British in 1762 had made Charles III aware of some of the weaknesses in Spain's colonies, causing him to institute certain reforms. The intendancy system, which he first tried in Cuba in 1765 and later extended to other colonies, established a parallel administrative hierarchy charged with defense and fiscal matters. Intendants even replaced governors as chief executive officers in some areas where civil rule was paramount.

Having come along under the old system and finding the intendant in Havana unresponsive to the needs of East Florida, Zéspedes acknowledged only the captain-general as his immediate superior and addressed all of his requests and reports to him. The problems that this system created were compounded by the deaths of José de Gálvez and Bernardo de Gálvez, Zéspedes' principal patrons. These men, an uncle and nephew, had occupied respectively the key positions of minister of the Indies and viceroy of New Spain.

As Tanner indicates in her 1989 preface, the letter from Nathaniel Greene to his wife affords a slightly different picture of Zéspedes. Also John D. Ware (1969) concluded from documentary evidence that the governor resorted to a bit of subterfuge in seeing that his own residence was renovated first while assuring higher authorities that Government House would be the last on the list of shabby public buildings to receive attention.

To an eighteenth-century gentleman, all of the hallmarks of status were important in presenting himself in an official role. In accord with this view, Doña Concepción, the governor's wife, maintained the proper tone of colonial society in the small provincial capital. Each colonial administration was a representative, a microcosm, of the Spanish court itself, demonstrating to the world the eminence of the Spanish king and his dominions. Tanner gives us colorful glimpses of the entertainments and fêtes in this "little court" in a remote corner of the Spanish sovereignty. An entire chapter is devoted to the fiestas in 1789 that celebrated the succession to the monarchy of a new king and queen and, incidentally, provided a memorable ending to Zéspedes' tour of duty in Florida.

Indeed, one of the outstanding qualities of Tanner's book is the way in which she makes the colonial milieu come alive. She helps us to picture the disordered nighttime life in the military barracks fostered by the "dingy glow of a candle stuck in an empty wine bottle" (187) or the disgraceful and unmilitary condition of the horses as the new commandant, Lt. Colonel Ignacio Peñalver, inspects them and notices how "the leather was mildewed on the badly worn saddles and halters, and buckles and stirrups were rusty and corroded" (183). While describing in vivid detail the Delaney murder case, a case that occupies many folios in the official papers, she says in an inspired sentence about one of the suspects that "the young man evidently scampered along the side roads as much as he followed the straight and narrow path" (73). Tanner discusses the details in a 1965 article.

Bishop Cyril de Barcelona's visit to inspect the religious life of the province, to which Tanner devotes a chapter, is scarcely the dry recital that one might expect. It provides a window from which to view a whole year in the life of the province, just as the chapter on the fiesta did for another year during Zéspedes' tenure. While he dreaded the visit beforehand because of an unpleasant experience during his visit to Louisiana, the bishop found religious matters in relatively good order in East Florida. After he completed his official duties, the salubrious climate and agreeable society lulled him into an extended stay. Under the pretext of avoiding bad weather and maintaining that he was learning English to help in his impending West Florida visitation, he managed to stay for almost a year. We see him enjoying the company of the five other clerics gracing the little capital at the time, a group whose diverse backgrounds lent a cosmopolitan tinge to their sociability.

Zéspedes' term of office was the honeymoon period of the renewed Spanish regime. He envisioned carrying forward the commendable plantation system instituted by the English. Already resident were the "Minorcans," remnants of a large colony of Mediterraneans brought to East Florida as plantation workers during British times, and an almost equal number of blacks, both slave and free. To these the governor expected to add many *Floridanos* (returnees from the First Spanish Period), newly recruited families from Spain and the Caribbean, and perhaps a sprinkling of Anglos-turned-Catholic. He envisioned peaceful trade with the Indians and free trade in world markets. He expected that such a growing and prospering colony would be its own defense against the encroaching Americans: in his own words, "the best fortification would be a living wall of industrious citizens" (Lewis 1984, 202).

Yet those initial years foreshadowed the colony's destiny; as Tanner said, "The plot was set for the whole Second Spanish Period during the Zéspedes years" (pers. comm. March 1989). Attempts at effective colonization of the province failed, two major crises over the intruding

Americans were dress rehearsals for what was to follow, and the Indian trade buffer zone was insecurely established. Trade with other than Spain and its dominions, although carried on to some extent, continued to be frowned on by higher authorities, and the neglect of the colony by those in charge in Spain, Mexico, and Cuba became chronic.

The Spanish did not anticipate the Napoleonic Wars and their impact on the fate of the Floridas and Louisiana. News of the French Revolution had reached the Floridas by the end of Zéspedes' term, alarming him because of the ground swell of republicanism infecting the New World. But Zéspedes could not have foreseen the imperialism of Napoleon in the wake of the French Revolution, or that New World revolutions and attempts to repel the French from Spain would keep the Iberian peninsula in turmoil and lead eventually to the treaty by which both Floridas were ceded to the United States.

To an aristocrat such as Zéspedes it was unthinkable that the notion of liberty as a national ideal could replace loyalty to a monarch. Yet in his own administration he embodied many ideals that were progressive for his time. He established one of the first free public schools in the Spanish colonies, and his concern for the welfare of the black population, including those who fled from the north to seek freedom, led him to see that black boys, slave and free, were allowed to attend the school. His notions of free trade, of benign treatment of the Indians, of settlement as a means of landholding in opposition to the strong-capital–weak-hinterland characteristic of the First Spanish Period, which his superiors still favored for the Floridas, all speak of an enlightened administration.

Tanner's book was written at a time when "top down" historical writing was in fashion. In that framework, past times are detailed through description of great men, national fortunes, and sweeping events. Her choice of topic was in that genre, yet her development of the subject foreshadowed the ascendency of "bottom-up" history writing—emphasis on the common man and woman, everyday life, and ethnic and racial cultures and their influence on the commonweal. The drift in this direction in the writing of history has been steady during the seventies and eighties. Recent writing on colonial Florida has reflected that interest by placing center front such groups as blacks, Indians, women, Minorcans, "Conchs," Greeks, Italians, and Cubans. Tanner's *Atlas of Great Lakes Indian History* (1987), as well as the many hours she has spent preparing for and testifying in Indian land-claim cases, demonstrates her own development along these lines.

While to many historians this book read like a novel when it was published, by now its substance is apparent. How often can one say of a twenty-six-year-old book that it is as fresh as the day that it was written?

Patricia C. Griffin

References

Arnade, Charles W. 1961. Review of "Vicente Manuel de Zéspedes and the Restoration of Spanish Rule in East Florida, 1784–1790," by Helen Hornbeck Tanner. *Florida Historical Quarterly* 40:391–94.

Bolton, Herbert Eugene. 1921. *The Spanish Borderlands: A Chronicle of Old Florida and the Southwest.* New Haven: Yale University Press.

———. 1964. "The Cession of Louisiana and the New Spanish Indian Policy." In *Bolton and the Spanish Borderlands*, edited by John Francis Bannon. Norman: University of Oklahoma Press.

Cabot, Ramón Romero. 1983. "Los últimos años de la soberania española en la Florida, 1783–1821." Tesis doctoral, Universidad de Sevilla.

Fretwell, Jacqueline K., and Susan R. Parker, eds. 1988. *Clash between Cultures: Spanish East Florida, 1784–1821.* St. Augustine: St. Augustine Historical Society.

Gold, Robert L. 1965. Review of *Zéspedes in East Florida, 1794–1790*, by Helen Hornbeck Tanner. *The Americas* 21:310–11.

Harlan, Rogers C. 1971. "A Military History of East Florida during the Governorship of Enrique White, 1796–1811." Master's thesis, Florida State University.

Lewis, James A. 1984. "*Cracker*—Spanish Florida Style." *Florida Historical Quarterly* 63:184–204.

McWatters, D. Lorne; Bruce S. Chappell; and Michael Getzler-Eaton. 1978. "A New Guide to Sources of Spanish Florida History." *Florida Historical Quarterly* 61:495–97.

Miller, Janice Borton. 1981. *Juan Nepomuceno de Quesada: Governor of Spanish East Florida, 1790–1795.* Washington, DC: University Press of America.

Murdock, Richard K. 1951. *The Georgia-Florida Frontier, 1793–1796.* Berkeley and Los Angeles: University of California Press.

Norris, L. David. 1981. "José Coppinger in East Florida, 1816–1821: A Man, a Province, and a Spanish Colonial Failure." Ph.D. dissertation, Southern Illinois University.

Patrick, Rembert W. 1954. *Florida Fiasco: Rampant Rebels on the Georgia-Florida Frontier, 1810–1815*. Athens: University of Georgia Press.

————. 1964. Review of *Zéspedes in East Florida, 1784–1790*, by Helen Hornbeck Tanner. *Ethnohistory* 11:292–94.

Powell, Thomas. 1924. Thomas Powell to Col. Stephen F. Austin, October 24, 1827, in *The Austin Papers: Annual Report of the American Historical Association for 1919*. 2 vols. Washington.

Tanner, Helen Hornbeck. 1949. "The Transition from British to Spanish Rule in East Florida, 1783–1785." Master's thesis, University of Florida.

————. 1961. "Vincente Manuel de Zéspedes and the Restoration of Spanish Rule in East Florida, 1784–1790." Ph.D. dissertation, University of Michigan.

————. 1965. "The Delaney Murder Case." *Florida Historical Quarterly* 44:136–47.

————, ed. 1964. *General Greene's Visit to St. Augustine in 1785*. Ann Arbor: University of Michigan Press.

————, ed. 1987. *Atlas of Great Lakes Indian History*. Norman: University of Oklahoma Press.

TePaske, John J. 1965. Review of *Zéspedes in East Florida, 1784–1790*, by Helen Hornbeck Tanner. *Florida Historical Quarterly* 43:276–77.

Ware, John D. 1969. "St. Augustine, 1784: Decadence and Repairs." *Florida Historical Quarterly* 48:180–87.

Whitaker, Arthur Preston. 1970. *The Spanish-American Frontier, 1783–1795*. Lincoln: University of Nebraska Press.

Treasury Street

I

The Appointment

SITTING at his desk in Havana, Cuba on March 3, 1784, Don Vizente Manuel de Zéspedes y Velasco carefully drafted a short letter acknowledging his appointment as governor of St. Augustine and the surrounding province of East Florida. The formal and modest phrases he penned scarcely revealed his inner sense of pride and satisfaction in accepting this appointment. For two years, he had sought a governorship in the Spanish colonial administration. Now he eagerly looked forward to beginning his régime. He was already formulating plans for taking the reins of government from the British, who had held St. Augustine for the past twenty years, and re-cementing into the Spanish empire this former possession, first claimed by Juan Ponce de Leon in 1512. Spain had ceded Florida to England as part of the peace settlement in the First Treaty of Paris in 1763, but regained the province in the Second Treaty of Paris signed in 1783 at the close of the general European war growing out of the American Revolution. In St. Augustine, Zéspedes would assume command of the Castillo de San Marcos, the important fortification located just fifty miles below the border of the new American nation, whose independence was formally recognized by England and other European powers in another provision of the Treaty of 1783.

1

The newly-appointed governor felt perfectly confident that his own background and experience amply qualified him to re-store Spanish rule in Florida. His self-assurance partially stemmed from the fact that he had been reared in Spain; and he knew the home government preferred to give higher administrative posts in the overseas empire to native born Spaniards. In addition, he had a backlog of fifty years in the army, for the most part spent on the Island of Cuba but including special assignments on the American mainland. During most of his military life he had actively opposed British schemes in the Caribbean area, serving with varying fortunes through three major wars and the inter-vening periods of tension. In March of 1784, he found it grati-fying to be definitely on the victor's side, delegated by the king to reclaim Florida and remove the traces of brief British occupancy.

The appointment to the post in St. Augustine capped a long and honorable career in the royal service. Looking back over his past history, Zéspedes realized that he had progressed far since he left the country where he was born in 1720. His homeland, Almagro, was in the district of La Mancha on the southern margin of New Castile. The vast and arid grasslands where he spent his childhood resembled the rolling prairie of the western plains region of North America. There were no mountains, ravines, rivers or trees to accent the landscape, only an occasional church tower and the windmills identified with the region since the days of Don Quixote. The history of this part of Spain is as colorless as the landscape. It was a wasteland until the period of reconquest when Christian princes forced retreating Moslems south of La Mancha to the coastal area of Andalucia. The first settlements grew under the protection of military orders of chival-ry to whom the frontier was entrusted in the thirteenth century. The tradition of the medieval knights remained strong in the eighteenth century. A typical masculine representative of these Spanish plains was a lean and weatherbeaten figure, generally un-demonstrative, but easily aroused to fight for principles of honor, religion and human justice. The Almagro district did not form a municipal organization until 1803. By that time, it was known only for joyous holiday festivals and for the beautiful pale lace made by local women.[1] As a child, Zéspedes' contacts were limited to this community of widely-scattered clusters of rural

---

[1] Ceferino Palencia, *España Vista por los Españoles* (Mexico, D.F., 1947), pp. 214-215, 231.

hidalgos and their farm workers, who were dependent on crops of wheat and barley.[2]

These drab and unpropitious surroundings nevertheless provided Zéspedes with two assets of great value to a man destined to serve in the Indies. In the first place, he enjoyed a privileged position in colonial society because he was born in peninsular Spain. Moreover, he was born in Castile, the core of the Spanish nation which continued its hegemony over the peripheral provinces. Secondly, he was an *hidalgo*, a man of upper class birth, though on a social rung far below the *grandees*. In a rank-conscious society, these two distinctions were more valuable than monetary wealth.

Zéspedes' early training followed a trend common to sons of the lesser nobility whose prospects at home were discouraging. Wealthy nobles could go to Madrid and promote their interests in court circles; the lesser nobility often sought advancement in the army. Young Vizente Manuel de Zéspedes was enrolled as a cadet in the Infantry of Granada when he was only fourteen years old. Three years later, he was assigned to the garrison at the Algerian port of Oran, 220 miles east of Gibraltar. Spain originally occupied Oran in the sixteenth century because it was a pirate stronghold, but lost the city to a local Moselm leader, the Bey of Mascara, during the War of the Spanish Succession (1702-1713). The Spanish army retook Oran in 1732. Zéspedes' first overseas experience consisted of thirty months in this busy North African city, where his regiment protected shipping in the port, preserved order in the casbah—the native quarter clinging to the steep hillside—and guarded the ancient citadel overlooking the harbor.

In retrospect, Zéspedes could see that his subsequent career was determined by the course of eighteenth century European warfare, during which England emerged as Spain's principal colonial adversary. Hostility toward England was already deeply ingrained in the Spanish military and diplomatic corps when he became involved in the eighteenth century phase of the great European rivalries. This antipathy was rooted in the sixteenth century wars when religion was the vital issue. In that early period, Protestant England aided the Dutch provinces engaged in a dual rebellion against Spanish political control and the Roman

---

[2] Leonardo Martín Echeverría, *España, el País y los Habitantes* (Mexico, D.F., 1940), p. 400.

Catholic religion. The Elizabethan "sea dogs" raided most of Spain's ports in America. In retaliation, the great Spanish Armada made its dramatic but unsuccessful attack on England in 1588.

In the seventeenth century, the conflict broadened as additional European nations gained foothold in the New World. The English, French, Dutch, Danes and Swedes all established settlements in North and South America and previously unoccupied Caribbean islands, but in the course of this century, France and England became the leading contestants challenging Spain's early domination of the western hemisphere. As the Hapsburg dynasty in Spain weakened, inroads into Spanish colonies increased. Spain had staked out a large area in America, but occupied only a small portion. France, a rival Catholic power, seized the western half of the Island of Santo Domingo and other minor islands in the Antilles in addition to founding a vast empire extending from bases on the St. Lawrence river through the Great Lakes and down the Mississippi river valley. La Salle reached the Gulf of Mexico by this route in 1689, greatly alarming authorities in Spain, intent on keeping the Caribbean a private monopoly and fearful for the safety of the mines in Mexico. Although La Salle's colony did not survive, France secured a hold on interior North America after the founding of the New Orleans in 1718 as the administrative center of the province named Louisiana.

English people swarmed to America in the seventeenth century, following the establishment of the first two permanent colonies on the Atlantic coast, in 1610 in Virginia, and in 1620 in New England. During the Puritan Revolution, Cromwell's forces took Jamaica in the year 1655. Spain maintained the *mare clausum* theory until 1670, the year of the treaty recognizing English occupation of Charleston, as well as Bermuda and the Bahama islands. The Spanish king, and his courtiers, deeply resented all these incidents of foreign intrusion into the royal domain. The Spanish monarch based his personal claims on the decision of the pope, who in 1497 divided the newly discovered parts of the globe between the kings of Castile and Portugal. By papal bull, the Spanish portion included all of North and South America except the eastward projecting hump of Brazil.

The element of equilibrium in the seventeenth century triangular struggle between England, France and Spain was destroyed in 1700 when a member of the French royal family claimed the Spanish throne. The absolute nadir of Spanish civilization had been reached by the turn of the eighteenth century, when the last Hapsburg king died without leaving an heir to the throne. The crisis had been foreseen by all the powers of Europe, and each felt a personal interest in the choice of a successor. Ultimately the choice was reduced to an Austrian and a French contestant. The dying king's will, written under rather dubious circumstances of influence and pressure, designated Philip of Anjou, grandson of Louis XIV, Bourbon king of France. Neither England nor Austria was content to see the Bourbon family occupy the thrones of both France and Spain, and a large segment of the Spanish population, particularly in Catalonia and Aragon, was antagonistic to the thought of being ruled by a Frenchman. The selection of Philip of Anjou disrupted the balance of power in Europe and precipitated the War of the Spanish Succession (1702-1713), the first of a series of eighteenth century wars gradually involving all Europe in military operations on a global scale.

When he entered the army in 1734, Zéspedes' superior officers included many veterans of the War of Succession who still recalled the years when foreign troops battled on Spanish soil aided by local factions supporting either the Austrian or French forces. While the fighting was in progress, England gained control of the Island of Minorca, one of the five islands in the Balearic group, an area favoring the Austrian pretender to the Spanish throne. England also seized the great rock of Gibraltar, a serious strategic loss for the Spanish army and an unforgetable blow to the national pride.

The Treaty of Utrecht in 1713 at the end of the War of the Spanish Succession contained provisions which foreshadowed the subsequent eighteenth century conflicts, with their fluctuating alliances and complicated motives. Among other provisions, the treaty acknowledged Philip of Anjou as king of Spain, but at the price of granting England the Island of Minorca, Gibraltar, and a commercial privilege called the asiento—the right to bring slaves and a limited consignment of goods once a year to the Spanish Indies. In practice, the Treaty of Utrecht marked the dominance of French influence in the Spanish court, including the stimulating effect of the French enlightenment. The treaty also marked the beginning of Spain's persistent effort to regain Gibraltar, and Minorca from the English, and to prevent British contraband trade facilitated by the asiento.

French military experts brought in by Philip rapidly improved the quality of the decadent Spanish army. One of the early signs of Spain's reviving strength under Bourbon leadership was the recapture of Oran, Zéspedes' first overseas post. His regiment was well-trained before facing the British for the first time at the beginning of the War of Jenkins' Ear (1739-1743). Immediate cause for the war was the contraband trade which greatly increased in volume during the quarter century following the Treaty of Utrecht. In order to curtail the illicit commerce of English merchants, Spain began searching vessels on the high seas. This irritating procedure, though legally justifiable, was a major factor influencing England to declare war in 1739. Zéspedes' regiment immediately sailed to reinforce the garrison at Cartagena de Indias, the Spanish stronghold on the Caribbean coast of present-day Colombia. By the time he arrived, the British fleet under Admiral Edward Vernon had already seized Portobello, eastern terminus of the trade across the isthmus of Panama. Vernon's next objective was Cartagena, key point in Spain's defense of northern South America. The recently strengthened garrison and the forty-foot thick walls ultimately rebuffed the British attack in 1740, although destruction was severe.

Zéspedes arrived at his next station, Santiago de Cuba, in 1741 in time to fend off Admiral Vernon a second time. Guerrilla warfare and fever played an important part in thwarting the admiral's projected attack, following a preliminary landing at nearby Guantanamo. In Santiago, Zéspedes became a lieutenant in a unit called the *Piquetes de Vitoria,* and evidently his ability came to the attention of the local governor, Francisco Cagigal de la Vega. When Cagigal was promoted to the position of governor and captain general of Cuba in 1747, Zéspedes accompanied him to Havana and served as his secretary of government for the next seven years.[3]

In this period, Havana really became Zéspedes' home. He married Maria Concepción Aróstegui, whose family of Basque origin ranked high in the local Creole oligarchy, and soon the first of their six children arrived.[4] Rising up the military ladder, he became captain of Grenadiers, an élite corps of the Havana Regiment. These were years of exceptional peace and well being in Cuba, as they

---

[3] Ramiro Guerra y Sánchez, Jose M. Pérez Cabrera, Juan J. Remos, Emeterio S. Santovenia, *Historia de la Nación Cubana* (10 vols. Havana, 1952), II, pp. 27-38.

[4] Roman Catholic Records, *White Marriages, Book A* (Jacksonville, 1937), p. 8. Entry names parents of Maria Josepha de Zéspedes.

were in Spain, when the empire was ruled from 1747 to 1759 by stoutly pacifist Ferdinand VI, the second Bourbon king.

After fourteen years in the urban environment of Havana, Zéspedes left the island in 1761 to subdue Creek Indians attacking Pensacola, an isolated garrison on the Florida Gulf coast. The little town had maintained a tenuous existence since its founding in 1698, continually menaced by Indian hostility, food shortages, and poor leadership. Reports of La Salle's activities, and general French interest in harbors along the northern edge of the Gulf of Mexico, originally led to the establishment of the base at Pensacola bay. Several years' intensive investigation of the shoreline preceded the selection of a site. When the new settlement was only three weeks old, ships bringing French colonists appeared outside the beautiful harbor. Finding this highly desired location already occupied, the French moved to the next large bay and founded the town of Mobile.

Since the establishment of Spanish Pensacola, French Mobile and British Charleston, the southeastern portion of the continent had been a focal point for the triangular contest of the major European empire-builders. All three nations were rivals for superior influence among the southern Indian tribes. In 1719, French forces from Mobile with their Indian allies captured Pensacola, but later returned the outpost. When Zéspedes and the two companies of Grenadiers under his command arrived at Pensacola in the spring of 1761, the garrison was besieged by warriors sympathetic to the English. Frequent sorties against the Creeks over a period of seven months finally induced them to make peace.

Zéspedes was back in Havana when Spain became involved in the most decisive of the eighteenth century conflicts, the Seven Years' War (1756-1763), or the French and Indian War, as it is known in American colonial history. Although the international policies of France and Spain became closely related through a series of "Family Compacts," Ferdinand VI preserved Spanish neutrality during the early engagements between England and France. Charles III, who came to the throne in 1760, was naturally as pacific as his older half-brother Ferdinand but was exposed to stronger pressures. Among these was the personal influence of the French minister, who with masterful finesse urged him to cooperate in a war that might regain Gibraltar. Furthermore, Charles III felt goaded into action by British infringement on trade and insolent insistence on cutting valuable logwood along the Honduras coast. Spain entered the war in 1761, and in consequence her overseas empire became a target for British forces already in a position of supremacy over the French. This great imperial contest was fought on many widely-separated battlefields: Quebec, the Ohio river valley and Cherokee hunting lands in America; from Netherlands to Portugal in Europe; along the frontier between the Spanish and Portuguese possessions in South America; India and the Philippine Islands in the Orient; and finally in the Caribbean, where Zéspedes played his small but heroic role.

Although rumors that Spain had entered the war against England came to Havana from nearby French islands, official word of the declaration of war in December, 1761, never reached Cuba. The captain of the packetboat bringing the dispatches dropped them overboard when facing capture by an armed British vessel. Spain's entrance into the conflict gave England a long-awaited opportunity to try to seize the Spanish Caribbean empire. The ultimate goal was the wealth of Mexico, but the first military objective was Havana, crossroads of commerce for the Caribbean and center of the defense system. On the day of the Holy Trinity, June 6, 1762, *Habaneros* were completely surprised to see the British squadron sailing toward the city. The ships had cleverly approached by way of the Old Bahama Channel, along the north coast of Cuba, guided by an old Spanish map and by pilots skilled in illegal trading.[5] The usual sea route was round the southern coast of Cuba, approaching Havana from the west.

The British could have sailed right in and taken the city, whose walls were much thinner than those of Cartagena, but instead they adopted the methodical siege procedure used in fighting in the Low Countries. The overall plan of attack, on file in the British War department since 1756, had been devised by Sir Charles Knowles after examining the defenses of Havana when he was in Havana as guest of Captain General Cagigal. Sir Charles made a "state visit" to Cuba near the end of his term of office as British governor of Jamaica.

The Grenadiers under Zéspedes' command played a conspicuous part in prolonging the defense of Havana, during which British losses from disease greatly exceeded their battle casualties. Morro Castle, the fortress guarding the entrance to Havana harbor, was the first object of British attack. Its speedy reduction was prevented by a constant supply of reinforcements and supplies brought around

---

[5] Eduardo Martinez Dalmau, *La Política Colonial y Extranjera de los Reyes Españoles de la Casa Austria y de Borbon y la Toma de la Habana por los Ingleses* (Havana, 1943), pp. 55-57.

the bay from the town.[6] Zéspedes' Grenadiers braved enemy fire five times to take reinforcements to the fort. On June 29, they made a dramatic pre-dawn rally to spike enemy mortars already in place to begin battering the Castle walls.[7] Havana finally capitulated on August 2, 1762. At the beginning of the eleven month English occupation, Zéspedes left on the first transport of troops for Cadiz. He was honored with a citation from the king in recognition of his brave actions. A few months in 1763 were his only visit to Spain during all the years following his initial trip to the Indies in 1740.

Spain's participation in the Seven Years' War was short but disastrous. By the terms of the Treaty of Paris in 1763, the situation in the Caribbean area was radically changed. British forces had captured both Pensacola and Havana, as well as distant Manila, and the cession of "The Floridas" to England balanced the return of the two more important cities at opposite ends of the Spanish empire. After some delays, France turned over to Spain the western half of Louisiana as compensation for her ally's losses. From France, England received Canada and the part of Louisiana lying east of the Mississippi river. As a result of these territorial exchanges, France lost all her empire in North America. Victorious England gained control of the Gulf shoreline east of the Mississippi river, and secured possession of the entire Atlantic coast from Nova Scotia to the tip of the Florida peninsula. The Mississippi river became the interior border zone between the Spanish and English colonies. The diplomats negotiating in Europe conveniently ignored the rights of the American Indian tribes to their own towns and hunting lands.

Charles III had found unexpected weakness in his American colonies, and immediately he began to reform the army and colonial administration. The fall of Havana was partially attributed to lax military discipline and a lag in the construction of additional fortifications near Morro Castle. It was in Havana that his comprehensive reform program first took effect. In 1765, he introduced into Cuba the intendency system, later extended to other colonies, with the general purpose of improving defense and increasing royal revenue. The intendant ranked on a level with the captain general, taking over such matters as army finance and the inspection of troops. The creation of a second hierarchy of

---

[6] Account of the siege of Havana from June 7, 1762, author unknown, dated July 14, 1762. MS, Howe Papers, William L. Clements Library.

[7] Francis Russell Hart, *The Siege of Havana* (Boston, 1931), p. 42.

officials led to many incidents of friction in the future, but under the new system revenues increased.

The reform program brought to Havana Mariscal del Campo Alejandro O'Reilly, a highly successful officer in the Spanish army's Irish Brigade, who supervised reorganization of the local regiments. When the French inhabitants of Louisiana showed signs of rebellion against Spanish authority, O'Reilly took a new governor and the pick of his troops to New Orleans in 1768.[8] The speed with which he secured evidence and punished leaders of the conspiracy later earned him the name "Bloody O'Reilly," but his dramatic arrival brought an initial reaction of awe and admiration. Zéspedes accompanied this expedition as executive officer of the first batallion of the Havana Regiment.

For the people of New Orleans, O'Reilly's arrival was a grand show, beginning with the parade of 2,000 soldiers marching off the ships to the roll of drums. In the procession, a silver mace, symbol of authority, was prominently displayed. During the formal ceremonies acknowledging Spanish rule in Louisiana, there were shouts of "Viva el Rey!," and the thunder of fifty cannon. At the conclusion, O'Reilly went to the parish church to receive the blessing of the vicar and join in chanting the *Te Deum*. Zéspedes was among the officers attending O'Reilly later when he received a delegation of Indian chiefs. To present a regal impression, O'Reilly was seated under a red silk canopy, surrounded by his officers. Following an exchange of speeches, O'Reilly gave individual attention to each visiting chief, touching each one on the breast and shoulders with his sword then making the sign of the cross overhead. But the chiefs were even more impressed by the sham battle presented in the afternoon by the Spanish soldiers. All in all, Zéspedes witnessed an effective use of pageantry to establish authority.

The next threat of general war with England occurred the following year, 1770, as a result of British activities in the Falkland (Malvinas) islands off the coast of Argentina. War never materialized, but the situation in the Caribbean remained tense. The British garrison in Pensacola was alarmed when O'Reilly took such an over-powering force to New Orleans, and immediately requested additional reinforcements. Zéspedes commanded the second batallion of the Havana Regiment transferred in 1770 to Santiago de Cuba, a garrison which feared attack from British Jamaica. In

---

8 John Walton Caughey, *Bernardo de Gálvez in Louisiana* (Berkeley, 1934), p. 22. See also Chapter X.

1771, he advanced to the rank of lieutenant colonel. After the crisis passed, Zéspedes returned to Havana in 1774 to become colonel of the Infantry Regiment of Havana, an important promotion.

Although war was narrowly avoided in 1770, Europe again became embroiled before the decade was over. The uprising of the English colonies on the Atlantic coast in 1775, soon followed by their demands for complete independence, invited the support of anti-British powers on the continent. In the opening years of the American Revolution, when Spain remained neutral, Zéspedes was occupied with the protection of Havana. New fortification built since the Seven Years' War gave the capital a reputation for impregnability. Havana was free from attack in the American war.

Military leaders in the Caribbean became increasingly alert after France added her support to the English colonists' cause in 1777, and made extensive advance preparations before Spain reluctantly allied with her fellow Bourbon power in 1779. Spain did not form an alliance with the rebellious colonies. Charles III believed that Spain could profit from the disruption of the British empire, but on the other hand he knew a successful war for independence set a bad example for the Spanish colonies. The Spanish court sent letters to colonial officials on May 18, 1779, advising them of the forthcoming war with England, but delayed formal declaration until June 21. A conservative monarchist, Zéspedes could not share wholeheartedly the local enthusiasm which burst forth as soon as the decision became known. Cubans willingly paid a special head tax levied by the crown to pay for prosecuting the war against England. Havana society belles sponsored bazaars and auctioned their jewels to cover the back pay of French sailors whose fleet was anchored in nearby Matanzas (Cuba) harbor.

In joining the Revolutionary War, Charles III's only objective affecting America was to recover Florida and regain control of the Gulf coastline. The king assigned this task to Bernardo de Gálvez, youthful governor of Louisiana, who was rising rapidly in the colonial service through the sponsorship of his uncle, José de Gálvez, minister of the Indies. Florida under British rule comprised a larger and more precisely defined area than the former Spanish province. The British first of all divided the province at the Appalachicola river into two separate jurisdictions, East Florida governed at St. Augustine, and West Florida whose capital was Pensacola. In the early years of British occupation, the northern boundary of West Florida was moved northward from the thirty-first parallel of latitude to thirty-two degrees, eight minutes. On the west, West Florida extended across a portion of former French Louisiana to the left bank of the Mississippi river. The new West Florida boundaries included the Natchez district, an area fast growing in popularity with English colonists, as well as Mobile and a few other isolated French settlements. Both East and West Florida remained loyal to the British monarch and fought against the thirteen rebellious colonies.

As soon as he decided to enter the American Revolution, Charles III dispatched a royal order to Bernardo de Gálvez instructing him to conquer Pensacola, Mobile and the British posts along the Mississippi river. Gálvez received notification of impending war with England before the news reached British Florida. Taking advantage of his prior knowledge, Gálvez organized a surprise attack in August, 1779 and during the fall he seized all British posts on the left bank of the Mississippi from Natchez to the delta. He followed up his initial victory with the conquest of Mobile in March of 1780, and concluded a successful onslaught against Pensacola in May, 1781.

Zéspedes was remote from the early phase of Spain's participation in the American Revolution. As commander of the regiment guarding Havana he was on the sidelines, while a younger generation of soldiers carried fighting into British territory. But he became directly concerned with the progress of the West Florida campaign when his son Fernando joined the expedition against Mobile. Lieutenant Fernando de Zéspedes was one of fifty men from the Havana Regiment, part of a total force of 754, who left New Orleans with Bernardo de Gálvez on January 11, 1780, and captured Mobile on March 14. The conquest of Mobile proceeded with eighteenth century gallantry. Before opening the attack, Gálvez sent ahead an aide, who was also a personal acquaintance of the British commander of the fort, to request immediate surrender. Dining together in Mobile, the two men drank to the health of their opposing sovereigns, and discussed the relative advantages in the prospective battle. The British commander politely declined to surrender, but graciously sent Gálvez gifts of mutton, chickens, fresh bread and wine. Gálvez returned the compliment with Bordeaux wine, tea, biscuits, corn cakes, oranges and Havana cigars. During the exchange of fire from March 9 to March 12, seven Spanish soldiers were killed. After resistance ceased at Mobile, the French and English citizens took an oath of loyalty to the Spanish king.

News of the victory, and his son's safety, reached Zéspedes when he was preparing to leave for Santiago de Cuba to serve as interim provincial governor. The captain general, an exceptionally conscientious man himself, persuaded Zéspedes in April of 1780 to take the temporary position even though at considerable personal sacrifice. As soon as he received the necessary papers, Zéspedes set out for Santiago. It was not an easy destination to reach, located over 600 miles away on the southeastern side of the island. The land route was used principally for carrying mail on horseback and driving farm animals to market. The road was always difficult for wheeled vehicles, and in the rainy season it was utterly impassable. Zéspedes spent several weeks en route, the discomfort of daily rough riding eased by the pleasures of famous Cuban hospitality at night. Inns were unknown but the proprietors of haciendas along the way maintained guest houses for occasional travelers who ventured through the interior of the island.

In returning to Santiago for the third time, Zéspedes was surprised to see how the city had changed. In 1770, the area still bore the scars of the terrible earthquake which shook the surrounding mountains in 1766. Ten years later, he found the rubble removed, the beautiful cathedral rebuilt and new residences constructed. Zéspedes bought a home suitable to his rank as district governor, the second most important political office on the island. His family soon joined him. Santiago, older than Havana, was really Cuba's most cultured community. A primary school, the first in Cuba, had been in operation since 1754. The city had a strong musical tradition, fostered by the choirmaster who had transformed the cathedral into a conservatory of music since his arrival in 1766. Talented citizens wrote music performed at religious services by an orchestra consisting of violins, double bass, bassoons, in addition to the organ and harp. Social evenings were spent singing Christmas carols during the holiday season, and by the more popular forms of *canciones* with titles such as "Disdain is a deep abyss" and "Passion is an inferno."[9]

The generally charming atmosphere which Zéspedes found in 1780 was unfortunately marred by complex local economic problems more formidable than any danger from the current state of war in the Caribbean. The Santiago garrison was theoretically supplied by a single annual shipment that often proved insufficient. Under the Spanish system of restricted trade, the city was

[9] Guerra y Sánchez, *et al., op cit*, II, pp. 301, 322.

not open to legal commerce with other Caribbean islands or the mainland. As a natural consequence, contraband trade had grown in volume, particularly with Jamaica, and constituted a serious problem to local authorities.[10] The illegal trade continued in spite of the war between Spain and England.

Monetary matters created further difficulties during Zéspedes' brief régime in Santiago. For about twenty years, Cuba and New Spain had suffered from currency devaluation. The milled edges of silver pesos coined in Mexico City had been pared off—some said for the use of silversmiths. The defaced money, called *macuquina*, was ordered withdrawn from circulation and replaced by new coinage in a royal order of 1771. But the following year the garrison at Santiago was paid with eighteen thousand pesos of *macuquina* brought from Vera Cruz. During these years in Cuba, there were actually two types of currency, the local currency and that of the rest of the empire called *moneda fuerte*. Santiago suffered from a scarcity of all types of coinage in 1780. In the wartime emergency which arose soon after Zéspedes' arrival, he consented to the printing of temporary paper bills called *papeletas* and the issuing of copper coins called *vellón*. Old copper coins minted locally in 1738 were reissued from the treasury and circulated for a brief period. These were temporary expedients to facilitate local trade, for the currency instability affected business life of the community for another decade.[11]

Zéspedes really expected that his interim appointment as governor of Santiago would be extended, but, in the general shift of positions on the island in 1781, his replacement arrived bearing a permanent commission signed in Madrid. In March of 1782, after only fourteen months of actual service in Santiago, he was back in Havana. Transportation to and from his temporary office had cost him over 5,000 *pesos fuertes*, more than a year's salary.

The status of the Revolutionary War had altered during Zéspedes' brief absence. He had left Havana during the high tide of excitement over Bernardo de Gálvez' triumphant march from New Orleans to Mobile in the spring of 1780. The exuberance over Gálvez' victory was tempered by the news of universal British success in Georgia and South Carolina in 1779 and 1780. While Zéspedes was in Santiago de Cuba, Gálvez successfully completed the West Florida campaign with the capture of Pensacola in May,

---

[10] Ricardo Rousset, *Historical de Cuba* (4 vols. Havana, 1918), vol. 3, p. 102.
[11] Guerra y Sánchez, *et al.. op. cit.*, p. 257

1781. Spanish military strategy called for Gálvez to attack Jamaica immediately following the fall of Pensacola, but a series of misfortunes combined to make this project unfeasible. In the first place, Gálvez was delayed in organizing the Jamaica expedition by a rebellion of English subjects in the Natchez district. He did not reach Havana until August, 1781. Next, an uprising in New Granada, known as the *Comunero* revolt, called away seven ships and a regiment of soldiers, depleting the available military force. Plans for the conquest of Jamaica came to a standstill when the British gained naval supremacy in the Caribbean by defeating the French fleet.

By the end of the year 1781, the significant phase of the warfare arising out of the American Revolution was concluded. The British surrendered at Yorktown in October, 1781, although they did not withdraw from Charleston until December of 1782. In Europe, the Spanish army abandoned the siege of Gibraltar in 1781. With all the manifold problems of his empire, Charles III was ready to make peace, for there was an Indian uprising in Peru that year as well as the revolt in New Granada.

Although the principal engagements of the American Revolution were over when Zéspedes returned to Havana in March, 1782, a final spurt of military activity was just beginning in the Caribbean. He found a bustle of activity at military headquarters and in the harbor. Bernardo de Gálvez, unable to carry out the Jamaica campaign, was completing final arrangements for a lesser expedition to seize the Bahama islands, headquarters for British privateers preying on Spanish shipping. As a result of his victory at Pensacola, where the siege ended shortly after a lucky shot exploded a British powder magazine, Gálvez became the great Spanish hero of the American Revolution. The king granted him the title of count, promoted him to the rank of lieutenant general, and commissioned him governor of West Florida as well as Louisiana. But with all his honors and increased prestige in the army, Gálvez could not secure sufficient aid from the navy to launch the attack on the Bahama islands. In desperation, he finally used ships from the South Carolina colonial navy to convoy the Spanish transports to the Bahamas. The military force was under the command of Captain General Juan Manuel de Cagigal, son of Francisco de Cagigal for whom Zéspedes had served as governmental secretary from 1747 to 1754. Although the troops had been ready to leave since January, the expedition did not sail until April 22, 1782. The British governor at New Providence surrendered on May 6.

Thereafter, Bernardo de Gálvez again turned his attention to plans for an attack on Jamaica, but the project had to be abandoned when word arrived that a preliminary peace treaty was signed in Europe in January, 1783. The conquest of the Bahamas was scarcely a worthwhile victory. Bernardo de Gálvez' use of the South Carolina navy drew severe criticism from government officials in Madrid who deplored direct cooperation with the American rebels. The Bahamas remained in Spanish control for less than a year. Ignorant of the preliminary peace terms, a band of South Carolina Loyalists sailed from St. Augustine and secured the surrender of the Spanish garrison in April, 1783. Under the Treaty of Paris in 1783, the Bahama islands returned to British authority.

During this last anticlimatic phase of the Revolutionary War, Zéspedes again was occupied with the defense of Cuba, but with greater responsibilities. While Captain General Cagigal, who had led the Bahama expedition, was in Guarico on the island of Española preparing to attack Jamaica, Zéspedes had charge of the government in Havana. From July to December, 1782, he held the position of *Teniente del Rey* and served as inspector of troops on the island. He also commanded a group of mobile units prepared to resist British invasion of the coast near Havana. The two governmental posts were distinct honors, but entailed heavy expenditures. Zéspedes found that his salary as inspector of troops was insufficient to pay the couriers. The summer of 1782 he was one of the Havana citizens who loaned money to the army during a financial emergency. A man of exceptional patriotic zeal, he liberally expended his personal funds in the royal service, accepting the situation as one of the sacrifices made by a good Spaniard in order to prosecute the war against the English.

The year following Zéspedes' return from Santiago was probably the most discouraging in his entire career, since he had no prospect of a position other than colonel of the Havana regiment with the beginning of the year 1783. Nevertheless, he was confident that his meritorious record would ultimately receive recognition, and he used every possible means to bring his case to the attention of the minister of the Indies, José de Gálvez. In July, 1782, he wrote directly, mentioning the financial outlay required by his recent temporary appointments, and pointing out that his predecessor in the regimental hierarchy had lately become governor and captain general of Puerto Rico. The position of colonel of the Havana regiment was usually the springboard for advancement to political office in one of the governmental regions of the Caribbean area. In November, he sent a more personal message by his son, Fernando, whose battalion apparently was transferred to Spain near the end of the American Revolution.

Zéspedes' ambitions were also furthered by Luis de Unzaga, new governor and captain general of Cuba, who arrived in Havana late in 1782. Unzaga felt well-qualified to recommend Zéspedes. As a superior officer, a former colonel of the Havana regiment, he had observed Zéspedes' qualities during his "formative years" in the regiment. Zéspedes had not seen Unzaga since the expedition to New Orleans in 1769, when Unzaga became governor and captain general of Louisiana after O'Reilly subdued the French inhabitants. Since Zéspedes had left New Orleans in 1770, Unzaga had served as governor of Louisiana until 1776, then transferred for a term as governor and captain general of Caracas in Venezuela before returning to Havana. Unzaga had a high opinion of Zéspedes and in March, 1783 wrote the minister of the Indies recommending him for a governorship, suggesting the district of Cumaná in eastern Venezuela.

Probably the most potent aid Zéspedes received came directly from Bernardo de Gálvez. After Zéspedes returned to Havana in 1782, the two men met frequently at military *juntas.* A common interest in Fernando de Zéspedes promoted their friendship. In April and May of 1783, Bernardo de Gálvez was engaged in healing the diplomatic wounds of war by entertaining the British Admiral Hood and Prince William of Lancaster in Havana. By this time, knowledge was current that East Florida as well as West Florida would go to Spain in the final peace settlement. The round of social functions honoring the British visitors provided many opportunities for personal conversation. In the course of numerous official and private contacts, Gálvez began to appreciate the old colonel's ambitions and decided to award him the governorship of East Florida. They came to an understanding on the subject even before news reached Havana of the signing of the definitive treaty of peace in June, 1783. When Bernardo de Gálvez arrived in Madrid in the fall, he brought with him a letter from Zéspedes to José de Gálvez mentioning the prospective appointment. The highly-favored young general enjoyed great influence over policies and appointments in the Florida provinces he had regained for Spain. The royal order, dated October 31, 1783, naming Zéspedes as governor at St. Augustine, with a promotion to the rank of brigadier of the armies, was delivered in Havana late in February, 1784.

In summary, this was the full story behind the royal order Zéspedes was acknowledging on March 3, 1784, the first day he corresponded with José de Gálvez in his new capacity of colonial governor. The letter from Spain that lay on his desk was obviously no surprise. Yet it was a distinct relief to receive formal confirmation of the appointment discussed the previous summer with Bernardo de Gálvez. Zéspedes knew that the post in Florida was no great prize, but at the age of sixty-four he was grateful for a governorship, and for a chance to prove that his usefulness in the royal service had not ended.

Actually, the newly appointed governor and the province he was chosen to rule had much in common. The ancient European rivalries that molded Zéspedes' attitudes and the eighteenth century wars that controlled his personal career, also determined the fate of the land called Florida. In the sixteenth century era of religious wars, the first town in Florida was established after reports reached Spain that heretic Frenchmen had settled on the east coast of Florida in 1563. Philip II, who relentlessly opposed the Reformation, designated Pedro Menéndez de Aviles to remove the French from Spanish territory. In 1565, Menéndez located the struggling Huguenot settlement near the mouth of the St. John's river. With the fury of religious fanaticism, he slaughtered all the French he could round up, giving the Indians their first bewildering view of Christians massacring Christians. To insure Spanish occupation of Florida, Menéndez immediately founded a settlement of his own, named St. Augustine, at the inlet he had used as a military base.

St. Augustine maintained a continuous, but usually hazardous, existence throughout colonial history. The early inhabitants fled to the pine woods when Sir Francis Drake, most famous of the Elizabethan "sea dogs," burned their half-built wooden fort in 1586. At the end of the sixteenth century, St. Augustine was one of about two hundred Spanish towns in the new world, and the only one within the present limits of the United States. It was the provincial capital governing an Indian mission system protected by outlying forts, similar to other frontier areas in Latin America. Grandchildren of the first Spanish inhabitants were born and baptized before the English founded Jamestown and Plymouth. The mission villages, supervised first by the Jesuit and later by the Franciscan orders, extended west of St. Augustine to the Gulf of Mexico, and north along the Atlantic coast, briefly reaching as far as Chesapeake bay. In the sixteenth century, all eastern North America was included in the vague geographic term "La Florida."[12]

During the seventeenth century era of colonial expansion, the British advanced steadily southward along the Atlantic seaboard toward St. Augustine, while the French limited their interest to the Gulf coast, a region of Florida always more closely tied to the development of the Mississippi valley. After the founding of Charleston in 1670, the influence of British Indian traders weakened the Spanish mission system, already frequently imperiled by Indian uprisings. The southeastern tribes soon developed pro-British and pro-Spanish sympathies and were thus drawn into the conflicts of the rival European powers. As early as the 1680's, South Carolinians made raids on the Florida Indian villages and sold the captives as slaves to West India planters.[13]

Florida's direct participation in the clash of European empires began with the eighteenth century's first major international conflict, the War of the Spanish Succession, called Queen Anne's War in English colonial history. Between 1702 and 1704, the Spanish mission system in Florida was completely destroyed, and the Indian population killed, captured or dispersed by the attacks of Governor James Moore of South Carolina. The raids extended to the Lake Okeechobee area by 1711.[14] Moore's invasion reached St. Augustine, where the inhabitants took refuge in the partially constructed Castillo de San Marcos while their homes were burned to the foundation.[15] The Spaniards retaliated by unsuccessfully attacking Charleston in 1706.

Later wars in the eighteenth century heightened Florida's role as a province on the border of rival empires. When Georgia was founded in 1733, carved out of original Spanish Florida, that border was marked at its present location, the St. Mary's river, just fifty miles north of St. Augustine. During the War of Jenkin's Ear, Governor James Oglethorpe of Georgia made two attacks on

[12] Claudius Ptolemaeus, *La Geografia di Claudio Tolomeo* (Venice, 1574). A copy of this atlas in the William L. Clements Library contains an excellent example of this early phase of cartography. The map showing the western hemisphere and expansive "La Florida" is obviously the most recently drafted of the maps in this edition. It is the only map that uses hemispherical projection and longitudinal lines. Others appear like flat wood cuts.

[13] Verner W. Crane, *The Southern Frontier, 1670-1732* (Ann Arbor, 1929 and 1956) pp. 23, 24, 114

[14] Charles H. Fairbanks, "Ethnohistorical Report of the Florida Indians." MS. P. K. Yonge Library of Florida History.

[15] Charles W. Arnade, *The Siege of St. Augustine in 1702* (Gainesville, 1959).

St. Augustine in the 1740's, using both land and naval forces. Florida residents also sent ships to try to capture Savannah. At the end of the Seven Year's War, Florida became one of the pawns in the peace settlement when European diplomats met in Paris in 1763 to resolve the military action in both hemispheres. In 1764, St. Augustine, still the only European settlement in the Florida peninsula, was turned over to England, Spain's traditional enemy, and the three thousand inhabitants evacuated to Havana.

During the twenty year period of British control, East Florida experienced more sweeping changes than during the previous two hundred years as a Spanish colony. A combination of royal land grants, crop subsidies, and private investment promoted a plantation economy that spread along the seacoast and rivers within a radius of fifty or sixty miles of St. Augustine. Communication with Savannah and Charleston improved with the extension of the King's Road from the Georgia border to St. Augustine.

When the Revolutionary War broke out, raids and skirmishes commenced along the Georgia-Florida border. In 1778, the year France entered the war, Florida began to contribute to the overall strategy of the British army. The British immediately determined to seize Savannah and Charleston, the ports from which Congress was shipping tobacco, rice and indigo to repay loans secured from continental bankers. In September of 1778, a British contingent marched overland from St. Augustine and captured Savannah in December. Georgia remained in British control for the balance of the war. The same regiments from Florida advanced to Charleston in 1780, and sent back to St. Augustine as prisoners forty of South Carolina's leading citizens. Between 1778 and 1782, a deluge of five thousand whites and eight thousand Negroes fled from northern colonies to take refuge in East Florida, the only Loyalist territory south of Canada. After Spain entered the war in 1779, Florida was in a defensive rather than offensive position. The British realized that Bernardo de Gálvez might include the conquest of St. Augustine in his Caribbean campaigns.

The Second Treaty of Paris ending the American Revolution was signed in 1783, redrawing the map of North America for the second time in twenty years. The new map limited England to Canada, and recognized the existence of the first independent nation in the western hemisphere. Spain regained both East and West Florida, and the Island of Minorca which the British had taken in 1713. She would have preferred to recover Gibraltar, yet East Florida was worth possessing for two reasons. First, in other hands, Florida might become the first stepping stone in the conquest of Cuba and the rich kingdom of Mexico. The proximity of the Florida coast to Cuba had always been a factor in Spanish defense plans. Second, the ocean route by which the wealth of Mexico, Peru and the Orient reached Spain, followed the Gulf Stream along the Florida east coast. For this reason, it would certainly be dangerous to have enemy settlements continue to expand in Florida. Under the terms of the Treaty of 1783, British residents of East Florida were given eighteen months to depart.

If the officials in Madrid attached rather negative values to East Florida, Zéspedes nevertheless believed the province possessed real potentialities, particularly in view of the rapid strides made by the British. In the previous Spanish era, before 1763, no official with power or influence had ever been interested in Florida. Zéspedes knew that far more auspicious circumstances prevailed at the outset of his own régime. It was a period of high morale in public administration. Capable and progressive members of the cabinet in Madrid were aided by an unprecedented group of admirable viceroys and lesser officials in the Caribbean and other colonial areas. More than any previous colonial secretary, José de Gálvez believed in strengthening the Spanish border provinces. He had actually visited Mexico in 1769, gaining valuable insight into colonial problems.

Zéspedes' contemporary officials were congenial men, sharing a common background of wartime experience and other ties, most of them connected with Bernardo de Gálvez, whose meteoric career was still in ascendancy. In 1784, the governor of West Florida was Arturo O'Neill, an officer Gálvez had placed in charge of Pensacola when the town surrendered in 1781. The governor of Louisiana, Estevan Miró, had served Gálvez admirably in the attack on Mobile and in quelling the rebellion of English subjects in the Natchez district in 1781. Like Gálvez, Miró had married the daughter of a famous French family in New Orleans, an added qualification for handling his province successfully. In the administrative hierarchy, Bernardo de Gálvez, governor and captain general of Louisiana and the Floridas, was directly above the three governors of the individual provinces.

The web of relationships including Bernardo de Gálvez extended far beyond the three border provinces under his immediate jurisdiction. Luis de Unzaga, governor and captain general of Cuba in 1784, was a brother-in-law of Bernardo de Gálvez. The two men had married sisters in a leading French family of New Orleans during their contiguous terms of office as governors of Louisiana. Reference has already been made to the fact that Zéspedes accompanied Unzaga, his former commanding officer, on the expedition to New Orleans in 1769 at the beginning of Unzaga's governorship. At the highest level in the colonial administration, Bernardo's father, Mattias de Gálvez, was viceroy of New Spain, a post secured through his brother, José de Gálvez, one of the most influential figures in the court of Charles III. The viceroyalty of New Spain included the Floridas and Louisiana, Cuba and Puerto Rico, Texas, California, Mexico and Central America.

Before 1763, St. Augustine was a rather inconsequential settlement, so remote that it was almost insular. Pensacola, founded a century later had the same limitations. Both were lonely outposts on the southeastern American continent with no Spanish settlement on the hinterland closer than the Texas frontier. In the post-Revolutionary War world, however, St. Augustine's position was vastly different. By retaining the Louisiana territory and regaining the Floridas, Spanish possessions on the American mainland now extended from the Atlantic ocean along the Gulf coast, and spread west of the Mississippi river to the Pacific. In 1784, the Spanish empire achieved the peak of expansion in the New World. St. Augustine, protected by the Castillo de San Marcos, lay at the eastern end of a chain of fifteen smaller forts along a thousand mile frontier ending in the Illinois country. On that frontier, Spain no longer faced a familiar colonial rival, but a new independent nation of uncertain future and as yet undetermined characteristics. Considering these new factors, Zéspedes found a definite challenge in the Florida governorship. The old army officer approached his task with youthful vigor and determination to distinguish himself in the royal service. In trying to strengthen the border province of East Florida, Zéspedes utilized every facet of his background and experience: his prestige as a native Spaniard; his long record of military service; and his knowledge of British strategy, Indian warfare, the colonial economy and time consuming governmental procedure.

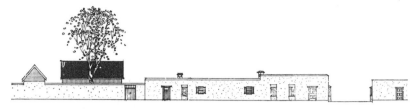

II

Arriving In East Florida

GOOD weather in Havana on June 19, 1784 forecast a pleasant journey to St. Augustine for Governor Zéspedes and the occupation force selected to re-establish Spanish mandate over East Florida. Before the morning heat settled on the city the previous day, the last officials and their families had hastened to the ships ready for departure. Zéspedes had arranged to close his Havana residence, pack the necessary household possessions, and take his family to his new post. The older sons, Fernando and Thomas, were with army regiments in Spain. The two younger sons were still under his immediate supervision in the Havana Regiment, Vicente Domingo as a sublieutenant and Antonio as a cadet, and both were included in the troops destined for the St. Augustine garrison. The young men were elated because Captain General Unzaga had recommended them for promotions as soon as their father received official notification of his governorship. Other members of the family accompanying him were his wife, Doña Maria Concepción, and his two attractive daughters, Dominga and Josepha, who were all excited over the prospect of their first voyage away from their island home. With their small pieces of personal luggage, they went by carriage to the wharf through deep-rutted streets crowded with the heavy traffic of drays loaded with boxes of sugar. In some of the narrower passages, the air seemed particularly oppressive with the rancid odor of *tasajo*, the salt meat serving as the

23

staple food for the poorer folk of the city.[1] In a short time they
perceived the forest of masts in the busy Havana harbor, and uti-
mately were escorted to their quarters aboard the *San Matias*.

The little armada heading for East Florida included fifteen vessels carrying five hundred troops, ammunition and supplies, and
the members of the military, hospital and treasury staffs who with
their families totaled several hundred additional government dependents. The brigantine, *San Matias*, mounting eighteen guns
led the convoy commanded by her captain, Pedro Vásquez. As
they moved out of the inner harbor, the passengers came in view
of a palm-bordered shoreline and small farming villages at the base
of the hills surrounding the broader bays of the trefoil-shaped harbor. Forming a line, the ships maneuvered toward the main channel
and the half-mile passageway providing access to the open sea. At
the ocean entrance, they passed beneath the rebuilt Morro Castle,
now guarded by new fortifications on La Cabana hill to the rear.
Sailing directly north until they sighted the first of the Florida
keys, they soon turned east, gaining speed as they entered the Gulf
Stream.

The swiftness of the current at this point results from the fact
that masses of water sweeping west along the north coast of South
America become bottled up in the Gulf of Mexico where sea level
is eighteen inches higher than at the equator. The so-called "river
in the sea" forces it ways through the narrow exit between the
tip of Florida and the northern coast of Cuba, disgorging a volume
of water equivalent to ten thousand Amazon rivers, moving at an
average speed of four miles an hour. In 1513, the Ponce de Leon
expedition encountered the remarkable current which became the
official route for shipping the wealth of the Indies to the Kingdom
of Castile. One of Ponce de Leon's pilots, who was later with
Cortés when the Aztec capital in the Valley of Mexico capitulated
in 1521, recommended the Florida strait as an obscure, pirate-free
route for sending gifts of Indian treasure to the king. Up to that
time, the common sea route was through the Old Bahama Channel,
along the north coast of Cuba. Throughout the sixteenth century
traffic increased on the portion of the Gulf Stream that swirled
through the Gulf of Mexico, rounded the tip of Florida, and carried ships out into the Atlantic Ocean where they could sail eastward to Spain. Precious metal from Peru was brought up the
western coast of South America and across the Isthmus of Panama

---

[1] Alexander von Humbolt. *The Island of Cuba*, with a preliminary essay by
J. S. Thrasher (New York, 1856), pp. 104, 106.

to Puerto Bello on the Caribbean coast, where it was put on board vessels joining the homeward bound fleets. After the Philippine trade developed late in the century, the Manila galleons brought silks and spices to Acapulco, on Mexico's Pacific coast. Goods from the Orient were then carried on mule-back across the mountains to Vera Cruz for transhipment. Spanish pilots were under oath not to reveal any information about the intricacies of the current, and knowledge of the Gulf Stream did not become general until about 1770, when the name first began to appear on maps.[2]

After skirting the keys, the course of the *San Matias* continued northward with the Gulf Stream, paralleling the Florida coast for over five hundred miles. With the aid of a spy glass, important landmarks were visible to the Zéspedes family and other passengers in the convoy. To a number of sailors, soldiers and staff members, this was familiar territory, for they had lived in St. Augustine before 1763, and some were returning with children reared in Havana while the British occupied East Florida. One of the first notable points was Cape Florida, located at the extremity of a key south of Biscayne bay, reputedly a favorite pirate lair. Near the entrance to the Santa Lucia river rose the hill called *"La Ropa Tendida"* by the Spaniards, and "The Bleach Yard" by the English, because its white-spotted surface gives the appearance of laundry spread out to dry in the sun. Further north, the forty-mile long island near Hobe inlet could be identified by cliffs of blue stone, the first rocks emerging high out of the water along the beach. Sandier sections of the island were the rendezvous of loggerhead turtles, who came in large numbers in the spring to lay their eggs. For this reason, the island became the resort of bears that came to eat turtle eggs. About twenty miles below Cape Canaveral, acute observers could detect an inlet to the Indian River, hunting area of the most southerly tribal group in contact with authorities at St. Augustine. The coast between this point and the Bleach Yard was the scene of one of the most disastrous losses in Spanish naval history in 1715, when fourteen galleons loaded with gold and silver were blown ashore during a savage northeast gale. As late as 1770, English surveyors observed that Spanish doubloons and pistareens usually washed up on the beach

---

[2] Edward W. Lawson, *The Discovery of Florida and its Discoverer, Juan Ponce de Leon* (St. Augustine, 1946), p. 36. See also, Hans Leip, *The Gulf Stream Story* (London, 1957), pp. 48-49, 57, 117.

during strong east winds. One of the wrecked ships, identified as
a hired Dutch vessel, lay in only twenty feet of water.[3]

Approaching Cape Canaveral, the *San Matias* tacked to the
east to avoid the principle hazard along the east coast of Florida.
Reefs surrounding the cape extend over twenty miles out to sea,
the shallow green waters flecked by whitecapped waves where
the ocean swells break over the sandbars. By noon on June
26, Governor Zéspedes could see Fort Matanzas, the outpost
fourteen miles from St. Augustine guarding the southern approach to the provincial capital. At this point the Matanzas
river enters the sea between the mainland and Anastasia island.
The fortified stone tower was built at the site where Menéndez
de Aviles ordered the massacre of the French settlers in 1565, and
the name Matanzas is literally translated "the slaughters." Sailing close to the outer shore of Anastasia island, the *San Matias*
and three other ships of the convoy anchored off the bar at two
o'clock in the afternoon of June 26, after a relatively short trip
of eight days.

Governor Zéspedes had made comprehensive advance preparations for a ceremonious arrival in St. Augustine, and for a smooth
transfer of the province to his command. In Havana, he began to
collect his staff and to gather pertinent information about the state
of affairs in Florida as soon as his first official communication arrived from José de Gálvez. Among other official papers he received
from the colonial secretary was a copy of an order, dated November 25, 1783, for Thomas Hasset, an Irish priest temporarily residing in Philadelphia, to proceed to St. Augustine. Since Zéspedes was concerned about the rapid or even safe arrival of the original
communication, he forwarded a copy of the order with a personal letter on February 28, 1784 in the care of one of his commercial connections, a captain sailing immediately for Philadelphia. Zéspedes hoped that Father Hasset, destined to be the principal religious figure of his province, might be awaiting him in
St. Augustine.

Of all the staff members, Zéspedes selected only the secretary
of government, Captain Carlos Howard, and his assistant. Captain Howard, a cultured individual in his middle forties, had served
with Spanish forces since 1761 in Portugal, Algiers, Brazil and
Santo Domingo. An officer in the Hibernia Regiment, one of the
units represented in the occupation force, Carlos Howard had

---

[3] Bernard Romans, *A Concise Natural History of East and West Florida*
(New York, 1775), pp. 286, 282, 266-267.

secured his captaincy in 1780 through the patronage of Bernardo de Gálvez. During the latter part of the American Revolution, he had aided the secretary to the captain general of Cuba with the translation of secret documents. The political understanding gained by this experience, his facile use of French and English, and general social skill, combined to make the talented Irishman a valuable member of the occupation force. Zéspedes had urgently requested a legal officer, called an *assessor* or *auditor de guerra*, for his staff, but to his great regret none was provided, although such an official was usually included in a military staff.

Before leaving Havana, Zéspedes gained a limited insight into the problems awaiting him in St. Augustine. The captain general's staff found a trunk full of correspondence from officials of the previous Spanish régime in East Florida. The trunk, which had been filed away in 1771 according to the inventory, was delivered to Zéspedes early in March, 1784. In the latter part of March, he discussed Florida affairs with Brigadier José de Ezpeleta, who had just received a packet of correspondence from Governor O'Neill in Pensacola. The most important letter, written by the British governor of St. Augustine to O'Neill in September, 1783, recommended that the British firm currently handling the Florida Indian trade be allowed to continue in business to prevent this commerce from falling into the hands of the Americans. A letter from a mestizo Creek chief, named Alexander McGillivray, solicited Spanish aid in maintaining the British Indian trade. In conversation, more candid information was secured from Ezpeleta, who had been one of Bernardo de Gálvez' principal officers in the West Florida campaign and had recently returned to Havana from Pensacola. Zéspedes learned that some of the British violently resented the re-cession of East Florida and were reluctant to leave the province. He also heard about the belligerent anti-Spanish faction among the Florida Indians, who might create trouble when the British departed. On the other hand, Zéspedes learned that the governors of Louisiana and West Florida were planning a spring Indian congress to lay the basis for friendly relations with the important Creek tribe.

In view of the uncertainties in the Florida situation, Zéspedes immediately arranged to send ahead an advance party to announce his prospective arrival in St. Augustine, to place buoys in the harbar channel, and arrange housing for the incoming troops and staff. With Captain Howard in command, Zéspedes knew that the advance party would also serve as a reconnaissance mission. Captain Howard, treasury official Dimas Cortes and chief engineer Mariano LaRocque, along with a few troops left Havana in early April.

Zéspedes expected to follow within a few weeks, but delayed departure because insufficient funds were available for him to take along. The Cuban intendancy was very short of cash, and the warship bringing money from Vera Cruz had not arrived on schedule. The departure date, June 19, had been set when further postponement of the expedition to St. Augustine seemed inadvisable. The intendant was able to supply only 40,000 pesos, but provided brandy, sugar and tobacco that Zéspedes believed would suffice for Indian gifts. No word from the advance party reached Havana before Zéspedes set out, and he felt a little uneasy as he neared the Florida shore.

As soon as the *San Matias* lay safely at anchor, Captain Vásquez ordered the firing of two cannon shot, the prearranged signal to summon the harbor pilot who had come with the advance party. From the pilot, Zéspedes received the distressing news that Carlos Howard was ill, that the main bar at St. Augustine was temporarily closed, and that all the vessels of the convoy drew too much water to attempt entry into the harbor. Although he had set his heart on a dramatic arrival, Zéspedes realized that circumstances forced him to set aside his plans, at least temporarily. Wind, weather, tide and current conspired to delay his formal assumption of the governorship by a series of exasperating contretemps.

Just after high tide the following morning, June 27, Zéspedes came ashore in the pilot's launch with Lieutenant Colonel Guillermo O'Kelly, commandant of the detachment, and his adjutant, Captain Eduardo Nugent, both veteran officers of the Hibernia Regiment. Bernardo de Gálvez had recommended Nugent for a captaincy because of his outstanding exploits during the siege of Pensacola. Rolling heavily in the high seas, the little craft brought them close to the north end of Anastasia island where a stone watchtower was erected long ago to signal with flags the arrival of incoming vessels. As they rounded the end of the island and entered the protected harbor, Zéspedes saw directly ahead, rising from the shore of the Matanzas river, the thirty foot height of the Castillo de San Marcos with white-washed walls and red-painted watch towers silhouetted against the clear blue sky. To his right lay a sandy neck of land called Point Cartel. A short distance within the bar, an opening in the swampy expanse marked the mouth of the North river, a stream originating twenty miles north of town and flowing gently behind the coastal dunes into the harbor. Turning to his left, he looked across the Matanzas river, really an arm of the sea separating the fifteen mile length of Anastasia island from the mainland. As the launch approached the dock a few hundred feet south of the Castillo, Zéspedes caught his first view of the town destined to be his headquarters for the next six years.

From the water's edge, an oblong area called the "parade ground" or "plaza" extended virtually the width of the town. A guard house and sheds and stalls for selling fresh meat and garden produce occupied a portion of the plaza on the river side. Along the north and south borders of the plaza were double rows of orange trees planted by the first English governor, James Grant. Between the lines of foliage, Zéspedes could see the high wall before the Government House at the opposite end of the plaza. Above the trees protruded the wooden lookout tower atop the house, added to the structure to provide a view of the harbor and surrounding landscape.[4]

Looking down the narrow streets opening off the parade, Zéspedes realized that the town resembled a village in Andalucia, except where peaked roofs replaced the flat *azoteas* of traditional Spanish and Arabic architecture. A solid line of walls and garden fences bordered the street, with wooden balconies projecting above the roadway. Within the enclosures were growing many varieties of citrus trees—lemons, limes, oranges and shaddock, ancestor of the grapefruit—but only the lean boughs of the fig supported ripening fruit at this season of the year. The carved oak doorways, opening off inner courtyards, were protected from the sun by grape arbors. With further attention to local wind and weather conditions, homes had large windows only on the east and south, small windows toward the west and often no openings at all on the north so that winter winds could not penetrate.

St. Augustine was about three-quarters of a mile long and less than half a mile wide, situated on a peninsula between the Matanzas river and Maria Sanchez creek, a rivulet entering the river in marshy land at the southern point of the town. The old defense line ran behind the Government House, provided with the additional protection of a *luneta*, or semicircular bulge in the line, directly at the rear of the property. The defense line had been built with redoubts approximately three hundred feet apart, or about

---

[4] George R. Fairbanks, *History of Florida* (Philadelphia, 1871) pp. 129, 165, 188 and 241.

the length of a musket shot. Earthwork fortifications were also
planted with a cactus hedge, whose spiny blade-shaped leaves gave
it the name of Spanish bayonet. St. Augustine at this time had
less than three hundred houses—and only half were in good condition—spread along the three main streets paralleling the river,
with a few dwellings located on the eight transverse alleys.

The more substantial buildings, including most of those Zéspedes saw near the plaza, were constructed of coquina rock. Coquina, as the name implies, was composed of layers of marine
shells compressed below the surface of the earth. It was soft and
easily cut, but hardened in drying to give the appearance of stone.
Coquina, quarried on Anastasia island and brought across the
Matanzas river by barge, was first used in building the Castillo
de San Marcos. Later it became the common material for other governmental buildings and better residences, as well as foundations
of wooden buildings. In two story homes, usually the first story
was made of coquina with the second floor constructed of a lighter
material of lime and oyster shells called "tabby." The term "tabby" is probably derived from the Spanish word *tabique* meaning
thin wall. Spanish descriptions of buildings in St. Augustine used
the term *tabique de hostion,* meaning "a light wall of oyster
shells." Heavier construction was called *mamposteria,* a Spanish
word defined as "rubblework masonry" and used in describing
typical houses of Andalucia. In St. Augsutine, cypress shingles
covered the slanted roofs of the more recent buildings. Poorer
structures, hastily erected for the British refugee population, were
of planks, split logs, or even of woven cane plastered with mud and
clay, with palm-thatched roofs and pounded earth floors.

The arrival of the Spanish delegation had already been announced when Zéspedes and his two officers landed. With the
minimum of formality, Zéspedes delivered to Governor Patrick
Tonyn the official papers signed by George III and forwarded from
London to Madrid and Havana before reaching their ultimate
destination. Among the letters was one from Luis de Unzaga mentioning the delicate situation regarding the Island of Providence.
According to the provisions of the peace treaty, Providence was to
be delivered to the British authorities at the time East Florida was
received by the Spanish governor. Diplomatic representatives in
Paris had never recognized the fact that the Island of Providence
was re-taken by Florida Loyalists uninformed of the status of
peace negotiations. As captain general of Cuba, Unzaga had tried
to send a Spanish governor to Providence to hold office until the

provisions of the peace treaty could be fulfilled properly, but the
English president of the Providence council refused to give up even
nominal and temporary control over the island. Zéspedes decided
it was wiser to ignore this problem, leaving it for solution by correspondence between other British and Spanish officials.

The first brief opening reception completed, Zéspedes went on
to inspect the Government House. He found the building in la-
mentable state to be called an official residence. The place had
been unoccupied for many years, but it had been used as a theater
the previous year for the presentation of a British comedy. The
broad balcony overlooking the plaza, and the handsome Doric entry
gate in the high masonry walls surrounding the property, gave a
hint of former grandeur. Besides the main residence, the block of
property included an assortment of outbuildings, a stable, servants
quarters, a large cook house with adjoining eating space, and a
row of privies behind the hedge of the rear patios. In the previous
Spanish régime, the governor's residence had been famous for its
spacious quarters and beautiful grounds, with many classic gate-
ways and ornamental porticos. Behind the patios, gates led to
the orchard of nineteen Chinese orange trees, ninety-five sour orange
trees, sixteen peach, eleven fig, six pomegranate, and quince, cherry
and grapefruit trees, and a grape arbor. In 1784, the former
orchard and garden were a shambles, as a result of a severe frost
in 1767, subsequent neglect and vandalism. Here, as elsewhere in
St. Augustine, British soldiers had cut down trees and ripped off
accessible wooden framework for firewood.

Entering the residence, the footsteps of Zéspedes and his attend-
ants resounded dully in the immense hall and salons on the first
floor. The incoming governor glanced around briefly before ascending the sweeping staircase, supported by three pillars, to reach
the second floor. Here he paused on the balcony to look down at
the plaza before climbing the observation tower. From this vantage
point, he could survey the entire town and environs. The skyline
at the northern end of town was dominated by the Castillo. A
line of earthworks and a deep ditch, similar to the defense line on
the western side of the town, extended from the Castillo across
the peninsula to the San Sebastian river. Near the middle of the
line was the city gate, guarded by two stone sentry towers, where
the main road from Georgia crossed a bridge to enter the town.
Outside the city walls to the west and north were garden plots,
groves and orchards, pastures, and a few small huts. To the east,
Zéspedes had a clear view of the watch tower on Anastasia island

and the harbor entrance. At the southern extremity of the town, beyond the district of residences and small shops, were the soldiers barracks. The old Franciscan monastery constructed on stone, with a British-built wooden addition, was the better of the two housing units. The second wooden structure put up at the beginning of the British régime was already badly rotted. Since the British troops had not yet left, Zéspedes understood that conditions might be crowded temporarily.

Zéspedes left the premises with the feeling that his wife and daughters would be utterly dismayed by the appearance of their new home. The stained walls and ceilings indicated a leaky roof, and indeed during the family's first weeks of occupancy, buckets stood in practically every room, for scarcely a day passed without a sudden shower or heavier storm. Considerable effort would be required to counteract the odor of mildew, and the spiders, roaches and lizards who ran freely through the empty building. But these were not his concern. Taking over the government of the province had to remain uppermost in his mind.

British authorities in St. Augustine offered their assistance with the immediate problem of unloading the vessels waiting outside the bar. Zéspedes chartered ten small sloops and schooners to speed the task, first of all delayed by a three day spell of bad weather that whipped up suddenly after the *San Matias* arrived. The night of June 29, the convoy rode out a severe storm, but the shuttle service began the following day and continued steadily for a week. Zéspedes was still concentrating on his plans for an impressive ceremony taking possession of East Florida. With this objective in mind, he had sent ahead four twenty-four pound cannons aboard the gunboats bringing Carlos Howard and the advance party. But the gun carriages and ammunition were buried deep beneath ordinance supplies in one of the convoy vessels.

When it became evident that another period of bad weather was approaching, Zéspedes tried to notify Captain Vásquez to proceed to safe anchorage forty-five miles north in the St. Mary's river. The bar at the mouth of the St. John's river, although closer, was also too shallow for the ships from Cuba. It was impossible to carry out this safety measure, however, because the crews celebrating ashore in the various taverns did not return promptly to their ships. In the second storm on July 8, scarcely a vessel escaped injury as hulls battered together in the fury of the gale and ships were dragged out of position by the strong current. The toll of damage included lost anchors, spars, portions of masts and rudders, and

some deck gear. By making temporary repairs, the Spanish convoy
was able to start for St. Mary's harbor on July 11. Zéspedes
estimated that an additional two months would be required to complete the transfer of supplies back to St. Augustine, but the charter
rates would be reduced because British supplies were being carried
to their evacuation fleet already waiting in St. Mary's harbor to
depart for the Island of Providence.

With the convoy dispatched to safety, Zéspedes was ready to
turn his attention to the duties of his new governorship. The British chief justice, James Hume, held the opinion that Zéspedes was
solely responsible for the province from the moment he presented
his official papers to Governor Tonyn. On the other hand, Zéspedes demanded possession of the fort as one of the requirements
for beginning his personal régime. Governor Tonyn tried to avoid
a pompous ceremony, but Zéspedes was unyielding. The British
soldiers finally vacated the Castillo on July 11 and the Spanish
garrison moved in the following day.

The Castillo was a marvelous construction, as Zéspedes noted
during an inspection tour. Set solidly on an ancient shell mound.
the Castillo was constructed over a period of twenty-five years beginning in 1672. Entrance was possible only by a bridge across
the moat on the south side. To the right of the entrance was the
high ceilinged guard room, with sleeping quarters consisting of a
wide wooden platform raised from the floor. All the rooms of
the fortress opened off the central open area, and few had any
opening other than the windows facing the courtyard. Space was
allotted for powder and ammunition, food storage, a chapel, treasury, and sleeping quarters for the soldiers. Beneath the ramp
leading to the artillery positions on the parapet, there was also a
latrine designed to be flushed by the ebb and flow of the tide. The
Castillo, with walls up to twelve feet in thickness, had been besieged but never captured. With sufficient supplies in the interior,
it was claimed that a thousand people could take refuge within the
walls. The self-sufficiency of the Castillo was also indicated
by the presence of a deep well in one corner of the courtyard to
provide an ample water supply.

At four o'clock in the afternoon of July 12, the townspeople
and officers of both governments gathered to witness the ceremony
in which Governor Tonyn and Brigadier General McArthur
handed over the fort to Governor Zéspedes. Melancholy though
the spectacle may have been for the British residents, for Zéspedes
it was magnificent to see the white flag with the red cross of St.

Andrew rising to the top of the flagpole. The Spanish emblem was saluted by three rounds of musket fire and fifteen thunderous volleys from the four twenty-four pound cannon whose presence he had taken such pains to assure. Next morning, the Spaniards gave thanks to God for returning the province of East Florida by attending the *Te Deum* service conducted by Father Pedro Campos, who had come to East Florida with a group of Minorcan settlers in 1768. Since the days of Columbus, every Spanish *conquistador* included this religious ceremony in taking possession of foreign soil, and in varying tunes chanted "We praise Thee, O God," a hymn whose origin was traditionally associated with the baptism of St. Augustine. The same day, Father Campos gave Zéspedes memorials of two groups of residents desiring acceptance as Spanish subjects. The seventy-nine signers of the two memorials included survivors of a large British colonial expedition recruited in Greece, Italy and Minorca. They represented a total of 460 inhabitants, according to the Minorcan priest.

Gradually becoming familiar with the new environment, Zéspedes was surprised by the evidence of wealth poured into St. Augustine and the surrounding countryside during the British régime. Dona Maria Concepción quickly realized that the latest modes in dress, furniture, livery and carriage equipment were followed by the tiny local representation of fashionable eighteenth century society. Both the governor and his wife were particularly impressed by three suburban estates and plantations carved out of the wilderness. One of the most famous belonged to the retiring lieutenant governor, John Moultrie, who had constructed a luxurious mansion called "Bella Vista" where Woodcutters creek enters the Matanzas river four miles south of St. Augustine. The one thousand acre tract included a deposit of coquina used in building his fifty-two by forty-four foot home. The lower story was described as "rustic style," but the exterior of the second floor, whose planning included six bedrooms, followed the classic simplicity of Grecian design. Six arches supported the ceiling over the drawing room and dining parlor.

Bella Vista boasted ten acres of pleasure gardens, in addition to three hundred fenced acres of plantation crops such as corn, beans, potatoes and rice. Part of the land had been cleared for agricultural use earlier by the Spaniards, but John Moultrie extended the acreage to a mile's length along the waterfront. Among the peach, plum and banana trees where peacocks roamed, gravel walks led to the bowling green, fish ponds, special pens for Poland geese and pigeons, and the aviary. Moultrie's hobby of bee-keeping deserves special mention. Honey bees were not native to America, but near the beginning of the British régime were introduced into Florida and into Cuba, where they were brought by Spaniards evacuating East Florida. Possible the first honey bees were imported from Italy, or from Minorca, an island famous for its honey. At any rate, the bees thrived in the new surroundings. By 1772, they had spread as far west as Pensacola and by Zéspedes' time the collection of wild honey had already become a profitable forest industry.

Four and a half miles north of town, "Oak Forest," owned by Chief Justice Hume, occupied the two-mile distance between the North river and San Sebastian river. Although the place included a grove of young orange trees, swampy rice land and dairy cattle, the principal economic asset was the stand of tall oak trees sold for firewood and transported from boat landings on the shores of both rivers. Part of the sixty-acre estate was devoted to parks landscaped with clipped hedges and canals crossed by high arched Chinese bridges. The oriental theme was carried out in the ornamental fencing around the house and a Chinese gate.

Across the Matanzas river on Anastasia island, Jesse Fish had taken over an old Spanish estate and developed a ten-thousand-acre plantation famous for experiments in raising dates and olives. This was the third place of exceptional interest in the immediate vicinity of St. Augustine. Mr. Fish was among the first to export oranges, as well as a spirituous beverage called "orange shrub." His residence, more in the traditional style of a southern country house, had a steep roof and porches on two floors running the width of the house.[5] Governor Zéspedes sincerely regretted that Bella Vista and Oak Forest would be vacant after their British owners departed, but was cheered by the knowledge that Jesse Fish expected to remain in Florida. After seeing the local homes, Zéspedes doubted that any prospective Spanish settlers could afford to purchase the most handsome British residences. The English owners eventually received partial compensation for the loss of homes abandoned because of Florida's re-cession to Spain.

Of the fifteen hundred British residents still awaiting evacuation, several hundred were in St. Augustine, and the leaders of provincial society feted the incoming Spanish administration with a succession of dinners and balls. The five top British officers were all

[5] J. T. Van Campen, *St. Augustine, Capital of La Florida* (St. Augustine, 1959), p. 53. Ruins of the Fish residence were sketched in 1867.

present when Governor Zéspedes arrived. In addition to Governor Tonyn and his old crony Chief Justice Hume, these were Brigadier General Archibald McArthur, Indian Superintendent Thomas Brown, and Lieutenant Governor John Moultrie, who was about to leave for England. William Panton and John Leslie, partners in an Indian trading firm, were both on hand to welcome Zéspedes and to press their claims for continuing in business in East Florida. Indians who were curious about the type of treatment they might expect from the Spaniards came immediately to see the new governor, each anticipating some form of gift. Zéspedes was dismayed to find that the brandy and tobacco he had brought were not satisfactory presents, according to the advice he received from British superintendent Thomas Brown. But William Panton quickly provided colored cloth, knives, small quantities of powder and ammunition, and other items appropriate for the occasion.

All in all, the first two weeks in St. Augustine provided many pleasant interludes to balance the distressing experience at the harbor and attendant confusion of unloading, unpacking, and getting settled. The climax of the first round of international social life occurred on July 14, when Zéspedes issued a proclamation announcing the beginning of his régime in East Florida. In the evening, the British residents gave a ball in honor of the new governor and his family, and members of the civil and military staff. There is no indication that any of the British understood Spanish, or that the Spaniards knew English. Consequently a heavy responsibility for social intercourse, as well as inter-governmental business, fell upon the Irish officers of the Hibernia Regiment.

It is interesting to note that a more elaborate celebration of the return of Florida to Spanish possession took place the same date in far off Madrid, although Zéspedes probably did not know of the event unless he learned through personal correspondence or the later arrival of a periodical such as the *Gaceta de Madrid*. Charles III tried to curb expenditure of funds for public amusement, a form of economy unappreciated by the people of Madrid. But the most spectacular public celebration of his twenty-nine year reign took place on July 13, 14 and 15 of 1784. The immediate occasion was general rejoicing over the conclusion of war with Turkey, and the birth of twins in the royal family, but the recovery of the Floridas and Minorca figured prominently in the parade.

Spain's victory in recovering the Floridas and Minorca formed the theme of the third in a series of five allegorical floats. Central figures in the scene were three matrons in flowing Grecian costume.

who represented the three geographical units of East and West
Florida and Minorca. The matrons were bowing and offering a key
and staff to a fourth figure, representing the Spanish monarchy,
seated on a gilded throne. Following the float, walked a Minorcan
leading a mule and a South American leading a horse, both animals
bearing an assortment of products native to the countries they
represented. Associating Florida with South America in this way
was typical indication of European misinformation concerning
the geography of the western hemisphere. Bands and fife and drum
corps marched between the floats to maintain a general spirit of
celebration. At nightfall the leaders of the parade, forty soldiers
dressed in Albanian and Irish costume, drew up to the main square
in Madrid, the Plaza Mayor. Here a large wooden platform
had been erected and the entire area illuminated with lanterns and
candles. The platform soon became the scene of a huge masquerade
ball, with music provided by an orchestra in the pit below
Twenty thousand visitors, a large supplement to the 150,000
population, thronged the streets of Madrid on this joyous occasion.
On the night of July 14, the royal family retired from the scene of
festivities at a quarter to eleven, but dancing in the streets of Madrid
and in the ballroom in St. Augustine continued later.

One unfortunate incident, equally distressing to British hosts
and Spanish guests, marred the spirit of celebration in the Florida
ballroom on July 14, 1784. Suddenly disrupting the atmosphere
of flute and violin music, graceful minuets, polite conversation and
languorously waving fans, servants brought news to one of the
sponsors of the ball, James Farley, that eight of his negroes had
just been stolen. As a ripple of comment spread around the assembly, Mr. Farley hurried away from the scene of dancing to the
residence of Carlos Howard, but Howard had retired and refused
to be disturbed since he was still battling a stubborn attack of fever.
Next morning, however, Governor Zéspedes and his staff were confronted with the responsibility for administering justice in the
province, a task often demanding the proverbial wisdom of Solo-
mon.

Treasury Street

III

Some Problems of Coexistence

T HE THEFT of eight Negroes from Samuel Farley's residence on
July 14, 1784, during the inaugural ball, introduced Governor
Zéspedes to matters that became the basis of altercations with Governor Tonyn and a few British citizens during their joint residence in East Florida, a period ending in September, 1785. From
his brief interviews with Carlos Howard, Zéspedes had learned
that East Florida harbored a lawless element who operated in open
defiance of Governor Tonyn. Howard's independent investiga-
tions had revealed that trouble might be expected from an outlaw
gang, headed by Daniel McGirt, and from Loyalists plotting to
regain control of the northern section of Florida. A few individuals appeared to have connections in both dangerous groups.
Anxious to achieve a settled state before Zéspedes' arrival, Howard
had tried to get word to the outlaws advising them to seek amnesty
from the incoming governor. At the same time, he convinced the
militant Loyalists that any reasonable proposition would receive
careful consideration by the new Spanish administration. In his
opening proclamation of July 14. Governor Zéspedes included
measures designed to dispose of both problem groups.

For all its ornate phraseology, the proclamation had a few simple objectives. First of all, it referred to the peace treaty signed on
June 3, of 1783 and ratified on September 19, whereby the British residents of East Florida were to dispose of their property or
remove it before March 19, 1785. Furthermore, as the treaty

rather obscurely mentioned, if they could not dispose of their property within the eighteen months interval, His Catholic Majesty would grant them some extension of time. Secondly, all British subjects who wished protection of the Spanish government, with the idea of becoming Spanish subjects, were both invited and required to register with Captain Howard within twenty days.

The other two important points in the proclamation of July 14 concerned the administration of justice within the province. Since the governor wished to begin his régime with clemency, he invited any citizen who had incurred the displeasure of the British government, by committing crimes of disturbing the peace, to report and secure permission to leave East Florida, By this measure, Zéspedes hoped to rid the province of the McGirt gang and the Loyalists who plotted rebellion. As for legal disputes between the British residents, Zéspedes decreed that these disagreements be settled by British arbitrators. He also advised the British to live in harmony with those of their nation under Spanish protection.

These first orders of the Spanish administration were posted publicly, with English translations, early in the morning of July 14, and flaunted that same evening. The theft of Samuel Farley's Negroes was scarcely a complete surprise. It was common knowledge that the theft of these particular Negroes was not an isolated event, but was linked to a series of episodes in a longstanding local contest between Governor Tonyn and outlaw leader Daniel McGirt. In the ensuing months, Governor Zéspedes repeatedly became entangled with the interrelated feuds brought into the open by the first crime of his régime. Because of the many complications, Zéspedes did not arrange the return of the eight Negroes until May of 1785. Ridiculous as it appears in retrospect, the matter became a central focus of controversy between the British and Spanish governors.

In view of his contemporary importance, Daniel McGirt's role in Florida history under the British and Spanish régimes merits a brief review. A native of South Carolina, McGirt served as a scout for the Continental army during the opening years of the American Revolution. His initial quarrel with society occurred when a superior officer tried to gain possession of his fine horse, evoking an outburst of disrespectful language. In retaliation, the officer ordered McGirt flogged, courtmartialed, and thrown in jail, but the former scout escaped and moved his family to Florida Loyalist territory. Although he had a plantation near the St. John's river, he also lived by highway robbery and questionable transactions involving the theft and sale of livestock and Negroes. He soon became the avowed enemy of Governor Patrick Tonyn, who invariably referred to McGirt and his cohorts as "the banditti." In April of 1784, shortly before Carlos Howard arrived in St. Augustine, Tonyn apprehended McGirt and imprisoned him in the Castillo. He charged that McGirt had attacked the coach in which Chief Justice Hume was riding toward the St. John's river, and tried to steal the coach horses. Not long afterwards, McGirt gained his freedom by bribing the sentry who fled with him into the backwoods.

While under arrest in the Castillo, McGirt sold forty-six Negroes, some cattle and plantation tools to Francisco Sánchez, a Spaniard born in Florida who remained on his ranch during the British period. Sánchez likewise had a feud with Governor Tonyn. On Tonyn's orders, the provost marshal seized from Sánchez thirty-five of the forty-six Negroes. Tonyn justified his action by claiming that the bill of sale was fictitious and obviously a device to transfer McGirt's property to Sánchez' protection and thus out of reach of the law. Tonyn also believed that thirty of this labor crew had originally been stolen from another St. Augustine resident. Of the Negroes taken from Sánchez and placed in the custody of the British provost marshal, eleven unaccountably disappeared and eight were sold to Samuel Farley. These were the eight Negroes whose theft created a flurry on the night of the inaugural ball. Although Farley was confident that McGirt was responsible for their disappearance, Howard advised him to keep quiet until they were located.

Zéspedes preferred to postpone any drastic action against Daniel McGirt, hoping that his proclamation would motivate the entire gang to report and secure passports to leave Florida. He was encouraged by the fact that five of the men associated either with McGirt or the plot to retain control of the northern section reported immediately, requesting permission to emigrate to Louisiana. Within a week, McGirt at least went through the formality of registering at Carlos Howard's office.

After Zéspedes learned that other members of "the banditti" were afraid to come to St. Augustine because they feared being drafted into the light horse troop controlled by Governor Tonyn, he took the initiative in coming to terms with them. He believed that Tonyn had rescinded the draft order prior to his own arrival in East Florida. About ten days after the proclamation was issued,

Zéspedes decided to send out emissaries to the desperadoes living in hiding along the St. John's river, and urge them to report to authorities in St. Augustine and then leave the country quietly. Lieutenant Colonel Antonio Fernandez, an officer during the previous Spanish régime, headed the delegation including his son and six dragoons. It was Fernandez' suggestion that Daniel McGirt and Francisco Sánchez guide them through the backwoods wilderness and assure other members of the gang that it was safe to go to St. Augustine.

On the morning of July 27, Lieutenant Colonel Fernandez and his band rode north through the city gates on their mission to establish peaceful relations between the Spanish administration and the British renegades on the St. John's river. The confusing events in which they were involved the next three days could be classed as a comedy of errors, except that they were to delay the creation of civil order in Florida for six months. A complicating factor was the presence on the St. John's river of a second law enforcement body, Tonyn's personal light horse troop headed by Colonel William Young. With Zéspedes' consent, Colonel Young's troop continued to guard British plantations in the vicinity during the period of evacuation. Governor Tonyn provided letters of introduction for Lieutenant Colonal Fernandez to take to Colonel Young, whose headquarters was their first destination. Arriving at noon July 28, they learned that Young was absent in search of missing Negroes. After waiting overnight, Fernandez left behind his letter of introduction and went on to McGirt's farm, where very disturbing news greeted him.

From servants, Fernandez learned that Colonel Young had stolen pigs from the farm while McGirt was in St. Augustine reporting to Spanish authorities. Furthermore, Colonel Young had vowed to return with a larger force to take the rest of the livestock, declaring all McGirt's property should be forfeited to the British crown. Fernandez and his companions also heard that, while they were waiting at troop headquarters the previous day, Colonel Young had attacked members of the gang gathered at the home of Daniel Melyard to receive representatives of the Spanish government. Details of the encounter included the fact that Colonel Young fired on sleeping inhabitants of the Melyard house, stole their clothes and roundly flogged a frightened youth of fifteen in an effort to discover where McGirt had hidden Negroes. In the course of the fighting, a servant was killed and a horse stolen. After hearing this tale of combat, Fernandez left a guard at Daniel

McGirt's farm to prevent further violence, and returned to St. Augustine without ever meeting Colonel Young.

In the meantime, Colonel Young returned to his station where he found Tonyn's letter asking him to cooperate and show every courtesy to Lieutenant Colonel Fernandez. Young was not entirely to blame for taking the offensive against the McGirt gang. He was unaware of the proclamation granting a twenty day period for offenders to report in St. Augustine. The only reports he received from Tonyn indicated that Zéspedes concurred with Tonyn respecting operations of the light horse troop to protect plantations along the river. Young had been roused to action by the rumor that James McGirt, brother of Daniel, had gone to Georgia to recruit a band of one hundred fifty rebels to come down into Florida and destroy the station maintained by Young's light horse troop.

This incident, the result of a general misunderstanding and poor communication, provoked an increasingly caustic exchange of correspondence between the two governors for the following year. Both Fernandez and Young soon gave accounts of their unfortunately coordinated actions to their respective chiefs. Colonel Young believed that his bold offensive against the McGirt gang had prevented the arrival of their cohorts from Georgia, and calmed the inhabitants of the St. John's area who were preparing to move from the hinterlands to islands along the seacoast. Lieutenant Colonel Fernandez believed that leaving a guard at McGirt's farm quieted the backwoods inhabitants, who were about to join the outlaws in the belief that they would not have security under the new Spanish government. Zéspedes was angry because Tonyn had given assurance that Colonel Young would only act in a defensive capacity. Tonyn was furious to learn that protection had been provided for McGirts' property. It was unfortunately true that the McGirt gang now had a genuine grievance. Both governors understood the incident at Melyard's home snarled up matters so that it was difficult to proceed immediately against the McGirts.

Zéspedes soon realized that McGirt and his henchmen were taking outrageous advantage of the situation. They had no intention of leaving the province in spite of their formal declarations. As soon as he felt immune from Tonyn's ire, Daniel McGirt singled out Tonyn's friend Samuel Farley for persecution. McGirt began to boast about the theft on the night of the inaugural ball, and insolently claimed he would get more of Farley's Negroes. Farley drew up his legal case formally on August 16, claiming that McGirt planned the robbery executed by a half-breed, Jack Kinnaird, who had kidnapped the servants from Farley's kitchen. Zéspedes refused to allow the evidence to be brought before the arbitration board because Farley had refused earlier to serve as one of the judges although he had been a justice during the British régime. Zéspedes thought that, in view of his refusal to cooperate, Farley should be denied recourse to the tribunal. Zéspedes originally held off Tonyn's demands for McGirt's arrest by claiming that since the Spanish government came into power, McGirt had committed no proven crimes. This contention became very weak in the face of McGirt's bragging. After he attempted to knife one of Farley's servants on the street in St. Augustine, Tonyn allowed Farley to place his servants under guard on board a British ship in the harbor. Even there they were not safe, and three more disappeared. Farley claimed that this last crime also was planned by Daniel McGirt. Fearing the loss of additional property, James Farley abruptly left the province in October, 1784. Governor Tonyn pressed his demands for justice on the Spanish administration.

Zéspedes knew he was far from candid in his exchange of correspondence with Tonyn concerning the McGirt gang. He hoped that as the evacuation proceeded, the number of troublemakers would diminish. Fearing that strong action against McGirt might provoke severe attacks on British plantation along the St. John's river, he settled on keeping careful watch on movements of the gang. He really wished that residents of the river plantations would remain in the province under Spanish jurisdiction. One of the members of the gang, John Linder, Jr., was hustled out of the province in November by an escort of Spanish dragoons. He was classified as incorrigible after uttering vulgar remarks to the effect that the Spaniards could wipe their backsides with their proclamation. James McGirt was the only one to redeem himself in the eyes of the administration. He and his family settled down in St. Augustine and joined respectable society. The former British governor was relieved to be rid of the primary responsibility for dealing with "the banditti." But as long as Daniel McGirt remained at large, Tonyn could not refrain from offering strongly-phrased advice concerning the proper course for Zéspedes to follow. He persistently urged Zéspedes to take action against Francisco Sánchez, asserting that the Sánchez ranch provided a hideout for "the banditti" close to St. Augustine. In this way, the merits of Francisco Sánchez and the nature of his connections with Daniel McGirt also became a topic of debate between the two governors.

In his conversations with Sánchez before Zéspedes' arrival, Carlos Howard secured information that made the association with "the banditti" seem less reprehensible. For two centuries, Sánchez' forebearers had operated a cattle ranch in the Diego Plains eighteen miles north of St. Augustine. Francisco Sánchez, the only Spaniard with large property holdings to remain in East Florida during the British régime, had profited from the sale of fresh meat to the British garrison. But he was conscious of the fact that Governor Tonyn regarded him with suspicion as soon as Spain joined the war against England in 1779. The real feud between Tonyn and Sánchez dated from 1782, when Sánchez aided Spanish soldiers shipwrecked in a storm off the St. Augustine bar. The Spanish soldiers were part of the expedition from Cuba sent to capture the Bahama islands. On the return trip, their vessel had been captured by corsairs from the Bahamas, and at the time of the wreck they were already poorly clothed, hungry, and some were suffering from scurvy. When Sánchez learned that his countrymen were prisoners of the British garrison, he offered to provide both clothing and food, since the British commandant refused to supply fresh meat from his own supplies. After the Spanish soldiers were freed, Sánchez furnished a brigantine with all the provisions necessary to take them back to Havana.

In 1783, Sánchez had been the first person to bring news to Cuba of the forthcoming re-cession of the Floridas to Spain. During the visit, he presented himself to Zéspedes, declared his perpetual loyalty to Spain, and offered to supply the incoming Spanish garrison with fresh meat. While he was in Havana, over 700 persons including Negro refugees and Indians camped on his ranch and destroyed 400 head of cattle. A band of four robbers, apprehended by Sánchez' friends while ransacking his farm, were arrested and, although all confessed, only one was punished. Without the protection of the British governor, Sánchez felt forced to be friendly with McGirt in order to prevent the "banditti" from stealing the rest of the cattle. He insisted that the British governor had bribed men to testify against him, although Tonyn moderated his attitude after Sánchez refused to supply the British with fresh meat pending the arrival of Spanish troops. Sánchez was convinced that Tonyn deliberately tried to ruin him financially, and plotted the destruction of his property.

In view of these explanations, Governor Zéspedes was reluctant to proceed against Francisco Sánchez or place him in the same category with the "banditti." The new year, 1785, was ushered in with a final crisis concerning the McGirt gang. On New Year's eve, Zéspedes received word that Daniel McGirt was gathering a band of Georgians to make a large scale attack on the plantations under Tonyn's protection. So great was the emergency that he dashed to Tonyn's home and, with his inadequate command of the English language, communicated this alarming information. He now decided that the arrogant rogue had passed all limits of toleration.

On January 20, Daniel McGirt and five associates were arrested and locked in separate cells in the Castillo. Two other ringleaders were William Cunningham, also active in the Loyalist plot, and Stephen Mayfield, whose inn provided refuge for the worst criminal element in the province. The rural community of north Florida and south Georgia joined in giving thanks to Governor Zéspedes for their apprehension. Forty-seven leading citizens of the St. John's area signed a memorial directed to Zéspedes. Landowners on the Georgia side of the St. Mary's river communicated their appreciation through the state governor, who added that remnants of the gang had fled to the Saluda river region.

In spite of all his efforts to force the Spanish government to arrest members of "the banditti," Tonyn's attitude altered as soon as McGirt was safely locked in the Castillo. The appeals of Mrs. McGirt, a decent, well-liked woman burdened with a sizeable family, gained the sympathy of both Tonyn and Zéspedes. Moved by visions of these British subjects sentenced to labor in Spanish mines, Tonyn begged that they be sent to British territory for trial, but Zéspedes felt they were clearly under the jurisdiction of Spanish tribunals. He sent the six men to Havana in May, 1785 asking Bernardo de Gávez not to impose any severe punishment, but to prevent their return to Florida. When McGirt left the country, Zéspedes finally felt safe in authorizing the transfer of Farley's eight Negroes to his local attorney, and thus concluded that lengthy argument. McGirt's contact with Florida did not end in the spring of 1785. His partisans and associates, only vaguely identifiable, threatened the Spanish régime long past Zéspedes' term of office. McGirt spent the last years of his life in South Carolina. Zéspedes confronted the unsuppressable rogue on two later occasions.

The man who escaped from the Continental army jail in Georgia and the British-held fort in St. Augustine easily outwitted Spanish authorities in Havana. McGirt, Cunningham and Mayfield were released from prison in September, 1785 with instructions never to return to Spanish territory. After securing passports for the Island of Providence, the three men and a crew of four sailed from Havana on September 31. Just outside the harbor, a small boat overtook them and placed on board two Spaniards to pilot the vessel to East Florida. Sensing some nefarious objective, two of the crew abandoned ship and reported to authorities at Jaruco the real plans of the three Englishmen. Zéspedes was notified in November, 1785 that McGirt intended to hide among the Indians south of St. Augustine until he could slip into town at night to learn the state of his family and property. Consquently, the governor was not surprised when McGirt and Cunningham showed up with passports, explaining that their vessel had shipwrecked on the Florida coast. Mayfield had transferred to an English ship in the Keys and sailed directly to Providence. Zéspedes deported Cunningham to Providence in December, but the vessel was too small to accommodate McGirt and his large family. Daniel McGirt was confined in the Castillo until January, 1786 when his family accompanied him to the Bahamas.

In March, 1788, Daniel McGirt returned to St. Augustine, ostensibly to discuss his business affairs with Francisco Sánchez. On this occasion, Zéspedes permitted the two men to hold a brief interview in the presence of officers of the Hibernia Regiment, then sent McGirt back on the "Mayflower," the ship that had brought him from Providence island. The "Mayflower" sailed out of Matanzas bay, but on March 27 entered St. Mary's harbor on the Georgia border. McGirt's presence on the south bank of the river was reported immediately to Henry O'Neill, a former British soldier acting as border agent for the Spanish administration. Henry O'Neill "took the people who was most handy," according to his account, and arrested McGirt while he was eating supper the following evening. When the captain of the "Mayflower" pledged three hundred Spainsh dollars as bail, O'Neill released the troublemaker on condition he remain aboard the sloop. The "Mayflower" remained in the St. Mary's harbor about a week, apparently without further incident. Zéspedes requested the British governor of the Bahamas not to issue passports for McGirt to make future excursions to Florida. The American frontier produced a colorful array of semi-outlaws, but few were more bold and elusive than the Florida renegade, Daniel McGirt.

Of the two major problems facing the incoming Spanish administration—the outlaw activities and Loyalist plot—dealing with the militant Loyalists proved much simpler than handling the

McGirt banditti. Zéspedes felt that Carlos Howard deserved the perpetual gratitude of the Spanish government for placating British groups opposing the return of Spanish rule. He still retained a vivid memory of his experiences in New Orleans in 1769 when General O'Reilly summarily executed five French creoles and imposed severe prison terms on six others opposing the transfer of Louisiana to Spain. Because of Captain Howard's adroit management, he was not forced to consider such distasteful measures in Florida. When Captain Howard arrived in St. Augustine, Governor Tonyn made no mention of the militant Loyalists' activities, possibly because a budding rebellion really challenged his own authority within the province. He had tried desperately to gain the peaceful acquiescence of the colonists to the wishes of the King concerning the disposition of East Florida. Although Tonyn later minimized the danger, he was sufficiently alarmed in April, 1784 to send a confidential message to Brigadier General Archibald McArthur, commander of British forces in East Florida, warning him that an outbreak might occur.

Captain Howard, a skilled undercover operator, soon became familiar with all phases of the British resistance movement. He learned that many residents along the St. John's and St. Mary's rivers clung to the hope of finding some stratagem to enable them to remain in Florida. In their plantations, they had the heaviest investment in buildings, livestock, slaves and equipment. A small percentage considered trying to maintain control over the area between the two rivers, without submitting to Spanish jurisdiction. A few were even bolder in considering a general protest of the entire province, counting on a group of two hundred St. Augustine residents to lead the opposition to Spanish authority in the capital. Howard contracted various Loyalist leaders, but concentrated his attention on John Cruden, the most outspoken representative. Cruden's wildest ambition, revealed in letters to the British ministry in April of 1784, aimed toward the recovery of "the revolted colonies in America" using East Florida as a base. Subsequent disunity in the underground movement aided Howard's task. Cruden enlisted the support of men associated with Daniel McGirt, but late in May of 1784 — after McGirt and the British sentry fled from the Castillo — he offered his services to Tonyn to pursue members of "the banditti."

Governor Zéspedes, who at first feared a general uprising of the British inhabitants, was relieved to observe the rapid disappearance of these symptoms during the summer of 1784. Mollified by Howard's apparent interest in his project, John Cruden addressed an open petition to Charles III, composed at St. Mary's in October 1784, requesting the cession of the St. John's-St. Mary's area to the "United Loyalists." Before sailing from St. Mary's harbor that month, he paid a sociable visit to Captain Pedro Vasquez on the neighboring ship *San Matias,* inviting the Spanish captain to join him in a toast on the birthday of Lord Cornwallis. The *San Matias* remained in St. Mary's harbor throughout the period of the British evacuation.

Although the Loyalist plot created scarcely a ripple in East Florida when the change of government occurred, both British and Spanish authorities felt varying degrees of apprehension concerning the peaceful transfer of the province. Apparently, the danger of uprising was very real before Captain Howard arrived. Fact and rumor spread rapidly through complicated international communication channels. Tonyn's confidential reports of the resistance movement, sent to the British colonial office June 14, 1784, somehow reached the Spanish ambassador in London, who sent copies of the alarming revelations to Madrid.

Rumors became even more factual while traveling through Georgia to Charleston. Charles Pinckney, member of Congress from South Carolina, brought his information to the Spanish diplomatic representative in Philadelphia, Francisco Rendon. In a confidential letter to José de Gálvez, written June 20, 1784, Rendon declared that the inhabitants of St. Augustine had taken up arms to resist delivery of the province to Spain, and had fortified themselves in the Castillo. In Spain, couriers rushed the report of uprising to Cadiz, where Bernardo de Gálvez was preparing to sail for Cuba early in September, 1784. Gálvez did not learn of the placid transfer of sovereignty in East Florida until February, 1785, when by a devious route he reached Havana to succeed Unzaga as captain general of Cuba. The spring of 1785, Zéspedes and Carlos Howard were still in correspondence with John Cruden, the eccentric leader of the Loyalist movement, providing a passport for him to interview Bernardo de Gálvez in Havana. Plans of the United Loyalists never passed the literary stage. When he returned to London, Cruden published a patriotic but visionary pamphlet and seriously considered persenting his ideas personally to the Spanish court in Madrid.

The numerous ramifications encountered in settling the theft of Farley's Negroes convinced Zéspedes that the Negro population constituted the most serious threat to local harmony and civil order.

Negro slaves were the most valuable movable and negotiable capital in the province, the object of the cupidity of unscrupulous individuals other than the McGirt banditti. Throughout the American Revolution, Negroes had been plundered, stolen, and shifted about like livestock, a part of the southern population displaced and uprooted during the period of hostilities. The Negro population in East Florida, also included many such refugees, and a small percentage who had been emancipated as a reward for service in the British army. Many fugitives, free and slave, received temporary protection, then were taken out of the province for sale in the West Indies. Even free Negroes and Mulattoes had little personal safety during the evacuation procedure, but were in danger of being seized and held under false claims of ownership.

Zéspedes tried to arrange for handling disputes concerning Negroes, and other property, by creating an arbitration board as one of the provisions of his first proclamation, July 14, 1784. Carrying out this provision, he appointed two highly-respected local merchants, John Leslie and Francisco P. Fatio, to serve as judges in disputes involving British subjects. Under these arrangements, he hoped to remain aloof from the host of minor squabbles bound to arise during the course of the evacuation period originally scheduled to end on March 19, 1785. Zéspedes gave instructions that in cases of property disputes, the arbitration board could assign temporary possession, and the losing party had the right to enter a formal suit to regain the property. In practice, the majority of cases brought before the board of arbitration involved questions of slave ownership.

With the idea of clarifying the status of the Negro population, Zéspedes issued a proclamation on July 26, 1784, which forbade embarkation of any passenger, white or Negro, without a license signed by the governor and imposed a fine of 200 *pesos fuertes* per passenger to be divided between the trial judge, the royal treasury and the informer; and any slaves whose departure was attempted without a license were to be forfeited. A second provision of the proclamation ordered all persons who had in their possession Negroes of indeterminate ownership to declare them within eight days if they lived near the city, or in twenty days if they lived far distant. Any person who harbored or procured the escape of a slave was subject to the laws of Spain. This provision applied equally to British subjects received under Spanish protection. Finally, all vagrant Negroes without papers to prove freedom were ordered to register with Carlos Howard within twenty days and procure permits to work and be hired, signed by Zéspedes. Any Negro apprehended without papers indicating his free status or a work permit would be declared a slave of the king.

Zéspedes thought this regulation would establish the status and ownership of every Negro and Mulatto in the province, and reduce the number of cases requiring a verdict from the British arbitration board. But the proclamation aroused a violent reaction from British Chief Justice James Hume, who received a copy two hours before it became public. Hume pointed out that enforcement ran counter to the treaty provisions guaranteeing the British residents the right to remove their property unhindered, and that many slaves changed hands without formal bills of sale. Furthermore, there were free Negroes who had lost their papers during the war who were illiterate and therefore not responsible for following the orders in the proclamation.

The provision of the proclamation that was an anathema to Hume was the one granting the judge and informer portions of the fine, and custody of forfeited slaves. Hume said such an arrangement was unthinkable under British law, but Zéspedes countered with the statement that there were many systems of law other than the British. Nevertheless, Zéspedes could see the difficulties of enforcing the proclamation if it conflicted with the provisions of the peace treaty. He did not attempt any strenuous enforcement program, but insisted on permits for taking slaves out of the province. He was satisfied to have some of the independent Negro population take advantage of the opportunity to secure work permits which protected them from false claims of ownership.

The board of arbitration had difficulty in maintaining a reputation for impartiality, and decisions made by Francisco Fatio were apt to draw severe criticism from Tonyn. In operation, the board had little formal legal procedure, not at all surprising since neither Leslie nor Fatio were lawyers. Most of the time, the judges knew the contending parties, and were able to arrive at a satisfactory agreement. Fatio was perhaps overimpressed by his new position as judge in the community, and on occasion took on the role of baliff and justice of the peace. But any judge can promote the miscarriage of justice by relying on circumstantial evidence. A single case of this nature aroused tremendous public sympathy in St. Augustine for over a month, beginning on September 24, 1784. The central figure in this particular controversy was Louisa Waldron, an illiterate woman of small property living about a mile north of town where an old wooden post defense line, known as the stockade, extended from the San Sebastin river to the North river.

The case concerned the disappearance of a Negro servant, Lucy, who was referred to in all testimony as "the wench." Louisa Waldron was sometimes called "Mrs. Welsh," but more often "Mrs. Proctor," with no apparent explanation. The servant in question was sold to Lorenzo Rodriguez, Spanish ship captain, when he returned to St. Augustine, because she twice ran away from her British owner and on both occasions was found with Louisa Waldron. When the servant disappeared from the home of Captain Rodriguez, she was rather naturally sought at Louisa Waldron's. First a party of Spanish sailors then a group of British sailors spied on the house and brought evidence to Judge Fatio which satisfied him that the girl was in hiding again.

On September 14, 1784, Francisco Fatio sent Manuel Solano and a Spanish comrade to bring in Louisa Waldron for questioning. Solano, whose family had been prominent in Florida since the sixteenth century, was one of the few Spaniards remaining in St. Augustine during the British occupation. When Louisa Waldron saw Solano approaching her home, the poor woman cast suspicion on herself by running out to hide in the tall grass and shrubbery. The soldiers forced her to ride into town and brought her to Fatio, who was leisurely sitting on the veranda of his home overlooking the bay. Fatio ordered Louisa Waldron placed in the custody of John Thomas, jailkeeper in the British régime, to await formal inquiry. Her maid brought clothing and personal articles, and remained with her. During the first two weeks of her imprisonment, Louisa Waldron was subjected to rather forceful interrogation by both Fatio and Francisco Sánchez, during which she became increasingly emotional. When her anguish reached a peak, she attempted to commit suicide and lay unconscious for more than six hours. Community interest in the case increased during all these dramatic events. The horse she had ridden to town was taken away by one of her Spanish captors and sold by the British vendue master for the inadequate sum of four shillings, and her home was robbed in her absence. Louisa Waldron was released, after insisting on her innocence for twenty-seven days, when the missing "wench" was discovered fifteen miles distant on another plantation.

When Tonyn protested the case, Zéspedes promised to investigate and prosecute the thieves who stole Louisa Waldron's belongings. But it seems unfair that the only form of restitution she secured was the inadequate price brought by her horse at public sale, and the return of the horse's bridle. Samuel Farley thought that he and Louisa Waldron were singularly abused while living under Spanish authority. He added her troubles to his own, and asserted that the servant who shared her imprisonment was a victim of false arrest.

In discussing the period of dual régime in East Florida, the sensational incidents call attention to discord between the British and Spanish in East Florida. Zéspedes was clearly over-optimistic in hoping that his first proclamation would give him a neat list of Florida residents who would remain under Spanish protection, and simultaneously force the troublesome element to depart. His well-intentioned measure to clarify the status of Negroes produced fraudulent bills of sale and unreliable testimony.

The friction between Tonyn and Zéspedes probably was increased because they were forced to use Captain Howard as interpreter and intermediary. Howard deeply resented the initial reception he received from Governor Patrick Tonyn, feeling he deserved more candid and courteous treatment as personal representative of the incoming Spanish governor. From the very beginning, relations were strained between the two Irishmen in the service of different monarchs. Zéspedes was at a further disadvantage because he had no legal official on his staff to compose suitable replies to Chief Justice Hume's lengthy contentions, full of Latin phrases and British legal vernacular. But Zéspedes' efforts toward law enforcement were most seriously curtailed by the shortage of cash. Had he been able to replace Colonel Young's light horse troop with a Spanish mounted force, Zéspedes could have avoided a great deal of discord, including the unfortunate handling of the McGirt banditti. But he considered the current price of horses, seventy pesos, absolutely prohibitive for the poor quality mounts offered for sale.

Actually, the majority of British and Spanish inhabitants in East Florida lived together for over a year with remarkable equanimity. Zéspedes' efforts to establish a rule of justice and humanity impressed the British residents. They could discern no manifestations of "the Spanish yoke" descending upon them, a dreaded fate widely forecast before Zéspedes' arrival. Zéspedes was too experienced to expect any degree of perfection during the transitional period in East Florida. The administration of justice in a community, no matter how carefully designed, is always susceptible to distortion and evasion.

Treasury Street

IV

A Year's Major Events

S T. AUGUSTINE had no newspaper to record the major events occurring during the joint residence of the English and Spanish governors in East Florida. A paper had been published briefly in 1783 by a refugee printer, who brought his press from Charleston and published a few issues of the "East Florida Gazette," but he departed for London before the Spanish occupation force arrived.[1] Since Zéspedes had no facilities available for printing, his proclamations and other important announcements were posted in the plaza for the townspeople to read. Yet there was plenty of other news to be exchanged at the market place in the plaza. Items of local interest generally centered around the arrival and departure of vessels, the brief visits of Americans coming from Georgia and South Carolina to settle property claims, the cases before the arbitration board, and a few more sensational incidents of crime and shipwreck. In addition to the problems of creating civil order and organizing some form of governmental machinery in the province, Governor Zéspedes found enough newsworthy events to be reported to Havana and Madrid to keep him writing late at night on many occasions.

In July, British emigrés sailing to Pensacola returned a week after departure, to report the wreck of a Spanish troop ship two

---

[1] Three surviving issues of the paper are in the Public Records Office, London. Photostatic copies are in the P. K. Yonge Library of Florida History, Gainesville. See *Escribano*, No. 33, October. 1959, p. 4.

hundred miles down the coast. They brought back an officer of
the Asturias Infantry Regiment, who said that the Catalonian
settee transporting his regiment to Spain had left Havana on June
1, and run aground on June 5. A rescue mission was organized
immediately to bring the stranded soldiers and officers to St.
Augustine, where they remained about a month before resuming
their homeward journey. Of the fifteen ships bringing the Spanish
occupation force to St. Augustine, twelve were scheduled to return
to Cadiz, the others to Cuba. After supplies were unloaded at St.
Mary's harbor, two of the vessels transported the infantrymen of
the Asturias Regiment back to Spain, departing August 19 and
August 28. St. Mary's harbor was a busy place during the late
summer of 1784, with the arrival of Spanish troops and the departure of the British forces proceeding simultaneously. The first
stage in the British evacuation of East Florida was completed on
August 14, when Brigadier General Archibald McArthur and his
military personnel sailed for Nassau in the Bahama islands.

Late in August, 1784, Governor Zéspedes received his first diplomatic visitor from the American states. Braving oppressive heat and
insect life, William Pierce journeyed through the swampy fever-
ridden lowlands from Savannah to bring personal greetings to
Zéspedes from John Houston, governor of Georgia. Major Pierce
had served as aide to General Nathanael Greene during the American Revolution, and three years after his visit to Florida he became
one of Georgia's delegates to the constitutional convention at
Philadelphia.

Americans frequently came to East Florida to settle business
affairs with British merchants or to seek runaway slaves, but Pierce
was the first prominent American to arrive in any official capacity.
Another well-known Savannah resident, John McQueen, visited
St. Augustine in early December. He evidently was impressed by
the opportunities there, for six years later he moved to East Florida
and became a Spanish subject. During the same month, Richard
Howley of Savannah made a religious pilgrimage to St. Augustine
to confess his sins. His death occurred three weeks after his return
to Georgia.[2]

An important news event for the month of September was the
arrival of the first ship from Cuba since the change of government.
Father Hassett finally reached Florida on this ship, which brought
passengers and mail but no cash, the one item desperately needed

---

[2] Michael J. Curley, *Church and State in the Spanish Floridas, 1783-1821.*
(Washington, D. C., 1940), p. 98.

in St. Augustine. Father Hasset, who had been trying to reach Florida since 1778, had a remarkable odyssey to recount to Governor Zéspedes. He was originally assigned to East Florida after news reached Cuba concerning the existence of the Roman Catholic Minorcan colony, located on Mosquito inlet about sixty miles south of St. Augustine. Father Pedro Campos, who accompanied the Minorcans to Florida in 1768, was anxious to secure renewal of his missionary orders, originally granted for only a three year period. In 1769, knowing that British authorities in Minorca prevented exchange of letters with the bishop on the neighboring Spanish island of Majorca, Father Campos took advantage of the opportunity to contact the bishop of Havana when a Cuban fishing vessel anchored off Mosquito inlet.

Lorenzo Rodriguez, master of the fishing vessel, was very likely the same man who returned to Florida with Zéspedes' occupation force as captain of one of the troop transports. The name was a common one in Florida during the first Spanish era. Lorenzo Rodriguez of St. Augustine served as pilot for ships evacuating Spanish troops in 1764 from Fort St. Marks, at Apalache on the Gulf Coast.[3] Father Campos' first letter, brought to Havana by Lorenzo Rodriguez, surprised officials both in Cuba and in Spain. They frankly doubted the valid existence of a Catholic colony in British Florida, but this fact was finally substantiated in 1771 by papal authorities in Rome.

In 1778, José de Gálvez appointed Father Thomas Hasset and Father Miguel O'Reilly to minister to the Catholic families in British East Florida. By that time, Father Campos was eager to return to Minorca. Both Father Hasset and Father O'Reilly were young men, recent graduates of *"El Real Colegio de Nobleses Irlandeses,"* established by Philip II in 1593 to train Irish clergy. Early in 1779, before Spain entered the American Revolution, the two Irish priests left Spain. By the time they arrived in Havana however, the southern campaigns were in progress and the Florida coast was blockaded. Father Hasset was reassigned to Philadelphia, but did not get there until May, 1782 when hostilities had ceased. Father O'Reilly remained in Cuba as a troop chaplain and accompanied the Spanish occupation force to St. Augustine in June, 1784.

---

[3] Mark F. Boyd, "From a Remote Frontier," *Florida Historical Quarterly*, vol. XIX, No. 3, January 1941. Quotes letter from Don Bentura Diaz in Apalache to Count of Ricla in Havana, January 19, 1764: "The only pilots experienced in this river are Miguel Lopez and Don Juan de Hita, and sailor Lorenzo Rodriguez, all three of St. Augustine."

The American Revolution did not change the original plans made by José de Gálvez, but merely delayed their execution.

As soon as Father Hasset received Zéspedes' letter, sent February 28, 1784, notifying him to proceed to St. Augustine, he tried to make arrangements for the voyage. Since he was unable to find a ship destined directly for Florida, he took passage with Captain Miguel Iznardy on a Spanish frigate departing from Philadelphia June 10 for Havana. The storm buffeting the ships outside the St. Augustine harbor on June 29 brought disaster to Iznardy's vessel. At three o'clock in the morning the frigate ran aground in the Keys, forcing Father Hasset and the crew to scramble ashore to safety. All his books, clothing, and even the King's orders were lost with the ship. Though severely battered by the surf, Father Hasset was thankful to escape with his life. After spending six days recovering on the key, the priest and twelve weather-beaten crewmen set out for Havana in the single small boat to survive the tempest. They reached their destination after six days of navigation, and immediately dispatched aid to Captain Iznardy and the remaining crewmen. Father Hasset left Havana in September, 1784 and was enthusiastically welcomed by Father O'Reilly on his arrival in St. Augustine. But the Spanish authorities had overlooked the linguistic problem in selecting a replacement for Father Campos. The Irish priests did not understand Minorcan, a language differing markedly from Castilian Spanish. Consequently, old Father Campos decided to stay in St. Augustine with his parishoners until a priest arrived who understood their speech.

Governor Zéspedes was glad that Father Hasset arrived in time to be present at the first formal Indian congress, September 30, easily the most important event scheduled for the early fall. Zéspedes wanted to be surrounded by as large a staff as possible when he received native visitors on this ceremonious occasion. His guests at the first formal Indian congress were the chiefs and head warriors of the Seminoles, the only tribe living exclusively in East Florida. The Seminoles comprised a population of close to two thousand people distributed among villages in half dozen locations in the central part of the peninsula.[4] Zéspedes understood that in numbers alone, their warriors could easily match the strength of the Spanish garrison. Before Zéspedes reached Florida, he had been rather worried about the Indian situation, but his anxiety subsided on learning that Cowkeeper, chief of the Seminoles and in-

---

[4] John R. Swanton, *Early History of the Creek Indians.* (Washington, D. C., 1918), p. 440.

veterate enemy of the Spaniards, had died about the time the change of government occurred. The new leader, Payne, appeared more pacifically inclined.

Although the conference with the Seminoles went off satisfactorily, Zéspedes felt that the relationship between the new Spanish government and the Indians was not firmly established until he had a conference including representatives of the Lower Creeks, living in western Georgia and in the Apalache district of northwest Florida. Since his arrival in St. Augustine, he had come to appreciate the importance of the unusual figure, Alexander McGillivray. He hoped the capable Creek chief would be able to attend a second congress in St. Augustine early in December, but an injury prevented McGillivray's appearance.

Zéspedes suffered through a period of extreme nervous strain prior to the second Indian congress. In September, he received a royal order sent June 20, permitting Panton, Leslie and Company to remain in East Florida if they traded exclusively in Spanish goods. Zéspedes knew that the Indian merchants could not continue in business if this restriction were enforced. He also felt it was impolitic to reveal the court's decision when he was dependent upon the firm to supply gifts for the Indian congress in December. Yet it bothered him to conceal important information from men who had consistently helped him out. In his own personal administrative problems, this quandary coincided with the hubbub over Louisa Waldron's controversial imprisonment, Samuel Farley's angry departure, and John Linder, Jr.'s expulsion from the province. At the time, Tonyn suspected that Linder, a most objectionable member of the banditti, was leaving with stolen property in his possession, and offered to secure Indian assistance in recovering the goods. Since Linder was traveling overland to Louisiana, he could easily be detained by the Indians. But Zéspedes had no desire to stir up the natives on any pretext when the chiefs were preparing to attend the congress. All these vexatious problems contributed to the governor's severe attack of colic, an ailment troubling him in late October and early November. He recovered his health in time to greet the Indian visitors on December 8, 1784.

Although Zéspedes was disappointed in not securing the attendance of McGillivray, Mad Dog, or other Upper Creek chiefs at his second Indian congress, many chiefs of the Lower Creek and Seminole towns accepted his invitation to come to St. Augustine. They encamped outside of town, and entered only for the formal conference held in the plaza across from the Government

House. A colorful delegation assembled to exchange "talks," the standard term in referring to Indian diplomatic messages. Most of the Lower Creeks displayed the typical tribal hair cut, a narrow band commencing at the crown and widening across the back of the head. Around their heads they wore folded headbands about four inches wide in which were stuck three of four feather plumes. Their white ruffled shirts were English importation. A few chiefs had silver chains around their necks from which were suspended silver medals presented at British Indian congresses. Since the weather was by now quite brisk, their legs were protected by deerskin breeches made by the women of the tribe. The beaded moccasins were similar to those of all American Indian tribes. More unusual were the red and blue blankets decorated with braid, coarse gold lace, and tiny brass or silver bells. Every chief carried a massive leather tobacco pouch slung over one shoulder and resting on his chest in handy position to refill a pipe.[5]

To make an impressive show of strength, Zéspedes was accompanied by all the officials of the garrison and the Catholic priests. In the course of the meeting, he displayed the portrait of Charles III so that the Indians would retain a mental picture of their new ally and benefactor. The general tone of the governor's message, delivered through an interpreter, assured the Indians that the Spaniards would continue the policy of the English, since the kings of Spain and England were now bound together by ties of friendship and brotherhood. As in the earlier congress, he indicated that Panton, Leslie and Company would continue to supply their needs for European articles.

The Indians, in turn, asked for the maintenance of stores on the St. John's river, Apalache (St. Marks), and Pensacola. They pointed out that the store at Apalache would cut down on the number of spirited and less reliable young men coming to the St. Augustine vicinity, and promised that the older men would try to control the younger men of the tribe. The Indians also mentioned that four of their horses had been stolen since they arrived in St. Augustine at the governor's request, and asked for their return or for monetary compensation. The horses, if found, could be returned to the nation through Mr. Leslie. For the majority of the chiefs, this was their first contact with representatives of

---

[5] Thomas McKenny and James Hall, *The History of the Indian Tribes of North America, with Biographical Sketches and Anecdotes of their Principal Chiefs embellished with portraits from the Indian Gallery in the Department of War.* (3 vols., Philadelphia, 1842) Excellent collection of colored portraits.

Spain, and they were encouraged to find their treatment similar to that they received from the British. As a result, they announced specifically that they no longer opposed the transfer of East Florida to Spain.

The Indians and Spanish officers ceremoniously shook hands, or to be more accurate, shook forearms, an Indian declaration of friendship. They drank the *aguardiente* Zéspedes had brought from Havana, and in smoking their pipes they blew the smoke far overhead to indicate their high opinion of the hosts. Presents were distributed before they left for their villages. It was a great relief to Zéspedes to establish amicable relations with the Indians on the border of his province. This accomplishment undoubtedly increased his peace of mind during the Christmas season, a holiday celebrated in St. Augustine as in Madrid with a sumptous dinner of roast turkey and toasts exchanged among many guests.

The first big news of the new year, 1785, was of course the apprehension of Daniel McGirt and other leaders of the banditti. But their arrest in no way guaranteed that peace would reign in the province. On January 24, four days after McGirt's capture, the whole town was aroused shortly after nightfall by the sounds of gunfire at Jesse Fish's place on Anastasia island across the river from St. Augustine. The commotion on the river indicated that boats were leaving the island, and one soon drew up at the town wharf. Servants from the Fish estate were bringing a severely wounded prisoner, one of a band surprised during an attempted robbery. Francisco Fatio was summoned to the city jail immediately to take the testimony of the prisoner, Thomas Bell, who readily admitted his association with a pirate band. The captain and crew had left North Carolina three weeks earlier with a cargo of turpentine, but decided before reaching Charleston to turn to piracy. They had come ashore briefly at Matanzas, opposite the southern point on Anastasia island, prior to anchoring outside the St. Augustine bar two days later. Early in the evening the four men aboard the pirate schooner rowed to the landing at the Fish estate. Leaving Thomas Bell posted as sentry on the walk to the house, the other three broke in, but soon came dashing back with a bedsheet full of booty, pursued by servants firing muskets. Thomas Bell, in the direct line of fire, fell instantly to the ground, but his three companions escaped.

Two hours after making his declaration, Thomas Bell died. Next day his body was exposed on the gallows standing in the northeast corner of the Castillo courtyard, indicating the punishment he would have received had he lived. Governor Zéspedes' initial alarm at the appearance of pirates so close to the city was increased when he learned that the band was larger than Bell indicated. A Negro servant, released after a few hours imprisonment in the stocks beside Bell, emerged with the story that a large band of Bell's associates had landed at Mosquito inlet. They killed three Indians there to prevent knowledge of their presence from reaching authorities in St. Augustine. Bell also had told the Negro that more than fifteen ships were being fitted out in American ports to engage in piracy along the coasts of Florida and the Bahama islands.

Zéspedes immediately wrote Governor William Moultrie of South Carolina describing the pirate attack and identifying the crew members who had escaped. He was not sure how much faith to put in the report of imminent widespread piracy, but included this information for the benefit of the South Carolina governor. On March 3, 1785, the Charleston newspaper printed an account of the attack and the reward Governor Moultrie offered for the capture of the other three crew members. Only one man was apprehended, but he was released on the technicality that no accessory to a crime can be prosecuted before the principal figure is sentenced. The threats of future punishment were evidently sufficient to prevent any further incidents of piracy for several years.

From the beginning of the year 1785, it became increasingly apparent that the evacuation of the British residents would not be completed by the March 19 deadline. Sometimes it seemed to Governor Zéspedes that the day would never come when news could be posted that the British had left Florida. A request for six months extension sent to Madrid in February was answered in June granting four additional months, making the new deadline July 19, 1785. Because of the delay in evacuation, former governor Tonyn, a major general in the British army, was still residing in St. Augustine when leading American officers of the recent Revolutionary War visited Zéspedes in March. Tonyn was definitely angered by the cordial reception accorded the American officials, and by his exclusion from the entertainment in their honor.

Governor Zéspedes' important guests in the spring of 1785 were General Nathanael Greene and Colonel Benjamin Hawkins. General Greene had led the southern division of the Continental army during the final victorious phase of the conflict, that ended with the reconquest of Charleston in 1782. For his services, he had been given a plantation near Savannah. The trip to St. Augustine in March, 1785 was an extension of a tour inspecting his property on Cumberland island where British loggers from East Florida had cut valuable timber. When Governor Houston of Georgia had forwarded protests against unauthorized logging in December, 1784, Zéspedes replied rather curtly that he had no responsibility for such excesses during the interval granted for the British to remove their property from Florida. Now that he was host to an important citizen whose property rights had been violated, Zéspedes strove to dispel any previous impression of disinterest or lack of cooperation.

While they were in St. Augustine, the two distinguished Americans lodged with friends, but Zéspedes supervised their entertainment. The governor's house was sufficiently repaired and redecorated for Doña Concepción to plan a state dinner in their honor. Zéspedes' daughters joined their accomplished mother in serving as hostesses on this gala occasion, creating a spirit of hospitality always impressive to guests in their home. Captain Carlos Howard was on hand to facilitate the exchange of conversation. When General Greene and Colonel Hawkins departed on March 19, 1785, Zéspedes sent Lieutenant Colonel Antonio Fernandez and four dragoons as an escort to the boat waiting at St. John's Bluffs. Colonel Fernandez accompanied them on to the St. Mary's river, where they dined as guests of Captain Pedro Vasquez on board the *San Matias*, before continuing to General Greene's property on nearby Cumberland island.

The effusive letters of appreciation that Lieutenant Colonel Fernandez brought back aroused more suspicion than approval in Zéspedes' mind, and it did not take him long to discover that General Greene's trip to St. Augustine had objectives other than a simple diplomatic mission. The general was also investigating the possibility of securing British evacuees to settle on his Cumberland island property. Colonel Hawkins, who was anxious to promote a treaty between the United States and the Creek confederacy, was primarily interested in learning the extent of Spanish influence with the Creek and Seminole tribes.

In the spring of 1785, the center of gravity in the province shifted to St. Mary's harbor, and the news of the day featured the names of families leaving town and the exciting events occurring in the vicinity of the embarkation port. Passengers and goods from St. Augustine and the outlying districts steadily concentrated at the harbor, in close proximity to the Americans on the Georgia shore of the river. Until September, Zéspedes received reports of quarrels and waterfront brawls animated by the recent revolution or intra-provincial feuds. In several cases, individuals and property were returned to St. Augustine for decisions by the arbitration board. The remnants of the McGirt banditti, and others of their kind, were still active in the border area, creating further law enforcement problems.

St. Mary's harbor during this period was the scene of almost frantic activity. Logging was still in progress along the waterways connecting with the St. Mary's river, contributing to the confusion at the harbor. These operations should have ceased on March 19, according to the provisions of the peace treaty, but under the pretext that the wood was cut earlier, rafts of valuable oak, cedar and red bay continued to float downstream. Along the beach, neat piles of logs contrasted sharply with the clutter of oversize possessions refused cargo space in the transports. Many settlers reduced their dwellings to original lengths of lumber in order to take them along, but there was no room to ship the clumsy house frames intact.[6] When Tonyn discovered the Spanish government would not purchase the church pews, bells or fire-fighting equipment, he had these items added to the cargo so that they could be used in a Loyalist refugee town to be established in the Bahamas. The congestion in St. Mary's harbor temporarily decreased early in May when transports left for Nassau with 387 people aboard.

On May 29, Zéspedes gave a final ball honoring the retiring British officials, and on June 3, General Tonyn and his staff left for the embarkation port. Tonyn supervised the final phase of the evacuation from his headquarters aboard the British frigate *Cyrus,* commanded by Captain Robert Browne. Spanish authority at the port was represented by Captain Pedro Vásquez of the *San Matias,* the brigantine stationed at the river border from Zéspedes arrival until the British evacuation was completed. Occasionally tempers flared on both ships.

Tonyn claimed, with apparent justification, that runaway Negroes were harbored by Captain Vásquez, who denied their presence when questioned by Captain Browne. He further charged that the teen-age daughter of one of the evacuees, and a Minorcan woman were both seduced on board the *San Matias.* Zéspedes sent orders for the girl to be returned to her parents, if she was found on board the ship. In the case of the Minorcan woman, who ran away from her husband, he decided she should have the oppor-

---

[6] Wilbur Henry Siebert, *Loyalists in East Florida, 1774-1785* (2 vols., Deland, Florida, 1929), vol. I, p. 177.

tunity of returning to her native island by way of Havana if she preferred.

Zéspedes, in turn, protested to Tonyn concerning the treatment of a Philadelphia captain, David People, who stopped at St. Mary's harbor in July en route to St. Augustine with a load of flour. While at St. Mary's, one of Captain People's seamen deserted to a British schooner anchored nearby. To replace this crew member, Captain People enlisted the aid of a Charleston captain whose schooner was loading lumber at the port. A stroll along the waterfront involved the two Americans in a brawl when they tried to break up a fight between Captain People's deserted seaman and a stranger, whom they later discovered had a local reputation for "shanghaiing" sailors. Seeking some legal authority, Captain People hailed the officers of the *Cyrus,* who had viewed the entire scuffle, and a boat soon arrived to conduct all participants to the presence of Captain Robert Browne.

After a few simple questions, and a glance at the seaman's articles indicating that Captain People sailed under authority of the American congress, Captain Browne launched an apoplectic monologue against "infamous rebels." Seizing a large spyglass, Captain Browne beat Captain People over the head then knocked him down the gangway. Continuing his tirade, Browne ordered his guards to strip both American captains and tie them to the whipping post. He determined to give a British subject, as he classed the deserter, a chance to administer well-deserved beatings to the infamous rebel captains. The seaman first took whips to the Charleston captain, whom Captain Browne charged with sailing under false British register, but refused to whip his own captain, David People, though ordered to do so by Captain Browne. Captain Browne wound up this incident by ordering the American captains to move to the other side of the river. When Captain People refused, he threatened to beat him as a "lying rebel rascal" if he did not leave the port within twelve hours. After hearing Captain People's story, Zéspedes wrote Tonyn that Captain Browne must be a madman and a brute, and Tonyn replied that Browne was protecting a lawful British subject.

News of further troubles came to St. Augustine from Henry O'Neill, Spanish border agent, who lived at Newhope, several miles upstream on the St. Mary's river. Trying vainly to keep track of scoundrels operating on both sides of the border, Henry O'Neill found his task more difficult after Tonyn arrived at the embarkation port. O'Neill reported that the population had grown turbulent since Tonyn arbitrarily imprisoned a resident of the district on board the *Cyrus*. He also complained that a British official had fired on Americans who came peacefully to St. Mary's on business. These events made it difficult to maintain any standard or justice on the border.

Zéspedes became increasingly exasperated as reports of highhanded British actions continued to reach St. Augustine. After the July 19 deadline passed, he informed Tonyn that the British had absolutely no claim to authority in East Florida and could demand nothing but hospitality. Although he threatened to send Spanish troops to the border, he adopted a far happier strategy to keep peace at St. Mary's. For the prevention or prompt settlement of all unpleasant and potentially dangerous incidents, Zéspedes sent a liaison officer to attend General Tonyn. Zéspedes' first selection, an officer of the Hibernia Regiment, became ill, but his next choice from a Spanish regiment achieved notable success. The amiable personality and impeccably diplomatic manner of Captain Manuel de los Reyes moved Tonyn to write a letter of gratitude to the Spanish governor. Captain Reyes, to whom Zéspedes gave the title of lieutenant governor, preserved amicable relations between the two governments during the final hectic weeks of the evacuation process.

Zéspedes was in no position to force the British to leave. He was heavily in debt to British merchants, many of whom were postponing departure until they received payment for goods advanced to the Spanish administration for the past year. The provincial treasury had received absolutely no money since Zéspedes arrived in Florida in June, 1784 with inadequate financial resources. The added delay to British evacuation was one of the most agonizing effects of the acute financial crisis paralysing East Florida in the summer of 1785. So little money circulated that on many days meat and fresh vegetables remained unsold at the market in the plaza. Credit alone enabled the commissary department to distribute rations at barracks mess halls.

For over a month after the July deadline, the evacuation process was at a stalemate and misery prevailed at St. Mary's harbor. One sailor on the *San Matias* died of the fever and digestive complaints. Tonyn deserves a good deal of sympathy for the unhappy task assigned to him by the British government. Between 1782 and 1785, he arranged the virtual exile of ten thousand subjects who had already suffered heavy loss by remaining loyal to their king. The disagreements involving Spanish authorities were only a fraction of the problems with which he contended during his last sultry summer in Florida. Enduring complaints about bad bread and crowded quarters, he was responsible for securing passports, rations, clothes and transportation for over seven hundred people who left the province in May and September. Except for a few official families, the last transports carried off the dregs of the population, who had shifted their homes about the province owning no land and little personal property. Included were two insane men who had existed by community charity in Florida.

Tonyn's difficult project received scant cooperation from officials in the Bahamas, who felt their islands were unnecessarily crowded by these Florida refugees. The governor of the Bahamas frankly wished these Englishmen were headed for Nova Scotia or even the Mosquito shore in Central America. Little provision was made for the two final contingents of refugees, who suffered a high death rate during their first weeks at New Providence. After hearing reports of conditions in the Bahamas, many British families decided at the last minute to stay in Florida, an act of disloyalty in Tonyn's opinion. During his final weeks on board the *Cyrus*, Tonyn also devoted considerable time to correspondence, preparing in concert with James Hume a six-page letter, his "last word" to Zéspedes on the subjects of disagreement during the previous year. With it he enclosed twenty-four lengthy documents, memorials, declarations, depositions and extracts of previous letters, almost all concerning the familiar figures of James Farley, Daniel McGirt, Francisco Sánchez and Louisa Waldron. Tonyn arranged to have this literary production delivered to Zéspedes the day the transports left the province. Carlos Howard spent weeks on the translation.

To everyone's vast relief, money from Havana arrived on August 30 to clear British debts. This long awaited event made newspaper headlines in Charleston, location of some of the Spanish administration's principal creditors. Transports carrying 114 Loyalists and 249 Negroes, along with the *Cyrus* and three galleys, weighed anchor on September 4, 1785. The vagaries of wind and tide which had hampered Zéspedes' plans for a dramatic arrival in East Florida likewise interfered with Tonyn's plans for a grand exit. After the transports sailed out of St. Mary's harbor, the wind died suddenly, leaving behind the *Cyrus* and galleys. A second attempted departure on September 11 proved even more unsuccessful. Captain Browne maneuvered the frigate across the first bar shortly after noon, then encountered shifting winds and tried to re-enter the harbor. With the tide last-ebbing late in the afternoon, he decided to anchor with a short cable between the bars until the next high tide. A brisk east wind arose near sundown, driving the unfortunate ship backwards to sit upon her own anchor for an hour and a half. The *Cyrus* soon began to take water at the rate of six inches an hour and after temporary repairs proved inadequate she returned to the river harbor.

When news of the accident reached Zéspedes, he offered hospitality to all passengers in St. Augustine, but in view of his last barrage of correspondence, Tonyn felt unable to accept. Since he was equally unable to request refuge in Georgia, he was temporarily trapped aboard a leaky ship. After efforts to careen the vessel on the beach at St. Mary's proved unsuccessful, her passengers transferred to ships sent from Providence and Jamaica. Patrick Tonyn finally managed to leave aboard the damaged frigate on November 13, 1785.

Charlotte Street

V

Romantic Springtime, 1785

GOVERNOR Zéspedes expected problems to arise during the transition to Spanish rule in East Florida, but he never anticipated that the aftermath of the American Revolution would involve him in so many romantic tangles during his first spring in the province. As the days grew warmer and nights more balmy early in 1785, the universally tender influence of the spring season pervaded the atmosphere at St. Augustine. Even in a semitropical climate, the exhilaration of springtime, the season of new growth and new bloom, is apparent after the dormant winter. The heady scent of orange blossoms from the trees bordering the plaza and in private gardens suffused the air. Tall shrubs of oleander with their slender green leaves and pink or scarlet blossoms, growing from roots originally brought from Spain, were striking notes of color in the carefully-designed planting. Shaded corners provided shelter for Canary island jasmin, whose white blossoms exhale a gardenia-like fragrance. In open areas, patches of wild honeysuckle attracted the patient, hovering bees and darting hummingbirds. With the addition of the flowering annuals, the calendula, marigold and zinnia with tones from yellow to brick red, the gardens behind the fences became a profusion of color. In the quiet morning air, before the ocean breeze blew in about ten o'clock, turtle doves cooed and muttered under eaves and balconies, and out in the bay the porpoise leaped the gentle waves.

67

The young people of the British colony, though possibly not the first to succumb to this heart-warming atmosphere, were the first to seek the governor's aid in solving their romantic problems. A number of couples among the evacuees wanted to marry before leaving the province, and petitioned Governor Zéspedes to allow John Leslie to perform civil ceremonies. Although Zéspedes heartily approved of matrimony as a stabilizing influence in society, he was certain his governmental capacity as vice-patron of the Roman Catholic church did not authorize him to permit non-Catholic marriages. For this delicate problem he had no solution at all, except to urge the couples to depart for British territory as soon as possible. The last contingent of evacuees had to do without the spiritual aid of the Anglican rector, who had been one of the first to return to England after the peace terms became known.

The British couples were not the only ones to seek Zéspedes' aid in getting married. In February of 1785, he received a similar appeal in behalf of a pair of young lovers in Charleston, South Carolina, whose predicament — like those of the Florida evacuees — was the result of the American Revolution. Charleston lacked neither churches nor ministers in 1785, but there was no Catholic priest nearer than St. Augustine. Intense anti-Catholic feeling prevailed throughout most of colonial America. In the Carolinas, prejudice was so strong that individual Catholics kept their faith secret, and were not even known to each other. These violent sentiments modified slightly after Europe's two leading Catholic powers became allies of the American colonists, France in 1778 and Spain in 1779, but in Charleston, public worship did not begin until 1788.[1] The French consulate established in Charleston created the local romantic predicament Zéspedes was asked to solve. A young man of Catholic faith on the staff of the French legation became engaged to a niece of Alexander Moultrie, a member of one of the South's leading families. Both the French consul and Alexander Moultrie urgently requested a priest from St. Augustine, naturally with expenses paid, to perform a marriage ceremony. The only alternative seemed to be for the couple to go to France in order to be married in accordance with Catholic ritual.

Zéspedes readily understood that this was a union of considerable importance. Colonel Alexander Moultrie was a brother of William Moultrie, currently governor of South Carolina, and also of John

---

[1] John Gilmary Shea, *Life and Times of the Most Rev. John Carroll, Embracing the History of the Catholic Church in the United States, 1763-1815.* (New York, 1888), p. 316.

Moultrie, former lieutenant governor of British East Florida, who had abandoned "Bella Vista" and returned to England shortly after Zéspedes' arrival. The family, like so many in the colonies, had been split on political allegiance by the Revolutionary War. Alexander Moultrie had spent eighteen months in St. Augustine as a British prisoner of war before his exchange in 1782. In spite of their political differences, the fraternal ties of the brothers remained firm. The Spanish governor hesitated to send a priest into foreign territory without the approval of a higher authority. He immediately wrote the Bishop of Santiago and Bernardo do Gálvez in Havana, and in June the request was granted for Father Michael O'Reilly, Spanish troop chaplain, to make a trip to Charleston for this laudable purpose.

The British evacuation broke up many friendships as well as romantic attachments that had blossomed during the confusing period of changing political sovereignty. For example, General Archibald McArthur and Zéspedes were on very good terms during the short space of time before the British troops left for New Providence in August, 1784. A much closer bond of friendship and mutual esteem developed between Zéspedes and Colonel Thomas Brown, British army officer serving as Indian superintendent at the end of the British régime. Wives and younger generation of both families were equally congenial, creating a pleasant atmosphere of sociability and recreation, a welcome contrast to more troublesome official duties. With the exception of Antonio de Zéspedes, members of these two families accepted separation as an inevitable consequence of war and peace.

Antonio de Zéspedes was most reluctant to see the younger members of the Brown family leave for the embarkation port in the spring of 1785. Late in July, he ran away from home and made a surprise appearance at Brown's shipboard quarters in St. Mary's harbor. The colonel was delighted to see his impetuous young friend, although he knew the excursion was unauthorized. For several days, Antonio's talented singing and guitar playing provided entertainment for an audience of appreciative young women. His presence also diverted the colonel's attention from a digestive complaint, a medical problem common in the seaside lowlands along with malarial fevers. Almost immediately on arrival at St. Mary's, Antonio was taken under the protection of Captain Manuel de los Reyes, Zéspedes' personal envoy to General Tonyn. Antonio realized he had behaved in a thoughtless, juvenile fashion, and sent penitent letters to his parents asking each one to forgive his impulsive actions. The written pleas of Captain Reyes and Colonel Brown were also influential in helping him escape punishment for his disobedience. Late in August, a sloop owned by John Leslie took Antonio and Captain Reyes back to St. Augustine to report on the state of affairs at the embarkation port.

Not all infractions of military rules received such lenient treatment, particularly if they indicated escapades more serious than Antonio's brief absence without leave. Penalties for disobeying rules were imposed upon two other young soldiers swept beyond regulation bounds by the spring tide of emotion in 1785. The season produced a bumper crop of miscreants, but these were the only two meriting the governor's personal and official censure. The first case involved a sergeant in the artillery corp, Juan Sively, for whom Governor Zéspedes felt a measure of personal responsibility. The second and more serious case, including an Irish lieutenant and the governor's daughter Dominga, caused a tremendous sensation in St. Augustine and a mild stir in Madrid court circles.

Distinguished Sergeant Juan Sively had been personally recommended to Zéspedes before leaving Havana. For this reason, the governor felt rather *in loco parentis* so far as the artillery officer was concerned. The adjective "distinguished" indicated that Sively belonged to a social class higher than that of the ordinary noncommissioned officer. Actually, he hoped to win promotion to a lieutenant's rank during the course of his service in St. Augustine. Sively was prominent among the members of the military corp whose general behavior worried the governor during the spring of 1785. At the time, the local international community in existence since July of 1784 was being swiftly disrupted as British residents moved from St. Augustine to St. Mary's harbor at an increased tempo. The sense of imminent departure, the urge to make the most of each passing moment, lent an intensity to personal relations that might have proceeded at a more casual pace under other circumstances. By the traditionally merry month of May, Zéspedes could no longer ignore the fast-ripening friendship of Sively and Isabel Shivers, a servant in the home of General Patrick Tonyn.

On the afternoon of May 15, while Zéspedes was standing in front of the Government House, he was exceedingly vexed to observe Sively and Isabel Shivers cantering by on horseback, headed toward the city gate, the outlying meadows and shady groves. Furthermore, the guard stationed at the plaza, and other garrison personnel were at hand to observe his reaction to this scene. The sergeant was not in uniform, his only observable offense at the moment. Quickly taking command of a situation he wished he could ignore, the governor sharply ordered Sively to go to the Castillo and report himself under arrest for appearing on the streets virtually "in disguise" with no indication of his rank or profession.

After Sively's arrest, Zéspedes handled the rest of the case in a suitably aloof manner, using as an intermediary the commander of the artillery corp, Pedro José Salcedo. In the course of several confidental discussions, Zéspedes expressed the view that Sively's affair, by now a public scandal, had continued too long. His own stern actions were influenced by rumors that Sively had expressed the desire to have the young lady receive instruction in the Catholic Faith, and might try to accompany her to England. The governor thought Sively should realize that a woman who was Protestant, English, and a servant, had three serious counts against her, clearly indicating her family was unsuitable for a marriage connection. A man obviously blinded by passion needed some sobering experience. Zéspedes knew he had utilized a rather trivial offense to secure the sergeant's incarceration, but hoped that solitude would help him recover his sense of values. As he explained to Pedro Salcedo, he was punishing Sively as a father, not for lack of respect in passing the Government House in improper attire with improper company.

Sively had difficulty in appearing sufficiently contrite to warrant release from imprisonment. At first, he felt outraged at being placed in a cell with Daniel McGirt, banditti leader awaiting transportation to a Havana prison. Next day, he was moved to the cell of an accused murderer. The gentlemanly side of his nature resented being confined where there were no writing materials, where he was not allowed to feed himself, and where there were no bathing facilities. When he requested permission to get a little fresh air in the Castillo courtyard, he was transferred to imprisonment in his own barracks, a dishonorable location usually reserved for those accused of more serious crimes. In his own way, Sively was more concerned about his reputation than Governor Zéspedes. He feared that imprisonment, rather than his own scandalous behavior, might discredit his reputation in St. Augustine and Havana, and prevent his promotion. Furthermore, Sively insisted he was unjustly singled out for a punishment equally deserved by other soldiers, who had previously been infatuated with Isabel Shivers. He confessed only that he was one of the most recent of the many Spanish subjects who frequently had visited the house of Isabel Shivers.

For this impertinence, Zéspedes almost returned him to the Castillo de San Marcos. Finally, however, Sivelly indicated a more proper frame of mind. He admitted that he deserved punishment, but insisted that he did not want to appear negligent in his service to the king, lacking in respect for his parents or heedless of their instruction. Still, Zéspedes did not release him until after General Tonyn and his household staff departed for St. Mary's harbor.

The governor, who kept track of many things in his small province, learned with relief that Sivelly seemed to be turning his attention to other damsels in town. Nevertheless the personality characteristics creating a problem in the spring of 1785 were evidenced throughout Sivelly's career in East Florida. Six months after his release from imprisonment, he was back in the public eye as one of the principal figures in a murder trial that undeniably appeared to be a crime of passion.

On the night of November 20, muffled assailants fatally stabbed Lieutenant William Delaney of the Hibernia Regiment outside the house where an Anglo-American seamstress, Catalina Morain, occupied a rented room. The personal affairs of Catalina Morain immediately became the leading topic of local discussion, with frequent mention of the fact that one of her current admirers was Juan Sivelly. Catalina made her living in St. Augustine ostensibly by taking in sewing, and her principal clients were soldiers of the artillery corp quartered in a barracks near her residence. During the fall of 1785, obvious jealousy developed between two members of this particular unit, Sergeant Juan Sivelly and Corporal Francisco Moraga. Sivelly rather unfairly made use of his superior military rank and ordered Moraga to cease visiting Catalina Morain, a command which Moraga heatedly refused to obey.

All the early evidence in the Delaney murder trial indicated that Sivelly should have killed Moraga, or *vice versa*. In fact, the scant attention to Lieutenant Delaney gave the impression that his murder was an accident, a case of mistaken identity. In gathering the facts, Governor Zéspedes desperately wished that his staff included a member with legal training, a need he repeatedly voiced during his term of office in Florida. He even had a friend to recommend for the office, Don Josef Mariano de Céspedes Clavijo, native of Havana and a lawyer in the Royal Audiencia of the district. Identity of the assailants proved impossible, with only the vague description that they wore cloaks with large hoods. The garb was not distinctive in St. Augustine. Hooded cloaks, originally worn only by sailors, were adopted by all the soldiers to keep warm in the chilly barracks. On that particular night, other muffled figures on the streets were actors in a play being rehearsed for public performance in the town plaza. Several members of the comedy cast were costumed in Franciscan habit with large cowls. Moraga attended part of the rehearsal.

As the examination of witnesses continued, Zéspedes decided that the majority of evidence pointed toward Corporal Moraga, although he became increasingly suspicious of Catalina Morain's complicity in the crime. In her first testimony, she supplied evidence incriminating two other soldiers who were arrested immediately, then released after they were able to clear themselves satisfactorily. Sergeant Sivelly also successfully proved his innocence of murder, but not of reprehensible behavior. The governor finally released all suspects except Francisco Moraga and Catalina Morain, whom he retained in custody while 176 pages of confused and conflicting testimony from 57 witnesses were sent to Havana for decision by legal authorities.

Juan Sivelly seemed to be indiscreet, but not criminal in his general behavior. The sergeant acquired many friends in highly respectable families in St. Augustine. The baptismal register shows that he became godfather to several children, as well as the father of one illegitimate daughter born to a British girl in 1787. The young man evidently scampered along the side roads as much as he followed the straight and narrow path. It was a great relief to Governor Zéspedes to learn of Sivelly's promotion to a lieutenancy, although the good news did not come until December of 1789. The governor promptly advised Pedro Salcedo to arrange transportation for Sivelly on the next boat for Havana.

During Zéspedes' initial trouble with Juan Sivelly and Isabel Shivers in May of 1785, he also took decisive action regarding his daughter and an Irish officer, the second sensational case occurring during the course of that highly romantic season. Of all the local attachments to appear in the spring of 1785, the one causing the most far-reaching repercussions involved Dominga de Zéspedes and Juan O'Donovan, second lieutenant in the Hibernia Regiment. Although Dominga and Josepha de Zéspedes received courteous attention from all the officers of the garrison, they were carefully chaperoned and under the watchful eyes of their parents on all social occasions. According to the strict code enforced for señoritas in Spanish society, they held no private conversations with gentlemen. Romance could be encouraged only by means of the sign language of a cleverly-maneuvred fan observed across a crowded room, or by secret correspondence forwarded through a sympathetic intermediary.

Vincente and Antonio de Zéspedes, overhearing a conversation in the officer's quarters, brought home rumors of the attachment, including the disturbing report that O'Donovan boasted to fellow-officers that he would elope with the girl if her father refused to consent to the marriage. Subsequently Lieutenant O'Donovan brought Zéspedes a copy of a memorial he was considering sending to the king, through his commanding officer, requesting permission to resign his commission and return to Ireland. Zéspedes could not decide whether the motive behind this action was to mislead or to threaten, but he feared the lieutenant might actually carry off Dominga to a foreign country, under cover of the current evacuation.

From the hints of his wife and daughter, the governor understood the mission bringing Lieutenant O'Donovan to call on an evening in February when other members of the family melted away at the sound of boots crossing the long veranda of the official residence. Zéspedes tended to bluster through the interview, pointing out that nobility of birth was an indispensable requirement for anyone seeking his daughter's hand, and asking proof that O'Donovan could support Dominga in a manner appropriate to her status in society. Zéspedes intended to temporize and prudently postpone a definite decision, but O'Donovan received the impression that the governor was masking a denial of his request.

Early in March, Zéspedes requested Bernardo de Gálvez, currently captain general of Cuba, to arrange prompt replacement of O'Donovan in the St. Augustine garrison. By return mail, he learned that this action was underway. Private correspondence also encouraged him to believe that before long O'Donovan would receive official orders transferring him to another post. Even under duress, however, Spanish governmental routine moves too slowly to compete with the emotional drive of young love. In the succeeding weeks, Governor Zéspedes kept a close watch over his daughter. Temporarily, the whole family was absorbed in entertaining their important American guests, General Nathanael Greene and Colonel Benjamin Hawkins. During the state dinner in their honor, the governor was pleased to see his eldest daughter behaving with her usual gaiety, but he was conscious that she was only momentarily diverted.

On the evening of May 29, the Government House was the scene of a farewell celebration honoring British officials about to depart for St. Mary's harbor. Under cover of the bustle of the social occasion, Dominga managed to elude her father's vigilance. About nine o'clock, he realized she was missing and sent Vicente to locate her. Vicente returned shortly, followed by Father O'Reilly who corroborated the following story. He found the couple at the home of Chief Engineer Mariano LaRoque, who was out of town, but whose wife had taken the responsibility of promoting the romance. LaRoque's wife, Doña Angela Huet, a close friend of the Zéspedes family, was never suspected of a plot in her frequent visits to their home. On this critical evening, a Minorcan woman went to summon Father O'Reilly on the pretense that Doña Angela had suffered a serious accident. When he arrived, Doña Angela ushered him into an inner room where the couple stood together, joined hands, and repeated the marriage vows. This was termed a clandestine or secret marriage, but a valid ceremony in view of the fact that the vows were repeated in the presence of a priest and other witnesses.

In the commotion that followed immediately and continued for several hours that night, it is difficult to decide who was the most distressed. Doña Concepcion had an immediate emotional reaction, retiring from the party to have her tears comforted by Josepha, who was cautioned never to bring similar disgrace on the family. The commandant, Colonel Guillermo O'Kelly, arrested Lieutenant O'Donovan on the charge of marrying without the permission of his superior officer. The bride returned weeping to the custody of her father. Father O'Reilly was beside himself with anguish at being the unwitting accessory to so regrettable an event. Doña Angela Huet became remorsefully conscious that the governor believed she had severely abused the privileges of hospitality.

The governor himself, sensitive to all matters of personal honor, felt particularly aggrieved. Dominga was his favorite daughter. She had flashing dark eyes and spirited manner admired in his native province of La Mancha. In the local idiom of southern Spain, she had "plenty of salt." It was a grave disappointment to see her joined in matrimony to a foreigner with no source of income other than the miserable pay of a second lieutenant in the Spanish army. Moreover, it was embarassing to have his authority as head of the province flouted by an officer so low in rank and doubly humiliating for this to occur when British officers were on the scene. His honor had been offended in the eyes of a foreign nation.

With the bride and groom under lock and key, the governor sat down to smoke and for the first time began to consider the

larger aspects of the situation affecting his favorite daughter. He
dreaded the gossip and scandal that would circulate in the small
town next morning, and soon he began to worry about the validity of the marriage. His daughter's honor now assumed more importance than his own pride, and he concluded that above all he
wanted assurance that she was properly married. Later that night,
he took Father O'Reilly to the home of Father Hasset and asked
to have a second marriage performed immediately. Father Hasset
as ecclesiastical judge had doubts about this procedure, but acceded
to the governor's vehement demands and promised to report the
whole affair to the king, assuming full responsibility if this was
an improper course of action. Then Governor Zéspedes returned
home, to pace up and down while Father O'Reilly escorted Lieutenant O'Donovan from his quarters. After a second marriage ceremony had been performed under the supervision of Father Hasset,
the bride and groom returned to their separate imprisonment.
Zéspedes vowed he'd retain custody of his daughter until he learned
the king's orders concerning this unprecedented marriage.

The governor's difficulty in handling the marriage problem
stemmed from the internal conflict between two sides of his own
personality, the father and the commanding-officer. During the
next few days, separate conferences with his daughter and the
young lieutenant convinced him that both were motivated by unusual love and sincerity. He cleared up the basic misunderstanding
with O'Donovan, pointing out that he had not flatly forbidden
the marriage. He even began to appreciate his daughter's husband,
whose devotion had led him to risk his future military career.
Since the union was indissoluble, the governor now accepted
O'Donovan as a member of the family and tried to straighten out
the tangle for the sake of Dominga's happiness.

In a newly-established province, it would set a bad example to
allow the disobedience of Lieutenant O'Donovan to be unpunished.
Zéspedes decided that he would have to go to Havana to remain
under arrest until the decision of the king was received. At the
same time, the governor rushed letters to José de Gálvez in Madrid
and to military authorities in Havana asking that the young man
be forgiven. He wanted O'Donovan, who promised to devote his
life to the king's service, to receive all the consideration due the
son of a faithful subject. During the summer, the problem of sending the lieutenant to Havana was added to other transportation
problems occupying the province. On three occasions, strong south
winds forced the return of ships destined for Cuba with O'Donovan

as a passenger. While Patrick Tonyn was still detained at St. Mary's by the damaged *Cyrus*, the brig *Esclavitud* sailed out of the harbor on November 3, at last taking the governor's penitent but hopeful son-in-law to await justice in Havana's famous fortress, Morro Castle.

Subsequent developments in this rather sentimental narrative might as well be recounted at once. Out of consideration for Zéspedes' reputation and service to the crown, José de Gálvez acceded to his wishes and secured a royal order in June, 1786 releasing O'Donovan from imprisonment and restoring him to his former rank in the Hibernia Regiment. This long-awaited decision did not reach St. Augustine until November, 1786. Immediately Zéspedes wrote the bishop in Havana asking that ecclesiastical censure be lifted from his daughter, a request promptly granted. But not until March of 1787 did Lieutenant O'Donovan return to Florida, escorted by his comrade, Lieutenant Remigio O'Hara. Almost two years had elapsed since the bride and groom were forcibly separated on the night of their clandestine ceremony, May 29, 1785.

In preparation for the happy reunion, Zéspedes selected a house for the young couple, complete with servants' quarters and separate kitchen in the rear. This first home for the O'Donovans faced the bay, at the south end of town next door to the home of the surgeon in the royal hospital. Although the lesser outbuildings on the property remained somewhat delapidated, the doors, shutters, windows and roof of the two story coquina rock home were adequately repaired. Doña Concepción supervised the work of properly furnishing the interior, transferring tables, leather-seated chairs, candelabra and linen from her own generous household supplies. The gardener pruned deadwood from the fig and orange trees, transplanted roots of broad elephant-ear plants, started cuttings of scarlet hibiscus bushes and set out pots of bright azaleas. Soon the house, vacant since the departure of its British owners, achieved an atmosphere of warmth and hospitality from the freshly-polished wooden entry door to the sun-lit patio.

Although the O'Donovans' transgressions had been forgiven by their parents, the Bishop of Havana and the King of Spain. Dominga did not feel at peace until her marriage was further blessed in a nuptial mass. Often a nuptial mass was part of the marriage ceremony, but at certain seasons of the church calendar, the nuptial mass may not be performed. Father Hasset certainly declined to hold a nuptial mass for Dominga in the spring of 1785 while the validity of her marriage was in question. But in November of 1787, when Dominga was proudly pregnant, Father Hasset performed a nuptial mass, conferring on her marriage the Church's complete sanction. On February 9, 1788, the O'Donovans' son arrived and was baptized ten days later with the governor as sponsor. Both father and grandfather, relatives, saints and apparently Bernardo de Gálvez, were honored in his baptismal name, Juan Vizente Maria Bernardo Domingo Benigno O'Donovan.

At the time of the christening party for the new baby, the inner family circle and group of close friends included other recent additions who should be mentioned. Zéspedes acquired a second son-in-law on December 6, 1787, when Josepha married Captain Manuel de los Reyes, whose first local achievement was winning Tonyn's praise for exemplary liaison activities at St. Mary's. The young man also received Zéspedes' gratitude for this accomplishment, and for assuming the responsibility for Antonio on his jaunt to the port. Captain Reyes had indicated his ability as an officer and consequently received the approval of the governor, who fostered the military tradition in his family. The romance between Captain Reyes, a native of Naples, one of Spain's Italian possessions, and Josepha de Zéspedes developed while Reyes was in St. Augustine convalescing from a fever that forced his resignation as lieutenant governor of the St. Mary's area in September, 1786. Because Josepha's marriage took place during Advent, her nuptial mass had to be performed later, and was entered in the church records in June, 1788. Two days after Josepha's wedding, another important marriage united the O'Donovans' friend in Hibernia Regiment, Captain Didaco Brett, and Barbara O'Frey, daughter of Angela Huet at whose home the O'Donovan clandestine ceremony took place. Barbara was a stepdaughter of Chief Engineer Mariano LaRocque, one of the three officers in the advance party that Zéspedes sent ahead to East Florida in 1784.

In the interval between the romance of the governor's daughter in 1785 and the baptism of his grandson in 1788, St. Augustine settled down noticeably. Of course, a small community with a high percentage of rotating military personnel always has social problems. The Spanish occupation force arriving in 1784 was composed mainly of young men, who according to their individual nature might be described as "unattached" or "still on the loose." By the end of his governorship, most of those who held positions of responsibility had also acquired wives and children and become stable members of provincial society. Captain Pedro Salcedo, Juan Sivelly's commanding officer in the artillery corps, married in 1786 and purchased a home near the plaza, probably his family's property in the previous Spanish régime. The incidents receiving more detailed treatment in the foregoing paragraphs indicate one range of human drama in which the governor played a role while carrying out his administrative responsibilities. The vernal equinox naturally cast magic over Florida each year, but in Zéspedes' experience no season ever matched the emotionally tempestous spring of 1785.

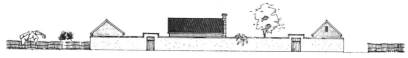

VI

Spaniards, Indians and Scotsmen

BECAUSE of the geographic location of Spanish East Florida, Governor Zéspedes was involved in foreign relations with three groups of neighbors: the Indian tribes to the west, the American states to the north, and the British inhabitants of the Bahamas islands to the southeast. As a general policy, he tried to avoid contacts with the Americans and British, but he held audiences for visiting Indians almost every week. In agreement with the Spanish governors of Louisiana and West Florida, Zéspedes considered Indian relations a matter of primary importance. He knew that the safety of the Spanish subjects on the American mainland depended on preserving peace with the numerically superior Indian towns. The proper method of dealing with the Indians was the subject of Zéspedes' first comprehensive proposal to the home government after his arrival at the provincial capital of East Florida. As soon as Tonyn left St. Mary's harbor in mid-November of 1785, he began composing a lengthy exposition of the Indian situation, addressed to Bernardo de Gálvez. Although his work was interrupted by the confusion arising from the murder of Lieutenant William Delany on November 24, he managed to complete his proposal by the end of the year.

In summarizing his views on the Indian problem, Zéspedes drew information from many sources: his knowledge of Indian relations in the previous Spanish régime, his conversations with Brigadier Ezpleta before leaving Havana, the intensive briefing from former British Indian superintendent Thomas Brown, and his own observations during his first year in Florida. Most vivid were his personal recollections of the hazards of living within reach of Indian enemies. Zéspedes clearly remembered the plight of the Pensacola inhabitants in 1761, beseiged by unfriendly Creeks until the grenadiers under his command forced the Indians to retreat and make peace. He also knew that in the previous Spanish régime, the residents of St. Augustine scarcely dared venture beyond the city gates, so great was the danger from marauding Indians. In 1762, the governor had organized all men and boys in a project to clear the brush for a mile's distance north of town to prevent Indians from taking cover close to the city walls. The semi-savage society that had menaced St. Augustine in 1762 still existed in close proximity to the European community on the coast in 1785.

Although the nearest Indian towns, those of the Seminoles, were fifty to seventy-five miles away, Indians hunted near the west bank of the St. John's river only twenty miles from St. Augustine. The principal Seminole town, Cuscowilla, was beautifully situated overlooking a lake in the fertile Alachua savanna. Surrounding the village were fields of corn, beans, potatoes, pumpkins and melons.[1] Part of the labor on these native plantations was performed by Negro slaves, and fugitive Negroes from the American colonies formed separate villages associated with the Indian towns. The luxuriant grass of the savanna provided succulent pastureland for Indian herds of domesticated horse and cattle as well as wild deer. Both the small, fleet Seminole horses and their horned cattle were descended from breeds introduced by the Spaniards in the early mission days.

In the Florida Indian towns as in other Creek communities, life followed a cycle determined by agricultural and hunting pursuits. The most important event on the southern Indian calendar, occurring in July or August when the first corn was ready for harvest, was the annual busk which might be considered an Indian New Year's celebration. At this season, a general amnesty was proclaimed for those who had committed minor crimes during the previous year, and offenders were permitted to return to town. In preparation for the annual busk, the Indians cleaned their houses and yards, then collected old clothes and household utensils for burning in a common fire in the town square. As a climax

---

[1] William Bartram, *Travels of William Bartram* (Philadelphia, 1791), pp. 168-171.

to the purification ritual, they took a special medicine and began
a three day fast, while all the fires in the village were extinguished.
On the fourth morning, the priest rubbed together two sticks of
wood, igniting a new flame to rekindle fires for all the homes.
The three days of fasting were followed by three days of dancing
and rejoicing, bringing in the harvest of corn. Everyone was
decked out in new clothes. In the evening, after a banquet of bear
steak, venison roasted in bear's oil, hominy, corn cakes and melons,
the Green Corn Dance began in the public square. All night long,
the dancing and singing continued, with monotonous chants to
the beat of drums and gourd rattles, and the dissonant melody of
reed flutes.

Following the harvest festival, Indians burned off the pasture
lands to promote the growth of tender new grass for grazing animals. Hunting was the principal occupation for Indian warriors
during the fall and winter. The women dried and preserved meat,
and cured the skins which were traded for European merchandise.
In the spring, councils to conduct the tribal business took place,
usually in April or early May. At the council meetings, emissaries from other southern and northern tribes were received and
decisions made regarding warfare against encroaching white settlements. Consequently, the danger of Indian attack was greatest in
the spring of the year. If the Indians did not attain their objectives
prior to the annual busk, they often continued hostilities in the
early fall, but arranged some form of peace or truce before the
hunting season began.

Although the Indians in Florida all followed this same mode
of life, they possessed no political unity. In 1785, the Florida
peninsula was inhabited by fragments from the twenty or more
tribes, speaking several languages, who comprised the Creek nation.
They had moved into Florida after the first decade of the eighteenth
century, at first filling the void left by the destruction of the Spanish
mission villages, then gradually moving south to the Keys. Wild
Indians and renegades were among the first to seek refuge in the
Florida wilderness, later followed by remnants of the former mission villagers. The pro-British Creeks occupying the Alachua
savanna had settled there after accompanying Oglethorpe's expedition to Florida in 1743 during the War of Jenkins Ear.

The word "Seminole" as an identification for part of the Florida Indians was still new when Zéspedes became governor. The
first written record is found in reports from the early years of the
British occupation of Florida. The term is derived from the

Spanish word "cimmaron" which means wild or runaway. The spelling is traceable to a peculiarity of the Creek or Muskhogean language, which contains no sound equivalent to "ro," so the Indians heard "cimmaron" and said "seminole," and the English in turn wrote what they heard.[2] Similarly, the English used casual phonetic spelling in writing Santa Fé as "St. Taffy," and Alachua as "Latchaway." The original Spanish name for the savanna contains the word *la chua*, the sink hole, and refers to an area where the land surface dropped several feet when the porous limestone substructure gave way.

Zéspedes realized that the advent of the British in Florida was actually the beginning of a new era for both the European and native populations of the peninsula. Before 1763, the Spaniards in St. Augustine had handed out several thousand pesos a year in Indian presents, but these gifts had not created peace with the nearby tribes. The British administration, on the other hand, received a more friendly reception. By treaty signed in 1765 at Picolata, an old Spanish fort on the St. John's river, the officials established boundaries separating the area of British occupancy from the territory reserved for the Indians. So far as European settlements were concerned, British East Florida was bordered by the St. Mary's river on the north, the St. John's river on the west, and on the south by a line from the entrance of the Ocklawaha river to the Atlantic coast. The British also introduced the system of Indian congresses, regular distribution of presents, and a supervised trade in European goods.

Zéspedes appreciated the wisdom of Colonel Thomas Brown's advice to continue the obviously successful procedures devised for handling relations with the Indians during the British occupation of Florida. To assure the Indians that the existing system would not be disturbed, Zéspedes held his Indian congresses in 1784 with the cooperation of British officials. General Tonyn had laid the basis for the smooth transition from British to Spanish supervision of Indian affairs in Florida through his "talks" in 1783 explaining that kings of England and Spain had "buried the hatchet" and become friends. Undoubtedly the transfer was simplified by the death, in March of 1784, of Cowkeeper, or Secoffee, anti-Spanish founder of the the Seminole tribe and Florida's most powerful Indian chief during the American Revolution. Zéspedes arrived

---

[2] Charles H. Fairbanks. Ethnohistorical Report of the Florida Indians. MS, P. K. Yonge Library of Florida History.

at a time when he could influence a new generation of Florida Indian chiefs, whose power was not yet established, and gradually
strengthen their attachment to the incoming Spanish régime. He
promised to observe the borders separating Indian and European
settlements established at the Treaty of Picolata in 1765. In
describing the Indian situation for the home government, Zéspedes
indicated that at this critical juncture, it was important to avoid
perceptible change in the system of administering Indian affairs.

Guided by British policy, Zéspedes established relations with
the different groups of Florida Indians. He met chiefs who attached great value to the silver medals they wore bearing the like-
ness of George III. These signs of distinction had been presented
at British Indian congresses. Other Indian families still cherished
a crucifix or rosary beads, handed down through descendants of
former inhabitants of the mission villages. A small percentage of
these Indians had observed European life in Cuba or the Bahama
islands. They returned with crews who came from Providence
to cut timber along the Florida east coast, or begged transportation
from Cuban vessels fishing near Mosquito inlet and the Tampa
and Apalache bay areas. Every spring, the fishing fleets anchored
along the coast to catch tons of mullet, bass and drum fish to sell
in Havana. In little smoke houses along the beach, they cured
fish over corn cob fires and preserved some varieties in barrels of
salt so that they would be in good condition at the end of a six
weeks expedition. As a sideline, the fisherman carried on a meager
Indian trade. The Indians also engaged in independent trading
ventures. In their canoes hewn from cypress logs, they could reach
Cuba in twenty-four hours from the Keys.[3] This regional economic activity began in the sixteenth century, and continued to
the mid-nineteenth century when Florida was an American territory.

During Zéspedes' governorship, remote Indian settlements far
to the south never sent representatives to St. Augustine, but followed a primitive and nomadic existence in almost complete isolation from all European contacts. Those living near the Indian
river, over a hundred miles south of St. Augustine, only occasionally came to see the governor. On the other hand, from the closer
Florida villages, chiefs and warriors came four or five times a year,
often bringing wives and children. Reports of good treatment at
St. Augustine spread through the back country and apparently had

[3] Bernard Romans, *A Concise Natural History of East and West Florida*
(New York, 1775), pp. 186-188.

a pacific effect on the entire native population, although there were a few malcontents. Some chiefs remained disgruntled because they had not been consulted before Florida was transferred from one European monarch to another. An unidentified group of Indians burned down "Bella Vista" soon after the handsome estate was vacated, but no general outbreak of Indian depredations occurred as the English residents had feared. Zéspedes found that the simple expedient of continuing the trading system and observing British boundary restrictions sufficed to smooth relations with his more immediate Indian neighbors in Florida.

The governor became involved in a vastly more complicated situation in dealing with the Indians of west Georgia and northern Alabama. Creeks from the Flint and Oconee river regions were frequent visitors to St. Augustine. Also, Zéspedes carried on a steady correspondence with Alexander McGillivray, whose home was near present day Montgomery, Alabama. Ties between St. Augustine and these more distant Indian towns had come into existence during the American Revolution. The complexity of Zéspedes' relations with this larger sphere of Indian diplomacy was the result of Spanish interest in the Indians on the American frontier and in the economic rivalry for the Indian trade. In both of these fields, Alexander McGillivray was a key figure.

Alexander's father, Lachlan McGillivray, was one of the first Scotsmen to develop the Indian trade in the southern hinterland. About 1738, he landed in Charleston without much capital except an excellent pen knife, which he bartered for goods to begin business. He established his headquarters, known as Little Tallassie, at the junction of the Tallapoosa and Coosa rivers, four hundred miles upstream from Mobile bay. The French had preceded him with a meager trade in this vicinity, and his own location was near an abandoned French outpost, Fort Toulouse. He married in a Creek ceremony a member of the powerful Wind clan, a young woman whose father was a captain stationed at Fort Toulouse. After Alexander was born in 1759, he remained entirely under his mother's supervision during childhood, according to Creek custom.[4]

In 1773, Alexander McGillivray's education was taken over by his father, who insisted that he come to Charleston, a town with

---

[4] John Walton Caughey, *McGillivray of the Creeks* (Norman, 1938), pp. 9-13.

more than five thousand white inhabitants, and as many Negroes.[5] In this urbane environment, the young Creek lad acquired the dress and manners of an English gentleman. He was tutored in Greek, Latin, Engish history and literature by his cousin, a Presbyterian minister, the Reverend Farquahar McGillivray. His father also arranged for him to receive business training in the Savannah countinghouse of Samuel Elbert, but Alexander found accounting a distasteful occupation and soon returned to Charleston. By this time, Lachlan McGillivray had achieved moderate wealth and renown. In dedicating to him the *History of the American Indians*, appearing in London in 1775, James Adair strongly recommended McGillivray for the superintendency of the southern Indians. At the outbreak of the American Revolution, Lachlan McGillivray's Royalist sentiments led him to return to his native Scotland, and Alexander returned to the Creek nation. The Georgians placed the name of Lachlan McGillivray at the head of their proscription list, and confiscated his estate valued at $100,000.

Back in the Indian country, Alexander McGillivray immediately assumed his hereditary role as a chief of the Wind clan. Among the Creeks, descent is reckoned in the female line, and less significance is attached to paternity. Young McGillivray successfully used his position to maintain the allegiance of the Creek towns to the Royalist cause during the American Revolution. In recognition of his services, the British named him commissary to the Creek nation and accorded the rank of colonel in the army. These wartime positions brought McGillivray into contact with the British authorities and trading firms in St. Augustine. When war broke out in South Carolina and Georgia, an increasing volume of Indian trade was channeled through Florida. After Bernardo de Gálvez took Pensacola in 1781, St. Augustine became the sole outlet for the southern Indian trade with England, as well as the final haven for British Loyalist refugees.

Several years before Panton, Leslie and Company became an important trading firm in Florida, Alexander McGillivray knew William Panton as a friend of his father in Charleston. Panton came to America in the decade before the American Revolution and

---

[5] In 1770, the white population of Charleston was estimated at 5050 according to Mary A. Sparkman in the forward to *The Charleston Directory for 1782 and 1785* (Charleston, 1951), p. 4. The estimated white population for 1790 was 8085. These figures compare reasonably with a description of the town in 1763, when Charleston was said to have 1100 houses, 4000 white inhabitants and nearly the same number of Negroes. See B. R. Carroll, *Historical Collections of South Carolina* (2 vols., New York, 1836), II, p. 484.

owned land in both Charleston and Savannah by 1770. The Scotsmen in the southern colonies were as clannish in America as in their native heath. In Scotland, Panton had known relatives of James Spalding, a trader who settled at St. Simon's island, Georgia about 1760 and operated three Indian posts along the St. John's river in Florida during the British period. Shortly before the American Revolution, William Panton and John Leslie also entered the trading business with headquarters at Frederica, Georgia, while Thomas Forbes handled the firm's interests in London. At the beginning of the American Revolution, Panton and Leslie moved to St. Augustine, and by January of 1783 they secured a license granting them a monopoly of the Indian trade in East Florida.[6] Among the merchants whom they superseded was James Spalding, who conducted his future operations exclusively in Georgia, but they absorbed into their own organization Spalding's most experienced Indian trader, Charles McLatchy.

William Panton boldly proceeded with his plans for business expansion even after learning the terms of the Treaty of Paris, by which Florida was returned to Spain. While he retained only one of the original Spalding stores on the St. John's river, the so-called "upper store" south of Lake George, he began to extend his enterprise westward toward the heart of the Creek country. At the request of the Lower Creeks, he opened a new branch at St. Marks in 1783, with Charles McLatchy in charge, and he hoped to become established in Pensacola. Yet he planned to remain in Florida only on condition that Alexander McGillivray become associated with his firm. The Indian trade, like other branches of commerce, had been disorganized by the period of warfare, and several American merchants were eager to gain the upper hand in the Creek trade as soon as hostilities ceased. Alexander McGillivray's foremost desire was to secure adequate European goods for the Creek nation. Loyalty to his father's friends and to the Royalist cause moved him to favor Panton, Leslie and Company. His other alternative was to promote trade with the rebel merchants of Savannah or Augusta, pre-revolutionary center of Indian trading. This would be an uncomfortable solution, since the Georgians already constituted a menace as they pushed forward the frontier of pioneer settlements and encroached on the Indian hunting lands.

Alexander McGillivray made his first overtures to the Spanish

---

[6] J. A. Brown, "Panton, Leslie Company," *Florida Historical Quarterly*, XXXVII (1959), pp. 328-336.

government in 1783, when he began writing to Arturo O'Neill, governor of Pensacola. In January of 1784, as soon as he learned the terms of the final peace treaty, he outlined a definite proposition for placing his nation under the protection of Spain. He expressed his belief that an alliance with a great monarch such as the King of Spain was preferable to an association with a "distracted republic," as he termed the American Confederation. Spain would also benefit from the alliance since the Indians could provide a buffer between the American states and the Spanish colonies. He went on to explain that for the Indians, the true sign of friendship was the provision of adequate trade. He earnestly recommended that the Creek trade be placed in the hands of Panton, Leslie and Company adding that Mobile or Pensacola were preferable locations for carrying on the trade with the Upper Creeks. In conclusion, he mentioned that he had served as British commissary to the Creeks for eight years, and offered to assist the Spanish government in the same capacity.

This first important letter from Alexander McGillivray, sent on to Cuba by Arturo O'Neill, introduced the young Creek leader to Zéspedes. The letter came to Zéspedes' attention in March, 1784, along with Tonyn's first letter also recommending that Panton, Leslie and Company continue the Florida Indian trade. Tonyn's letter to O'Neill originating in St. Augustine in September, 1783, traveled four months before reaching its destination. It went by messenger through the Indian country to Alexander McGillivray, who redirected it on the path to Pensacola, where it arrived in January of 1784. Very shortly, colonial officials in Louisiana, Florida and Cuba were all writing and forwarding letters in behalf of McGillivray and the Panton, Leslie firm, beginning a correspondence that filled many fat bundles in the Spanish archives. In London, Thomas Forbes broached the same plan for continuing the Florida Indian trade to the Spanish ambassador, who referred the matter to Madrid.

While these streams of correspondence were converging on the home government, arrangements for granting the requests were being made in Florida. In March of 1784, Arturo O'Neill planned a conference with the Lower Creeks which took place in Pensacola on May 31 and June 1. On this occasion, Alexander McGillivray was officially named Spanish commissary to the Creek nation with a salary of fifty pesos a year. McGillivray was disappointed in securing a trading concession for his friend Panton only at the store already functioning at St. Marks, actually in East Florida. At a separate conference at Mobile, the West Florida trade was assigned to the New Orleans firm of Mather and Strother, in which Governor O'Neill and Intendant Martin Navarro reportedly had an interest. Mather and Strother subsequently offered McGillivray a partnership in their Mobile operations, to the chagrin and embarrassment of Panton. But McGillivray accepted in order to prevent the trade from going to Elijah Clarke of Georgia.

Zéspedes did not learn the results of the Pensacola congress until after he reached St. Augustine. His immediate support for Panton, Leslie and Company stemmed as much from his desire to cooperate with the new policy set by his fellow governors, as from his need for the supplies which Panton provided when he first arrived in Florida. During the first year of his governorship, Zéspedes began to gather pieces of information giving him an insight into the complex world of Indian trade and Indian diplomacy. He was interested to learn that Elijah Clarke, the leading Georgian trader whom McGillivray was trying to oust from Creek territory in 1784, was associated in business with Samuel Elbert, who became governor of Georgia in 1785. It was in Elbert's mercantile house that McGillivray had such a distasteful apprenticeship before the Revolution. Colonel Thomas Brown, British Indian superintendent, also had cause to combat any operations attempted by Elijah Clarke. As British commander of Fort Augusta during the Revolution, Colonel Brown had been forced to surrender to Continental officer Elijah Clarke at the conclusion of a brave and stubborn defense.

During his first year in Florida, Zéspedes also began to understand the unusual characteristics of Alexander McGillivray, a person far different from the Creek chiefs whom he had battled over twenty years previously at Pensacola. Not only was McGillivray well educated, but a man of property as well. Although the Georgians had confiscated his father's accessible real estate, he still had a comfortable home at Little Tallassie. Surrounding the residence were fields of corn, an apple grove and cow pen, tended by fifty or sixty slaves. McGillivray had another establishment, and a second consort, at Little River near Mobile, but Little Tallassie was the home where he raised his two children, Alexander and Elizabeth. Like their father, they wore European attire, although the nearby Indian village was an important part of their life. When Zéspedes became governor of Florida, McGillivray was only twenty-five years old, yet his physical strength already was beginning to diminish. He suffered from severe headaches, fevers, vene-

real disease, the wracking pain of gout and rheumatism, in short
from the entire battery of eighteenth century ailments. Among the
Creeks, he owed his influence to his recognized wisdom, generosity,
warmth of heart, and above all to his astute manner of handling
outsiders.[7] A most atypical Indian chief, McGillivray was no war-
rior. His real talent was for diplomacy.

As Zéspedes became acquainted with the Creek towns nearer
to Georgia settlements, he was surprised at the number of chiefs
with Anglo-Saxon names. A few of Alexander McGillivray's
mixed-blood contemporaries in the Creek nation were Joseph Cor-
nell, Jack Kinnaird, George Galphin, Alexander McQueen, Charles
Weatherford, Daniel MacDonald, and the Perryman brothers,
who often acted as McGillivray's personal representatives to Zéspedes. The more prosperous and influential chiefs owned Negroes;
for example, one of the Perrymans possessed forty slaves. The
Anglo-Saxon patronyms seemed less common among the Florida
Seminoles, although John Hambly, Panton's storekeeper at the
St. John's river trading post, referred to the rising Seminole leader
with obvious deference as "Mr. Payne." These evidences of blood
relationship are but one indication of the English influence among
the Creeks which increased so rapidly after the middle of the
eighteenth century, largely through the traders who lived in the
Indian villages.

In Zéspedes' time, these Indians no longer were dependent on
the bow and arrow, homemade earthenware pottery, crude agricultural tools, blankets fashioned painstakingly from bird feathers,
and deerskin clothing. They also had passed the stage where they
were intrigued with beads, mirrors and other minor European
trinkets. Creek warriors demanded knives, spades, guns, saddles,
broad-brimmed hats, white ruffled shirts, fancy woolen blankets,
shaving razors, red and blue paint, and "taffy," their name for
rum derived from the Malay word *tafia*. Their wives wanted copper kettles and iron saucepans, scissors, needles and thread, gaudy
materials, linen bloues and silk petticoats, silver earrings and brace-
lets, and clusters of bright ribbons for their daughters' hair.

Since the Indian trade appeared to be a lucrative enterprise,
Zéspedes naturally wondered why this commerce should not be
handled by a Spanish firm. In making casual inquires he learned
some of the problems involved. Bernardo de Gálvez had tried to
turn the West Florida Indian trade to his father-in-law, Gilbert

---

[7] Caughey, op. cit., pp. 3-4.

St. Maxent, who still held the title of Indian superintendent when Zéspedes reached St. Augustine. Monsieur St. Maxent had suffered virtual financial ruin as a result of his attempt to enter the business. Officials in Spain accused him of engaging in clandestine trade, and the British captured two shiploads of his merchandise.[8] When Arturo O'Neill granted title and trade privileges to McGillivray at the Pensacola Congress in 1784, he was confident that superior officials would approve his course of action. He knew Bernardo de Gálvez wanted to win over McGillivray, whose Indian warriors had given formidable opposition during the siege of Pensacola. Bernardo de Gálvez also realized that few firms had the financial backing to undertake the Indian trade, a business requiring long term credit and the ability to survive periodic losses. A second factor to the advantage of British merchants was the Indians' marked preference for goods of English manufacture.

Taking into consideration all the multifold aspects of Indian relations, Zéspedes concluded that contact with these important neighbors should not be entrusted exclusively to British individuals. Although he was committed to support Panton, Leslie and Company, an honest, reliable and useful organization, he would prefer to introduce Spanish representation into the Indian towns that formed Spain's principal buttress against a more alarming neighbor, the new American confederation. With this goal in mind, Zéspedes suggested some interesting modifications of the existing system of dealing with the Indians. The plan he devised in 1785 included very practical suggestions, and some other ideas showing his old-fashioned missionary zeal, a quality quite rare among officials in the Spanish colonies by the eighteenth century. Zéspedes composed his proposal for handling the Indian question in great secrecy, even copying the final draft of the three-thousand-word discussion in his own hand.

Zéspedes acknowledged that Panton, Leslie and Company would have to continue in the Florida Indian trade until a Spanish merchant could be substituted, one who knew this type of business enterprise and knew the native languages. Since a firm with these attributes did not seem readily available, Zéspedes proposed that a Spaniard be attached to the Panton, Leslie and Company organization as soon as possible. To be qualified for this job, a man should have a knowledge of commerce, know the English lan-

---

[8] Arthur Preston Whitaker, *Documents Relating to the Commercial Policy of Spain in the Floridas* (Deland, 1931) pp. xxviii-xxix.

guage, and possess good health and a genial personality. Zéspedes believed that this newcomer's participation in the established firm should be subsidized by the royal treasury, if necessary. The trading post appeared to be indispensable in dealing with Indians, and Zéspedes preferred to have these stores located far out on the frontier in order to keep the Indians away from the areas of European settlement. For these Indian stores, Zéspedes recommended the addition of Spanish apprentices, boys from twelve to sixteen years of age who had received a primary education and who could learn the Indian language while helping with the Indian trade. This was a reasonable suggestion, since the Panton firm used the apprentice plan in training new employees. These young men eventually could join a Spanish firm when it seemed feasible to supplant Panton, Leslie and Company.

In making his recommendations for modifying the existing system of Indian trade, Zéspedes realized that one of the most difficult problems would be to get the Indians to accept Spanish articles in place of the familiar English merchandise. In Zéspedes' proposal, this sales job, requiring time and gentle persuasion, was one of the tasks assigned to an Indian commissary. Zéspedes hoped that suitable goods, particularly in the textile line, could be provided by manufacturing establishments in Alcoy and Palencia. A similar suggestion for producing Indian trade goods in Spain was made by Martin Navarro when he was recalled to Madrid in 1788 to give expert testimony on Indian affairs. But the quantity production of standardized articles has never been characteristic of the Spanish economy, and the duplication of English or French sample items was never attempted.

The unique portion of Zéspedes' Indian proposal is the section recommending a method for resuming religious conversion of the Indians. He certainly opposed a return to the seventeenth century mission system. In surveying the net results of the missions, possibly he failed to comprehend the destructive effect of the early English raids into the Florida mission villages. At any rate, he merely cited that fact that in 1763, after almost two hundred years' effort, the Spanish priests had only forty-three Indian communicants, all living in the vicinity of St. Augustine. Zéspedes was not an admirer of the noble savage, but rather believed that the average Indian would be humble or insulting, according to his estimate of the power of the man with whom he was speaking. Neither did he favor mingling with the native race. All reports agreed that white men living in Indian towns were a depraved and degenerate lot. Although he recognized individual exceptions, he generally deplored the racial mixture as a dangerous combination of savage barbarity and European sagacity. Still, he could not ignore the challenge of a pagan population within his sphere of influence.

Considering Zéspedes' personal convictions regarding interracial contacts, it is rather curious that he recommended sending out orphan boys as heralds of Christianity to the Indian towns. He had the naive idea of placing orphan boys, eight to twelve years of age, with selected Indian families who would be paid four hundred pesos a year for taking care of the youthful boarders. These boys should be well-instructed in Christian doctrine before entering the native villages, and should come to St. Augustine once or twice a year to re-accustom themselves to their natural language and to fulfill their obligations to the Holy Faith. Once they were well-versed in Indian language and customs, the neophytes could take the religious habit and become useful missionaries, appropriate instruments for civilizing the Indians and attracting them to an understanding of the True God.

The part of Zéspedes' proposal outlining the basic functions of an Indian commissary could not wait the approval of superior officers before execution. Zéspedes needed immediate assistance in handling the delegations of Indians visiting St. Augustine. Soon after his arrival, he assigned this "public relations" task to Luciano Herrera, one of the Spaniards who had remained in Florida during the British era. Herrera was listed on the staff of the occupation forces as chief overseer of public works, but since the public works program was negligible, Zéspedes used his knowledge and experience in a far more important field. Herrera received the Indian leaders, who always encamped outside of town, and notified the governor of their presence. He kept the records of arrival and departure of the different groups, the articles from the Panton, Leslie warehouse distributed as gifts, and the supplies of provisions and munitions doled out from the king's stores. As official host and protector, Herrera had to see that the Indians' brief visit to the capital was free from unpleasant incident. He had to keep them away from the taverns, and report any tavernkeeper serving them liquor illegally. If, in spite of these precautions, a drunken Indian appeared in town, the commissary along with the interpreter had the responsibility of returning him to his companions, unless they had already retired to their encampment. As a last resort, an Indian was turned over to the guard corps, who had permanent orders to care for these unfortunates and prevent them from sleeping in the plaza.

Until his death in 1788, Luciano Herrera served as Indian commissary for the province. He was succeeded by Fernando de la Maza Arredondo, bearer of a name honored in Florida history during both the first and second Spanish régimes. Long after he took over his new responsibilties, Maza officially held only his original appointment, as an orderly on the hospital staff accompanying the occupation force. Although Zéspedes could put into effect only a small portion of his proposal for managing Indian affairs, he did not change his ideas on the subject. He submitted his plan a second time in 1787, and again in 1789 with little variation except to substitute Maza's name as Indian commissary and add some details about accounting procedure. The home government never took official action on the proposal

In actual practice, Zéspedes had only a *mestizo* chief and a trading firm, both of Scottish origin, to promote Spanish influence among the Indians. In spite of his deeply ingrained suspicions concerning Anglo-Saxon designs, he did not diminish the usefulness of these less-than-ideal agents by giving them half-hearted assistance. Yet in supporting Panton and McGillivray, he inevitably became involved in their efforts to achieve their separate objectives. Panton was primarily interested in business expansion and increased profits. McGillivray was trying to achieve a measure of cohesion among the forty-five autonomous Creek towns to improve their joint defense against the Americans who were usurping their valuable hunting lands. Zéspedes used his own goal, rather vaguely defined as "the good of the royal service," to justify his subterfuges and bold maneuvers aiding Panton's firm and McGillivray's Indian nation.

For the good of the royal service, Zéspedes suppressed the court's first reply to requests for Panton, Leslie and Company to continue the Florida Indian trade. The royal order directing the firm to use only Spanish merchandise arrived in the fall of 1784, shortly before Zéspedes' important Indian congress December 8. He revealed the contents of the royal order early in 1785, after Bernardo de Gálvez had arrived in Havana as new captain general of Cuba. Zéspedes was confident that the home government would be strongly advised by Gálvez to reconsider the unenforceable restriction. In March, 1786, permission finally was granted for Panton, Leslie and Company to bring British merchandise to East Florida for the Indian trade, paying a six per cent import tax. In 1785, when

Zéspedes learned of the shortage of Indian goods at Pensacola, because Mather and Strother's credit sufficed only to get a shipment for Mobile, he issued Panton a passport to bring supplies from New Providence. Govenor O'Neill mildly protested Zéspedes' action authorizing a shipment from a foreign port into a province outside his jurisdiction. With this emergency shipment, William Panton entered the Indian trade in Pensacola, his future headquarters and a far more profitable location than St. Augustine. Here, he built a substantial three story brick building, a combination residence, office and hospitality center for visiting Indians.

Alexander McGillivray needed all the support he could get in order to carry out the agreements made at the Pensacola congress in the spring of 1784 to insure the supremacy of Spanish interests among the Creeks. Although the Spanish authorities seem to have assumed that McGillivray enjoyed superior authority among the Creeks, actually he could exert only the force of his personal influence. By the terms of the Treaty of Pensacola, McGillivray was obligated to exclude the Georgia traders and channel all trade to Panton, Leslie and Company. In the fall of 1784, several of the towns still preferred to trade with Elijah Clarke on the Ogeechee river rather than with the Panton store at St. Marks. In spite of their preference, McGillivray warned Clarke to remove his supplies and possessions from the nation before December. Nevertheless, throughout the fall, Clarke's representatives in the Lower towns continued to intercept loads of deer skins originally destined for McLatchy's new branch store at St. Marks. McGillivray's difficulties were increased when Creeks complained that the first load of Panton's merchandise was more expensive than Clarke's and of inferior quality. These problems diminished after the opening of the Pensacola store.

McGillivray also faced constant pressure from the Georgians who wanted the Creeks to concede the right to occupy additional land. With confidence in forthcoming Spanish support, McGillivray refused to attend a Georgia-sponsored congress in the fall of 1784 where trade and land grants would be brought up for discussion. Still, he feared that some of the poorer towns might be bribed into signing land grants. In September, 1784, William Panton went to Little Tallassie and assisted McGillivray in phrasing a "strong talk" to John Houston, governor of Georgia, on the land question. McGillivray learned in November that Houston had forbidden settlements on the Oconee river, a policy restricting the frontier people. He was certain that this diplomatic victory was gained because Houston realized the Creeks were assured of British trade and Spanish government support after the Congress of Pensacola.

Clearly the young Creek leader had his hands full when he received Zéspedes' invitation to attend an Indian congress in December, 1784 at St. Augustine. He already had a request from Governor Esteban Miró to visit New Orleans. An accidental injury to his right leg provided a painful but convenient excuse for refusing both governors. Actually, he was afraid to leave the nation for the three months time required for a round trip to St. Augustine. Tribal business needed his constant supervision. During the next year, by ceaseless and adroit management, he increased his control over the Creeks. The Spanish governors helped in this process by giving presents to McGillivray's friends and messengers when they came to Pensacola or St. Augustine. McGillivray often provided Creek warriors with notes recommending the bearer a keg of "taffy," shirts, or a blanket. As these slips of paper brought the promised rewards, McGillivray became a man of consequence to more people in the Indian nation, and the number of his supporters grew steadily.

By 1786, Alexander McGillivray felt his people were in a position to take the initiative against the frontier settlers, who had ignored Governor Houston's attempts to keep them off the Oconee river hunting lands. After McGillivray called an early congress of the Creek towns in March of 1786, the Indians systematically began to clear the frontier of all settlements as far as the Ogeechee river, the boundry set by treaty in 1773. A special messenger came to St. Augustine in May, 1786 to make sure the Indians could get extra guns and ammunition. In reply to direct questions, Zéspedes unflinchingly stated his position. He believed that war was regrettable, but defending one's land was laudable. He praised McGillivray for limiting the war to the recovery of land usurped by frontiersmen without the permission of their government, and assured him that generous supplies would be available in St. Augustine "for hunting." Zéspedes was stating the same policy he had expressed the previous year when Tom Perryman asked what the Spanish policy would be in the event of war between the Indians and Georgians. In May and June of 1785, Perryman and a large entourage made an information-gathering safari, visiting state officials at Savannah, General Tonyn at St. Mary's harbor, and finally Governor Zéspedes in St. Augustine.

Throughout 1786, unusually large groups of Indians visited St. Augustine carrying away over 5000 pounds of powder, and corresponding quantities of balls and flints, as well as other presents. Between May 12 and June 7, to pick a sample period, 141 Indians received hospitality from Zéspedes' administration. The Creeks had made impressive victories. Unfortunately, their success alarmed rather than pleased Governor Miró and Governor O'Neill, and almost upset the three-way cooperation between McGillivray, Panton and the Spanish government.

McGillivray did not learn that the Louisiana and West Florida governors had begun to waiver in their support until after the council meeting held in early April, 1787 at Coweta, a Lower Creek town. At this meeting, McGillivray reached the zenith power among the Creek Indians. The military success of the Creeks in driving back frontier settlers contributed to his enhanced reputation among the tribes, along with his ability to insure adequate trade through Panton, Leslie and Company and to secure ammunition supplies from the Spanish government. The Seminoles for the first time joined in the alliance under his control.[9] The Georgians had contributed to the unanimity of the Creeks by antagonizing the two Upper Creek towns previously inclined to favor the Americans. Chiefs of the two towns were the only Creek representatives attending a Georgia Indian congress, against McGillivray's advice in November, 1786, at which they had been seized and held as hostages. The meeting in Coweta in April, 1787, was also attended by an American Confederation representative, James White, who had arrived with the naive notion of persuading the Creeks to cede territory to Georgia. He received a more accurate education in the history of the Creek-Georgia feud from McGillivray, who convinced him the hostages should be surrendered. The returning warriors led the joint offensive against Georgia in 1787 following the annual meeting.

As soon as the three-day session in Coweta was concluded, McGillivray sent a full report to Governor Zéspedes asking for powder and shot for future use, but his message did not reach St. Augustine until late October when Perryman came to confer with the governor. McGillivray also solicited a large quantity of ammunition from Governor Miró in New Orleans, and was baffled at the hesitant reaction his request received. He had little enthusiasm for war, but believed that if he could follow up his last year's victories with a big spring offensive, he could bring the Georgians to terms and conclude once and for all the quarrel over the bound-

---

9 Caughey, op. cit., p. 33, 167 fn. 116.

aries of Indian hunting lands. He also felt that his Indians were taking the responsibility for preventing American infiltration into Spanish territory, an objective meriting the sincere cooperation of Spanish officials.

Governor Miró's hesitancy to continue Creek military aid was the result of his genuine fear that the Georgians would draw the American Confederation into their struggle. Furthermore, he had originally agreed to provide the Creeks with ammunition for defense, and in the spring of 1787, the Creeks were turning to offensive operations. Miró reluctantly consented to supply McGillivray's warriors with ammunition in 1787, but tried to handle the distribution with secrecy. He instructed Governor O'Neill in Pensacola to try to hand out the powder and shot through Panton's warehouse, if possible in the dead of night, but O'Neill knew there was little chance to carry out secret operations in his small town.

Governor O'Neill himself objected to furnishing ammunition for McGillivray to increase his power, already over-expanded in the opinion of the Pensacola governor. O'Neill favored securing additional commissaries to represent Spain in the Choctaw and Chickesaw nations and in the Lower Creek towns, limiting McGillivray to the Upper Creek towns. He was deeply suspicious of McGillivray's connection with William Panton, fearing the two would subvert Indian sympathy to the British nation or that McGillivray ultimately would succumb to American diplomacy. O'Neill did not appreciate how zealously McGillivray defended the Indian hunting lands and William Panton combatted that low-class political innovation called "republicanism," both objectives fitting into their joint venture in the Indian trade. Georgia was never able to lure McGillivray with offers to restore his father's $100,000 estate.

William Panton was also greatly disturbed by the attitude of the Spanish government, and particularly Governor O'Neill, in the spring of 1787. At this time, he learned the terms under which the court would allow him to continue trading in West Florida; namely, trade restricted to the Talapuche (Creek) Indians, permits required from the Spanish consul in London, captain and two-thirds of the crew to be Spanish, local licenses obtainable only in New Orleans. He had hoped for permission to expand his business further west into Choctaw and Chickasaw county, his reason for the large capital investment in Pensacola. In an irate mood, he explained his intention to leave Pensacola by January of 1788,

and engage in business only in East Florida where he could operate
with less restriction. Charles McLatchy decided that in order to
be under Governor Zéspedes' jurisdiction, he would change his
location to the upper St. Mary's river where he could be within
forty miles distance of the Lower Creek towns. The Apalache
area had been transferred to West Florida in 1785 because communication with Pensacola was easier than with St. Augustine.

McGillivray hoped that Zéspedes could regain authority over
the Apalache section and remove causes for discontent. The Spanish
army reoccupied Fort St. Marks de Apalache in the summer of
1787. McGillivray felt he had performed a real service in securing
Seminole acquiescence to the new Spanish defense post located
within the Indian territory. He was exceedingly displeased to learn
that the commanding officer had instructions from O'Neill to
seize any ships landing at St. Marks from Providence, the source
of Panton's supplies for both the Apalache and Pensacola stores.
He roundly criticized the pitiful and foolish policy of embarrassing
the small volume of Indian trade through Apalache which gained
so much good will for the Spanish nation. The Indian leader also
could not understand why Miró could not ask him to make peace
with Georgia, if that seemed the most advisable move. One astute
Creek chief had suggested that the Spanish wanted to supply only
sufficient ammunition to bring strong retaliation from the Georgians, and defeat for the Indians. McGillivray turned to Governor
Zéspedes in his efforts to fathom the baffling behavior of the West
Florida officials.

There is small wonder that messages concerning policy, with
fine shades of emphasis were badly garbled in McGillivray's mind.
The West Florida officials communicated with McGillivray through
a complicated procedure. Miró usually sent his instructions in
Spanish, although O'Neill tried to get him to send English translations of his letters since McGillivray knew no Spanish. O'Neill
similarly was hampered by his inability to speak English. Though
of Irish parentage, he had been brought up in Spain, and lacked
the bilingual ability of so many officers in the Hibernia Regiment.
To carry messages to McGillivray, O'Neill relied on an illiterate
interpreter who also acted as an undercover agent, O'Neill's personal
spy in the Creek country. In delicate matters such as distributing
large quantities of ammunition, O'Neill was afraid to send any
kind of a written message, but had the interpreter transmit verbal
instructions. Spanish letters arriving in the Creek country had to

be translated for McGillivray, and often their content taxed the vocabulary of available interpreters.

The reports of misunderstanding and dissension in West Florida, certain to weaken Spanish influence with the Indians, reached Zéspedes in October, 1787, at a time when the Creek-Georgia warfare threatened to include East Florida. The war was definitely moving south. Although Upper Creek towns took the offensive in the spring of 1787, the Georgians retaliated by attacking the Lower Creek towns. Residents along the St. Mary's river, including settlers who had fled from less protected locations in the interior, were frightened at the prospect of Indian warfare spilling over into Florida. In 1786, the Indians had mistakenly attacked settlers far upstream on the south side of the St. Mary's river, and scalped a little girl who survived the ghastly experience. Informed by Zéspedes, McGillivray also was horrified by the atrocity. Creek warriors were sometimes uncontrollable. They also had trouble recognizing the different political sovereignties on opposite banks of the St. Mary's. In the course of the war, fighting got out of hand; Georgians as well as Creeks took scalps. In the fall of 1787, official toll of Georgia casualties included thirty-one killed, twenty wounded and four captured by the Indians.

By the fall of 1787, the Georgians were thoroughly enraged and threatened to vent their wrath on Spanish Florida, the suspected source of ammunition for the Indian incursions that had gained in strength in 1786 and 1787. George Matthews, currently governor of the state, gave orders to raise an army of three thousand men and sought financial aid from the American Congress. Mathews also sent messages to dissuade the governors of East and West Florida from giving military supplies to the Indians, an action he charged was contrary to the law of nations. While the Indians turned to fall hunting, after their final forays extending from Kentucky to Georgia, the Georgians began to organize military operations that appeared to focus directly at Zéspedes' province.

The commander of the Spanish post on Amelia island, looking across the mouth of the St. Mary's river to Cumberland island early in November, observed signs of military construction and heard the sounds of cannon honoring the arrival and departure of Georgia military officials. Some of them visited the Spanish outpost and inquired about Spain's stand on the subject of Georgia-Creek hostilities, mentioning plans to station one hundred and fifty men on Cumberland island and to erect additional fortification along the St. Mary's river. They also expressed the intention of visiting

Governor Zéspedes personally in St. Augustine. It was the latter plan that Zéspedes found most alarming. He knew he could not prevent the Georgia officers from reconnoitering north Florida, a territory already familiar to them, but he did not want them to see the weak detachment on the St. John's river or the delapidated state of the Castillo. Zéspedes instructed the commander of the Amelia island post to treat all visiting Americans with extraordinary civility, but to prevent them from journeying to the provincial capital, offering the excuse that facilities were insufficient to entertain them adequately.

Faced with the need to put the province in a state of maximum defense, Zéspedes could do very little. His only mobile force consisted of four gunboats, one of which was generally stationed at Amelia island. He sent a second to San Vincente Ferrer, used the third to carry emergency supplies to the outpost at Panton's Indian store, and retained the fourth for service at the St. Augustine bar. Panton's storehouse near Lake George was a possible military objective, since the Georgians knew the firm distributed hunting supplies on credit to the Creeks. In the provincial capital, a state of military preparedness was signified by orders to cease pasturing cattle near the Castillo and to refrain from sowing fall crops north of the fort between the hornwork defense line and the ruins of the chapel *Nuestra Señora de la Leche*. These orders cleared the area within the immediate range of the Castillo's guns.

No American officials managed to penetrate the province except James Seagrove, a special representative sent by George Matthews in November, 1787 to explain the justice of the state's aims in fighting the Creek Indians. The Georgia legislature insisted that the Indian nation must adhere to treaties signed in 1786 by the insignificant minority of the towns who had since joined the majority of the Creek nation in opposing Georgia's land claims. James Seagrove, like Benjamin Hawkins, was at the beginning of his career in southern Indian affairs when he visited Governor Zéspedes. Apparently he had some knowledge of the Spanish language, and may well have been the same James Seagrove who helped Francisco Miranda, an early promoter of South American independence, to escape from Havana to Charleston in 1783. Seagrove first appeared in Georgia politics in 1786, shortly after American traders were expelled from Havana. At any rate, he listened respectfully to Zéspedes' protestations of neutrality and friendship, then asked Carlos Howard to write an English translation of the official reply for the governor of Georgia. Fluent in his own diplomatic line,

Zéspedes assured Governor Matthews that he would not only abide by the law of nations, but also by the law of reason and natural law. He informed Matthews that he supplied the Indians with ammunition solely for hunting, and sympathized deeply with the shocking outrages suffered by the Georgians, cruelties that the Spaniards had experienced so often at the hands of savages in former years.

The amiable reception of Governor Zéspedes and smooth phrases of Captain Howard convinced James Seagrove that no menace existed in East Florida to endanger the state of Georgia. Personally, Seagrove believed that the governor of West Florida, rather than East Florida, was primarily responsible for the Creeks' recently increased ammunition supply. To Zéspedes' great relief, signs of military activity ceased on Cumberland island and along the St. Mary's river during December, 1787. He felt he had done his best to follow his superiors' instructions relating to the situation. By royal order of May 10, 1786, Spain was officially neutral in the Creek-Georgia warfare, a pronouncement that had been modified by Bernardo de Gálvez' advice to support the Indians as far as possible without arousing the Georgians. Zéspedes realized that the Spanish frontier governors had come perilously close to overstepping this boundary, but fortunately had avoided disaster.

Governor Zéspedes preserved at least outward equanimity throughout the brief border crisis in 1787. While coping with this more alarming outcome of Spanish policy toward the Indians, he was also trying to restore relations between Indians, traders, and government officials in West Florida. He felt that Spain had too much at stake to permit the disruption of the delicately contrived system for sustaining Indian friendship, an integral part of the empire's frontier defense. He assured McGillivray that he would straighten out matters with the captain general in Cuba as well as with the home government, but he also had some well-stated admonitions for the Creek chief. Zéspedes explained that the Spanish monarch, a man of peace, had enjoined his subjects in America to maintain neutrality, a concept that had been strained to the limit in aiding McGillivray's cause. Certainly it was against the royal will to promote continuous offensive Indian warfare. In dealing with McGillivray, and with Panton as well, Zéspedes had the incomparable advantage of Captain Howard's assistance with correspondence. He could count on Captain Howard to convey his views with utmost accuracy in proper English phrases.

To postpone any definite action on Panton's part, Zéspedes

strongly advised waiting until the King's will became known. He always had confidence in the procedure of waiting until a definite satisfactory decision could be forced out of the ministry in Madrid. Panton was prevented from taking any rash action by a sudden tragedy within his firm. Charles McLatchy, who had built up an understanding with the Florida Indians through fifteen years of trading experience, died in the fall of 1787, creating an emergency at Apalache. In a friendly fashion, Zéspedes counseled the commandant at St. Marks, whom he had known in New Orleans, to promote friendly relations with the personnel at the Apalache trading post. He assured the commandant that there was no reason to prevent the trade with Providence, but that the official instructions probably needed some adjustment. The Apalache store across the peninsula from St. Augustine supplied the Lower Creeks and Seminoles on the fringe of his province. Knowing Indian reliance on the store, Zéspedes was determined to prevent its removal.

In his wholehearted efforts to repair the damaged alliance between the Spanish government, Alexander McGillivray and Panton, Leslie and Company, Zéspedes directed his major appeal to superior officials. First of all, he urged returning Apalache to East Florida, since the defense of the province depended on preserving the friendship of Indians served by that store. Supporting his case with fine technicalities, he pointed out that the royal order granting permission to Panton, Leslie and Company to remain in East Florida was given in response to a memorial presented while Apalache was still part of East Florida. Minutely checking Bernardo de Gálvez' original letter announcing the transfer of Apalache to West Florida, he seized on the phrase "for the present" and used this indication of a temporary change to defend returning the important area to his own jurisdiction. He wrote forcefully to the captain general of Cuba and to the ministry in Madrid, explaining at length that the services of Panton and McGillivray were indispensable until some alternative arrangements were made for handling Indian affairs.

Although Zéspedes was unable to regain the Apalache district, his energetic campaign otherwise brought satisfactory results. His positive point of view was adopted by Captain General José de Ezpeleta, the old acquaintance who in December, 1786 returned from Mexico to govern Cuba and the subsidiary provinces, Louisiana and the Floridas. In his letters to the court, Ezpeleta reiterated Zéspedes' arguments recommending complete support of McGillivray and Panton's organization. In 1789, the Panton, Leslie and Company trading privileges were re-confirmed in more favorable terms and extended to Mobile, where Mather and Strother had been forced to retire for financial reasons. Clearly, Zéspedes played a major role in establishing the unusual triangular alliance by which Spain secured unanticipated backing from the Creek nation, while Alexander McGillivray rose to eminent influence among the Indians, and a Scotch trading firm became a quasi-official agency of the Spanish government handling Indian relations.

VII

Bare Subsistence

BARRELS of flour and salt meat, and the money to pay for them, constituted Governor Zéspedes' most fundamental problem throughout his administration. He was responsible for feeding the troops and the families on his staff, an estimated 1800 people needing 1800 barrels of flour per year. The basic supply problem, graphically expressed in the familiar adage "an army travels on its stomach," applies in peace time as well as war. For the St. Augustine garrison, maintaining adequate food as well as money, guns and ammunition, required the use of sea routes extending from New York City, Havana and Vera Cruz. Furthermore, royal authorization had to precede shipments of funds or military equipment from Mexico or Havana, and methods for securing provisions also required approval from Charles III's ministry in Madrid. Although Zéspedes faced continual shortage of money and periodic shortage of provisions and military supplies, he found his problem most acute during the year 1786.

While the British merchants were in the province, he made use of their credit and resources. In 1785, he began purchasing flour and salt meat from a Philadelphia firm with Captain Miguel Yznardy acting as the local contractor. Captain Yznardy, a new resident in St. Augustine, carried on trade using his own vessel between Florida, Havana, Philadelphia, and New York, but hesitated to renew his provision contract in 1786 because he had lost money during the previous year. Needing assurance that rations would be

available in April, Zéspedes in January, 1786 appealed for assist-
tance to Diego Gardoqui, Spanish chargé d'affaires who had arrived in New York in July, 1785 to negotiate a boundary treaty
with American officials concerning the northern border of West
Florida.

Gardoqui soon ascertained that the Philadelphia firm was unwilling to continue supplying meat and flour for St. Augustine at
the existing price schedule. In New York, however, he arranged for
the firm of Lynch and Stroughton to send a consignment to Florida
for the last of March, 1786. Gardoqui acceded to Zéspedes' eloquent
pleas only because he knew the governor's reputation of a fine
gentlemen and loyal servant of the king. He first sent food to St.
Augustine as an emergency measure, a method by which so many
procedures in the Spanish Floridas became permanent.

From long experience, Gardoqui had acquired all the contacts
necessary to achieve the most satisfactory results. His own firm in
Bilbao, Spain, traded with the American colonies for a generation
before the American Revolution, serving during the early years
of the war as the screen for Spanish government shipments of arms
and clothing while Spain was still officially neutral. He learned
English and acted as interpreter throughout the negotiations carried
on in Spain with American colonial representatives.[1] All his experience with international trade did not alter his conviction that
colonies should trade only with the mother country using that
nation's shipping facilities. He could not see why East Florida,
like other colonies farther south, should not be supplied from
Spain or other parts of the empire.

Gardoqui's confidence in the Spanish merchant marine nevertheless had been severely shaken during his voyage to America.
After leaving Spain, he discovered that the captain had sailed without inspection because he feared the vessel would be declared un-
seaworthy. Defects included a hull heavily covered with seaweed,
a leaky hold and broken water pumps, and rigging that broke
even in fair weather. Fearing shipwreck, the crew in a secret meeting
decided to put ashore for repairs at Puerto Rico, but almost ran
aground between two mountain peaks, actually on adjacent islands,
that they thought marked a harbor entrance. They were rescued
by a Catalonian vessel, and in Puerto Rico secured the aid of
American harbor pilots who guided them to Havana. Here, Gardoqui learned that the captain illegally had brought to Cuba flour

---

[1] Arthur Preston Whitaker, *The Spanish American Frontier* (Boston and
New York, 1927), p. 73.

and cotton goods, and had opened a store in the name of a servant to sell the smuggled merchandise. Following the urgent advice of the American pilots, Gardoqui refused to finish the trip on his original vessel. He arrived safely in New York, full of gratitude and respect for American seapower. From first hand observation during his voyage, he realized that the Spanish merchant marine might be incompetent to handle the empire's trade.

A major difficulty of the Spanish colonial administration was the conflict between the home government's mercantilistic policy and the economic trends actually developing in the Indies. Furnishing provisions for the St. Augustine garrison is an example of a problem in which national policy ran counter to sound economics. To maintain all trade within the empire, St. Augustine should receive supplies only through Havana, including Cuban beef, and Mexican wheat raised in the Puebla-Axtitla region. Several factors made this system both impossible and inadvisable by 1786. In the first place, Mexico suffered a serious drouth and crop failure in 1785, forcing Viceroy Bernardo de Gálvez to dash hatless through the street to see that public granaries were opened to provide grain for a starving, fever-stricken populace.[2] Under these circumstances, Mexico could not export much grain to other Caribbean colonies or to Spain. A second factor was the rapidly growing Cuban population, which increased from 190,000 in 1775 to 260,000 by 1790. In 1786, the island absorbed a larger proportion of Mexican wheat as well as local beef production, and in spite of official prohibition, importation of flour and meat for home consumption had already begun. Thirdly, the Mexican wheat deteriorated more rapidly than American grain, a condition aggravated by exposure to tropical heat and humidity during the long voyage via Havana.[3] The fourth factor was cost, an important consideration when Florida received limited funds. The price of flour in Havana was double the figure in New York or Philadelphia. Finally, Zéspedes could not depend on the Cuban intendant to dispatch shipments to arrive when needed, and once en route the supplies followed a transportation route more hazardous than the coastal shipping lane north of St. Augustine.

Since the beginning of the eighteenth century, colonial governors

---

[2] John Walton Caughey, *Bernardo de Gálvez in Louisiana* (Berkeley, 1934), p. 253.

[3] Ramon Guerra y Sánchez, Jose M. Pérez Cabrera, Juan J. Remos, and Emeterio S. Santovenia, *História de la Nación Cubana*, (10 vols., Havana, 1952), II, pp. 79, 241-245.

of Florida purchased flour from American ports, an arrangement
known to Spanish officials familiar with the situation. In the
spring of 1782, Bernardo de Gálvez experienced difficulty in securing bread and flour for the expeditionary force aboard ship in Havana harbor waiting to depart for the Bahama islands. Consequently, he readily approved Zéspedes' securing meat and flour in
the United States, at least until some contrary orders were received.
In spite of all the experience jusitfying shipment of flour and salt
meat from New York, the method incurred the official disapproval
of both José de Gálvez, colonial secretary, and the Conde de
Floridablanca, chief minister of state in Spain from 1777 to 1792.
Assuming that Cuba lacked neither flour nor meat, they directed
Zéspedes to secure supplies from Havana, and directed the intendant
to furnish whatever the Florida governor requested. Replying to
Gardoqui's inquiries on the subject, they instructed him to ship
supplies to St. Augustine only in an emergency. The ministry's
orders had little effect because St. Augustine usually could claim
a state of emergency.

Policy was a negligible problem in comparison with the practical
difficulties of delivering supplies to the port, a fact amply illustrated
by the experience of the year 1786. In arranging their first supply
shipment to East Florida, Lynch and Stroughton's staff had considerable difficulty locating a vessel in New York with sufficiently
shallow draft to enter the St. Augustine harbor. Since the firm
knew pilot charges at the port were high and return cargo scarce,
freight rates were correspondingly increased. In realistic Yankee
tradition, the firm specified cash payment on return to the home port
as part of the delivery contract. Gardoqui asked Zéspedes to send
the amount of 4397 pesos because money was scarce in New York
at the time.

Acting in good faith, Zéspedes expected to have the cash on hand
by the time the sloop reached St. Augustine with the first quarterly
shipment of 450 barrels of flour and 100 barrels of salt meat leaving
New York the last of March. Funds actually left Havana on March
17, 1786 and normally should have reached Florida ahead of the
provision ship landing the third week in April. But the storm
season coinciding with the vernal equinox brought tragedy to the
Spanish brigantine, La Esclavitud, which had taken the governor's
son-in-law to Havana the previous November. Severely damaged
by heavy seas, La Esclavitud returned to Havana for repairs before
attempting to navigate the treacherous Bahama Channel a second
time. This consoling news reached Zéspedes shortly in advance of

the provision ship which he consequently detained in Matanzas bay awaiting the momentary arrival of the necessary money.

On the afternoon of May 3, signals from the watchtower on Anastasia island indicated that two vessels were approaching from the direction of Havana. Officers on duty hurried to the parapet af the Castillo San Marcos, where the northeast bastion commanded a view of the ocean road beyond the bar. The brigantine *La Esclavitud* and a schooner came into view as gathering storm clouds rolled across the sky and gusty winds made immediate entrance into the harbor impossible. The entire garrison and debt-ridden community was vitally interested in the safe arrival of the two ships. Seven officers of the Hibernia Regiment were on board *La Esclavitud*, as well as supplies of rum, tobacco, sugar, and 40,000 silver pesos. Townspeople standing along the shore watched with growing fear as the winds increased, by night developing into the most severe to strike the coast in several years. Next morning both ships had disappeared, but after five days the schooner came back, reporting that the brig had been lost from view during the three-day blow.

After a week of growing despair, Zéspedes finally borrowed the money to pay freight and unloading charges, and sent the empty provision ship back to New York. He still hoped the officers and supplies on *La Esclavitud* were safe in a distant port delayed only by further ship repairs. The community gradually abandoned hope for the lost brigantine, the first of three supply vessels to suffer shipwreck along the Florida east coast during the year 1786. The governor immediately decided that in the future he would set aside money to finance a six months' advance supply of provisions. After the next large sum arrived in July, he followed this policy although it left troops, government employees, day laborers and local creditors unpaid. To explain the continuing need for American provisions and to assure Gardoni of prompt future payments, Zéspedes sent his personal aide, Sergeant José Fernandez, to New York in June. Gardoqui had been forced to advance government funds to pay for the first supply shipment until he was reimbursed by the Florida governor. As a result of Fernandez' lucid explanation, the Spanish representative drew up an annual contract with Lynch and Stoughton and shipments left for St. Augustine every three months.

The arrival of money from Mexico in July, 1786 guaranteed payment for the year's provisions, but provided only temporary relief for the monetary crisis in East Florida. Although Bernardo de Gálvez sent 100,000 pesos, the intendant in Havana deducted ten per cent of the total for supplies previously furnished from Cuba. Zéspedes protested that the troops in St. Augustine were a detachment of the Havana garrison and consequently the intendant was responsible for furnishing clothing and supplies. In spite of the fact that new army regulations laid the financial responsibility for colonial defense on the local population, Zéspedes insisted that East Florida, an infant colony, could not be expected to have resources to maintain its garrison.

As a last resort, the governor appealed to Bernardo de Gálvez who admitted that part of the cost for maintaining the troops should be borne by the Cuban budget. Ignoring the viceroy's directions and the governor's protests, Intendant Ignacio Urriza continued to discount every shipment of funds for the St. Augustine garrison. Zéspedes tried to secure replacement of the money lost on *La Esclavitud*, but the captain general refused to send another shipment unless the Florida garrison would assume the risk. By September, 1786, local shoemakers, tailors and dry goods merchants denied further credit extension to government personnel, and the governor felt obliged to issue a proclamation to quiet the exasperated population. As an emergency measure, Bernardo de Gálvez suggested issuing local bills of exchange, a device adopted in Pensacola, New Orleans, Mobile and the Caribbean islands. Zéspedes had instituted a similar temporary expedient while serving as governor of Santiago de Cuba, but realized that East Florida possessed no resources to back up provincial paper money. Local credit was already strained by the issuance of notes to the Panton, Leslie firm for Indian gifts, to Francisco P. Fatio for lumber to repair buildings, and to Francisco X. Sanchez for the garrison's fresh meat.

One narrow escape and two shipwrecks later in 1786 further emphasized the hazards of relying on shipments from Havana, his only source of military and hospital supplies, rum, sugar and tobacco. Always conscious of his responsibility for the defense of a frontier fortress in the Caribbean defense line, he insisted on maintaining certain minimum supplies of guns and ammunition. Although the local use of weapons was generally limited to target practice, and to shooting muskets on festive occasions, the military supplies were continually depleted by presents to the Creek Indians. These gifts were usually generous in the spring of 1786. Governor Zéspedes anticipated replacement of the vital powder and shot in the fall during the rotation of troops assigned to the St. Augustine garrison from headquarters in Havana. But troop rotation was far from a routine maneuver in the fall of 1786.

Since the loss of the brigantine *La Esclavitud* in April, awaiting the arrival of a vessel from Havana had become a nerve-wracking experience. After surviving a hazardous voyage, the main body of new troops reached East Florida with difficulty in September. The first ship sighted St. Augustine, but was driven north by strong winds, finally anchoring at St. Mary's harbor. About a hundred weary soldiers straggled into St. Augustine during the following week, after tramping the fifty miles from St. Mary's harbor. Small gun boats stationed at Amelia island had to wait a month for good weather to transfer the ammunition and artillery south to St. Augustine, repeating the tedious procedure used when Zéspedes first landed in Florida in 1784. Local troops replaced by the new arrivals also had to go to St. Mary's to embark for the return trip to Havana.

Only a portion of the troops and military supplies arrived safely on the first ship. A smaller group of two dozen soldiers and artillerymen were wrecked on November 4, after a three weeks' voyage along a course plotted by an inexperienced coastal pilot. On this occasion, fishing vessels rescued the soldiers and three Canary island families coming to Florida as new settlers. Zéspedes later chartered small boats to rescue some of the supplies from the clear, shallow water. The final supply shipment of the year from Havana came on a schooner with a competent Florida pilot, but the overloaded vessel ran aground in broad daylight on December 11, on the shifting shoals north of Cape Canaveral. Six of the passengers drowned, and the supplies plus a large volume of government papers and official correspondence were washed into the sea. After the wreck on November 4, Zéspedes became increasingly anxious about a shipment of flour and meat expected from New York sometime during the month. By Christmas, he feared the ship was lost or that an unknown royal order forced Gardoqui to suspend shipments to St. Augustine. Finding only a month's supply of rations on hand, he sent triplicate messages to Gardoqui by three different vessels and dispatched local captains to bring emergency supplies from Georgia. The schooner from New York was delayed only by rough weather, however, and finally reached Florida in January.

Zéspedes' experience in 1786 repeatedly illustrated the precarious quality of existence in a military post dependent on unreliable supply lines. During the course of the year's tragedies, the garrison lost friends and relatives, officers, money, food, ammunition, and official papers whose contents were unknown until duplicates arrived. The governor also realized that his local problem was aggravated by the commercial policy of the ministry in Madrid and by the financial policy of the intendant in Havana.

With all the discouraging events of the year, Governor Zéspedes received one letter in November, 1786, giving him hope that the financial element in his problem might be alleviated during the coming year. The encouraging letter came from Bernardo de Gálvez, who requested a list of salaries and estimated expenses for maintaining the garrison in St. Augustine so that he could establish the annual subsidy, or situado, as it was customarily called. After serving only four months as captain general of Cuba, Bernardo de Gálvez had left for Mexico on May 16, 1785 to succeed his father as viceroy of New Spain. The request from the viceroy of New Spain was enclosed with the even more heartening royal order sent by José de Gálvez, who sought Zéspedes' estimates of tillable land, natural resources, and additional population for East Florida. Assuming that the situado was already determined, the royal order directed the viceroy to send annually an additional fifty thousand pesos to be used for financing new immigrants for the province. The royal order dated May 8, 1786 announcing the supplementary funds for population development apparently called to Bernardo de Gálvez' attention the fact that the regular situado had never been established.

The appropriation for East Florida was one of the items lost in the shuffle of inter-colonial correspondence, and further confused by Bernardo de Gálvez' frequent changes of location. In May of 1784, a tentative budget, the basis for the situado, originated in Mexico City. Antonio José Lopez de Toledo, who had been an auditor during the first régime in Florida, drew up a list of staff members with suggestions as to the functions of each member and an appropriate salary. He was probably a relative of Lieutenant Colonel Antonio José Lopez de Toledo who arrived in East Florida with his son very early in the occupation period to try to secure the title to the property his father and uncle had possessed before 1763. The Lopez recommendations first went to José de Gálvez in Spain, but arrived after Bernardo de Gálvez had commenced his return trip to Cuba in August, 1784. José de Gálvez forwarded the budget to Havana, where it arrived in January, 1785, but Bernardo de Gálvez did not establish a situado for East Florida during his brief term as captain general of Cuba.

When Bernardo de Gálvez became viceroy of New Spain, living in Mexico City, he retained his title as captain general of Louisiana and the Floridas, and thus the problem of the Florida budget and situado returned to its geographical point of origin. In the meantime, Governor Zéspedes had made his own budgetary recommendations in December of 1785, but he had never received a decision from anyone in the colonial administration. Judging from the viceroy's letter arriving in November, 1786 that previous budgets had gone astray, Zéspedes immediately prepared a new financial statement. The inquiries of the two higher officials, Bernardo and José de Gálvez, produced a flurry of activity among the clerks assisting Gonzalo Zamorano, director of the royal treasury in St. Augustine. On the day before Christmas, the new budget was completed.

Before sending the voluminous financial report to the viceroy, Zéspedes checked the final estimates requiring a situado of 121,000 pesos. The minute calculations can be rounded out to the following figures:

1) Annual salaries and garrison expenses .... 53,000 pesos
2) Rations for 500 soldiers 35,000   ″
3) Indian presents and rations 13,000   ″
4) Urgent building repairs 18,000   ″
5) Medicine, linen, hospital supplies 2,400   ″

Total for current expenses: 121,000 pesos

To repay indebtedness, the provincial treasury required the additional sum of almost 57,000 pesos. The royal order of March 8 allotted another 50,000 pesos for population financing. Adding these two sums to the annual budget, the royal treasurer estimated East Florida's cash needs for the year 1787 at 230,000 pesos. Governor Zéspedes realized that this was a staggering amount to request from the viceroy, but he sent along documents to substantiate every estimate. Unexpected tragedy prevented Bernardo de Gálvez from every reading the report so promptly and carefully constructed to merit his approval. One of the last victims of the fever epidemic in Mexico City, the promising young colonial official died on November 30, when he was only thirty-eight years old. This news reached Florida the last of January, 1787.

The death of Bernardo de Gálvez, the only superior official with both personal interest and authority to assign definite funds for Florida, was one of a series of misfortunes which prevented Zéspedes from ever securing a definite situado. In March, 1787, the super-

vision of Louisiana and the Floridas, the territory young Gálvez
had regained, was transferred to the captain general of Cuba, José
de Ezpeleta. In Havana, Florida's financial problem became the responsibility of the ailing Cuban intendant, Juan Ignacio de Urriza,
whose policy of discounting funds assigned to the garrison infuri-
ated Zéspedes even more than his initial error of sending insufficient
money with the occupation force. Urriza took the papers relative
to the Florida budget with him when he left for Spain after his
successor arrived in Havana on May 6, 1787.[4] The problem
might have been settled in Zéspedes' administration if Urriza had
completed the budget promptly in Spain and referred it back to
his successor, Pablo José Valiente, an able official transferred from
Guatemala by one of the last orders signed by Bernardo de Gálvez.
Valiente had proved his ability when he accompanied José de
Gálvez on the tour of New Spain completed in 1770. In Cuba,
he managed to increase revenues so successfully that he was called
to Madrid for consultation in colonial matters, and left Havana in
November of 1788.[5]

Under the Spanish monarchy, colonial government was theoretically dependent upon royal authority in Madrid, but it was also
dependent upon the ingenuity of the individual colonial governors.
Faced with the inescapable reality of erratic shipments of money and
supplies from Havana, and orders to resort to Gardoqui only in
emergency, Zéspedes made adjustments. Far in advance, he announced his minimum needs to the intendancy, and when supplies did not arrive by a certain deadline, he advised the Spanish
minister in New York. His were not the only appeals. In March,
1788, they coincided with the emergency requests from New Orleans when the city was devastated by fire. To cut down on the
importation of salt meat, he increased the consumption of local beef
and in April, 1788 granted a larger contract to Panton, Leslie and
Company, successor to Francisco Xavier Sánchez as supplier of
fresh meat for the St. Augustine garrison. The Indian trading
firm's assets included herds of cattle on the St. John's river and
contacts to secure additional cattle from the Indians. The cattle
industry in the province had been virtually wiped out during the
American Revolution. Panton, Leslie and Company also could
grant extensive credit, a rare and valuable commodity in itself.

---

[4] Duvon Clough Corbitt, "The Administrative System in the Floridas,"
Tequesta, I, No. 3 (1943), p. 59

[5] Jacobo de la Pezuela y Lobo, *Historia de la Isla de Cuba*, (4 vols., Madrid,
1868-1878), vol. III, p. 205-206.

Zéspedes analyzed the problem of shipping to and from Havana, and determined that freight charges would be reduced by using only Florida pilots, who made the round trip in five to ten days less time than Cuban pilots unfamiliar with the coast. Lacking money to pay local labor, he asked for additional *presidiarios,* convicts sentenced to labor on public works.

Translated into human terms, one can see the stagnation and discouragement forced on the colony by the lack of money and the procrastination of higher officials. Probably the most unfortunate were the small tradesmen of the town, who furnished the garrison families with additional staple foods, spices, drygoods, and the like, and also served as tailors, carpenters, shoemakers and day laborers. Unless they could be paid for services to the government personnel, they, too, were without income. The governor was nearly overcome with compassion at the sight of an obviously pregnant Minorcan woman, carrying a small baby in one arm and steadying a toddling child with the other. He knew that the government owed wages to her husband, who would be without a job until some vital building and repair projects were put into operation in the province. In despair, a few Minorcans, British and Floridanos departed.

The scarcity of money enforced a partial subsistence economy on the St. Augustine garrison. Lacking the cash to buy fresh provisions in the city market, officers, soldiers and treasury clerks all raised vegetables on plots of ground behind the barracks at the edge of town. This was not an original or unusual undertaking, for soldiers in the previous Spanish régime had also raised food in specially assigned gardening areas. Actually, it was a customary method of supplementing government rations. A close look at any colonial frontier garrison—French, Spanish, or English—will reveal a body of men behind in their pay, with inadequate food, clothing, beds and blankets, scraping along with the aid of the scanty harvest provided by planting seeds near the fort they are guarding.

In many ways, therefore, the general picture in St. Augustine was fairly typical of the colonial scene and not a peculiar injustice suffered only in East Florida after the American Revolution. From his examination of correspondence from the previous Spanish régime, Zéspedes knew that even with an established situado, the money often simply did not arrive. He had coped with similar supply and monetary problems in Santiago de Cuba, second largest city on the island but far more remote from Havana than St. Augustine when transportation time is considered. He also realized that the supply problem was worse in Chile, for example, or for outposts of the Philippine islands. From long experience with army administration, he understood that his situation required extreme patience. He never doubted that the royal council in Madrid, fully informed of the province's needs, would make suitable arrangements.

Governor Zéspedes' only feeling of animosity was toward the intendancy, the office responsible for the controversial discounts from funds en route to the East Florida troops. In his attack on the intendant, he always operated through the captain general of Cuba, whom he expected to bring the intendant to terms. Zéspedes pointedly ignored decisions of the intendant unless they were reinforced by orders from the captain general, the only official he considered his immediate superior. After all, he had advanced in the army's line of promotion for over thirty years before the parallel hierarchy of intendants and super-intendants was added to the governmental administration in 1765. As a military officer, he flatly refused to be subservient to a financial efficiency expert, even if that official ranked on a level with the captain general of Cuba. Except for special royal orders, however, he was completely at the mercy of the intendancy, the office with complete monetary control.

Nevertheless, he continued to insist that the Cuban army budget contribute to the support of the detachment in East Florida, a claim he justified by citing the opinion of Bernardo de Gálvez. By 1788, the unauthorized discounts amounted to over one hundred thousand pesos, including 72,000 in cash and the balance in shoes, clothing and supplies. Zéspedes realized that with 72,000 pesos, Florida merchants could be repaid and the balance distributed to the troops, through whose hands the cash would filter to revitalize the rest of the province. Finally, the super-intendant in Mexico City, Manuel Antonio Florez, joined in the fray. He counseled Zéspedes to cease bombarding the captain general of Cuba with demands, since decisions about money in the entire viceroyalty were exclusively within his own jurisdiction. Writing in December, 1788, Florez acknowledged that the intendancy in Havana owed the East Florida garrison 120,000 pesos. In view of this potential source of income, he decided to send Zéspedes only the 50,000 pesos assigned by the royal order of May 8, 1786 for population development in East Florida. Florez recommended that Zéspedes extricate himself from debt by securing the money owed his garrison in Havana, then become adjusted to the annual receipt of the fifty thousand pesos population fund. Florez pointed out that the king was heavily in debt, and everyone must tighten his belt. Utterly dismayed, the governor felt that the super-intendant had somehow simultaneously backed him up and let him down.

Officials of the intendancy, whose attitudes Zéspedes found so heartless, had their own problems juggling finances for governmental units much larger than East Florida. In Mexico, for example, approximately 2,400,000 pesos were expended annually on troops and presidios. The super-intendant also had to meet the high cost of Spain's globe-encircling defense system, largely supported by the fabled "wealth of Mexico." The largest mint in the world was in operation in Mexico City. In the 1785-1789 period, three million pesos annually were appropriated for situados sent to Havana, Puerto Rico, Trinidad, the Philippines, Louisiana and the Floridas.[5] Of the total sum, 500,000 pesos were expended for the government of Louisiana and West Florida, while East Florida usually received about 100,000 pesos. Taking into consideration the entire viceroyalty of New Spain, East Florida's financial need was a very small concern. The intendant in Havana likewise had difficulty adjusting the Cuban budget to harsh reality. In 1775, the Cuban situado was 728,000 pesos. After rising rapidly to a wartime peak of 8,468,000 pesos, the situado dropped to 663,000 in 1786.[6]

Throughout his battle with the higher administration, Zéspedes' only weapon was his pen, and in the course of combat he composed increasingly dramatic letters protesting against the unjust treatment of the little colony that was his personal responsibility. At the beginning of his régime, he was content with simple, cryptic phrases to describe the physical deterioration of St. Augustine's public buildings: ". . . the troops without shelter, God without a temple and I without a home." In March of 1789, the news that he could count on only 50,000 pesos came just two days after he had written his annual budget message, as usual explaining the absolute necessity for 200,000 pesos. After receiving the discouraging message from the super-intendant in Mexico City, his sense of anguish and frustration pushed him to a peak of metaphorical declamation. Writing again on March 16, 1789 to the captain general of Cuba, José de Ezpeleta, he declared:

---

[6] Herbert Ingram Priestly, *José de Gálvez, Visitor-General of New Spain, (1765-1771)*. (Berkeley, 1916), p. 372.

[7] Guerra y Sánchez, *et al., op. cit.,* p. 276.

Money is the life blood of the body politic. If any part of the body is deprived of the required amount of the vital fluid, that part will first become torpid, then shrivel and finally perish. This has begun to occur and will increasingly occur in Florida if the colony is persistently denied what is rightfully hers. Though this may appear to be an exaggeration, such is not the case, as I swear by the loyalty I owe the King; for the cries, groans and wails of the unfortunates who are my immediate responsibility, under your superior control, oblige me to speak clearly. Therefore, with the utmost frankness, let me call your attention to the general unhappiness of these inhabitants, and beg immediate and effective relief.

One of the unfortunate side effects of the acute financial strain in East Florida was the friction between Governor Zéspedes and Gonzalo Zamorano, director of the royal treasury, after they received the super-intendant's shattering decision to decrease future funds for the province. Although details of the disagreement are lacking, trouble arose in July of 1789 when Zamorano disapproved of orders that Zéspedes had issued regarding the treasury and supply department. Zamorano's uncooperative attitude may explain a peculiar mission undertaken in August, 1789, by four military officers whom Zéspedes sent to Charleston. Correspondence does not reveal their precise objective, but while in Charleston they made some expensive purchases. They paid for the merchandise by means of a five hundred dollar loan from the South Carolina treasury, negotiated with the assistance of Governor Moultrie. In February, 1790, Zéspedes personally arranged repayment through Thomas Tunno, a British merchant in St. Augustine, whose brother Adam Tunno, was a prominent Charleston businessman. Zéspedes could be highhanded if he thought the royal service demanded it.

The tiff between Zéspedes and Zamorano in the summer of 1789 occurred when the governor was already annoyed by Zamorano's punctilious interpretation of royal orders. On a previous occasion, in 1787, the two men had disagreed over the title to be used in addressing correspondence to Zéspedes. Both men had read the lengthy royal order issued November 27, 1786, explaining when the honorary terms "excelentissimo" and "señor" could prefix a regular title in the various ranks of the colonial administration. After receiving the royal order, Captain General Ezpeleta instructed his subordinates to address him as "Señor Captain General," and Zéspedes desired to adopt the same title. Zamorano insisted that the royal order did not permit this unless Zéspedes governed both Floridas, the case when Bernardo de Gálvez held the title. In response to Zamorano's inquiries, the court decreed that Florida was subordinate to Cuba as it had been before the cession to England. The decision destroyed Zéspedes' claim to a fancy title. He disliked being thwarted where honor and status were at stake.

In July, 1789, Zéspedes probably had little basis for his open criticism of Zamorano, a conscientious and hardworking civil servant, with an exemplary twelve-year record, including service through the difficult siege of Pensacola. A native Spaniard, Zamorano had married in Havana shortly before sailing for Florida, and already had the additional responsibility of three daughters born in St. Augustine. For the sake of his future career, and his family's welfare, he sent a memorial to Madrid defending himself against charges that he had exceeded his orders. The difficulty was that Zamorano's special instructions came from the intendant in Havana, his superior. This second "unpleasantness," to use Zamorano's term, began when Zéspedes' successor was already selected. No hasty decisions are made in Spanish bureaucracy. After due consideration, a new governor in East Florida and a new intendant in Havana agreed in 1791 that Gonzalo Zamorano merited no censure.

While financial uncertainty was creating so many forms of distress in St. Augustine, some of the difficulties slowly were being resolved in Cuba. By 1789, Intendant Domingo de Hernani, who took office in Havana in November, 1788, had begun to grapple with Florida finances, a problem requiring some complicated intra-colonial bookkeeping between the Cuban budget, the royal expense account, and a hypothetical Florida appropriation. Zéspedes' successor, Juan Nepomuceno Quesada, was delayed in Havana in the spring of 1790 while the intendancy tried to clear up the monetary confusion, but the final audit was not completed until February, 1791. Until Zéspedes left St. Augustine in July, 1790, his colony continued a hand-to-mouth existence. As the governor repeatedly observed, life would have been immeasurably easier if the intendant had provided a reasonable amount of money in 1784 to handle the original heavy outlay of the occupation force. Throughout Zéspedes' administration, the royal treasury generally owed about 50,000 pesos in debts, the majority a year old but some dating from the preceding year, to the few remaining Florida planters and to American business men in neighboring states. Officers' pay was usually one or two years in arrears, and common soldiers seldom received their small monthly cash allowance. For his last three years in Florida, Governor Zéspedes regretfully but frankly fed the garrison soldiers and their dependents by using the 50,000 peso fund that José de Gálvez intended for investment in immigration.

VIII

The Grand Tour

ALTHOUGH Governor Zéspedes considered the men, women and children dependent on the military garrison as his primary responsibility, he also felt solicitous for the civilian population consigned to his protection by the diplomats in 1783. He regarded this small group of approximately 1,500 people as the root stock, whose natural increase gradually would fill the vacant houses in St. Augustine and populate new settlements in the hinterland. Throughout his first years in East Florida, he was amazed as he learned the variety of lands from which East Florida residents had emigrated. In a population so small he became acquainted with the past history and individual problems of the people, particularly those living in the provincial capital. Though few in number, they revealed intriguing information about their curiously cosmopolitan origin and recounted personal experiences during their periods of adversity.

No systematic records were collected concerning the population of the entire province until the winter of 1786-1787. After receiving the inquiries from José de Gálvez in November, 1786, Governor Zéspedes immediately assigned Father Hassett to compile a municipal census. Census taking, with pertinent information about children to be baptized and adults to be confirmed or converted, was traditionally the responsibility of the clerical authorities. To supplement the city records, Father Miguel O'Reilly listed the families living along the St. John's and St. Mary's rivers while accompanying Governor Zéspedes on a tour of the backlands early in 1787. During the four weeks' journey, the governor's party made a survey of arable land and commercial and agricultural prospects, in addition to completing the census information.

The core of Florida's civilian population were the 460 survivors of the New Smyrna colony established in 1768 at Mosquito Inlet sixty miles south of St. Augustine, by Dr. Andrew Turnbull, a Scottish physician, who named the settlement in honor of his Turkish wife. From his trading connections in the Mediterranean, Dr. Turnbull arranged to bring eight shiploads of immigrants, including 200 Greek mountain tribesmen, 110 unemployed Italians from the city of Leghorn, and 1,200 Minorcans forced to leave their island as a result of serious crop failures. Almost immediately on landing in Florida, the projected settlement was shaken by a revolt led by one of the Italians, whose three hundred followers tried to escape on a ship with a thousand pounds worth of merchandise. Under the system of stern supervision following the revolt, the colonists suffered at the hands of overseers who did not understand their language and treated them with a brutality acquired while managing primitive Negro slave gangs in other English colonies.[1] The exhausting effort of clearing trees from semitropical jungles, swampland fevers, and inadequate food prior to their first harvest, were the hardships reducing their original numbers.

The settlement became the object of political persecution in 1774 after Dr. Turnbull intercepted correspondence between Spanish authorities in Havana and Father Pedro Campos, the Minorcan priest whom he paid an annual salary of three hundred dollars to attend the spiritual needs of the Catholics at New Smyrna. The correspondence originated from Father Campos' attempt to secure renewal of his faculties as a missionary in Florida, originally granted for only a three-year period. On the eve of the American Revolution, the secret contact between New Smyrna and Cuban officials appeared treasonable to Governor Patrick Tonyn, who ordered the deportation of Father Campos' assistant and the execution of one of the colonists. Indications that they might not secure their own land after seven years of indentured labor further dispirited the Minorcans, who came from an island where honesty and mutual trust governed the behavior of a virtually crime free society.

---

[1] Carita Doggett, *Dr. Andrew Turnbull and the New Smyrna Colony of Florida.* (Jacksonville, 1919), pp. 15, 29-31, 46-51.

Governor Tonyn, at least partially motivated by a provincial political feud with Turnbull, broke up the colony in the fall of 1777 while the doctor was in England. The rainy season that year brought a heavy toll of deaths during a fever epidemic. The weakened New Smyrna residents obediently gathered together their personal belongings and began the three day march to St. Augustine, where they buried sixty-five more of their number during the first month in the city. The British overseers, who had denied Father Campos the use of the sacred vessels of his religion, held the priest in custody until Luciano Herrera managed to secure his release. After burying the last victims of the fall fever epidemic, Father Campos also trudged to the capital to console his flock, by now reduced to 600.[2]

In 1777, the year when the first Royalists sought refuge in East Florida, the New Smyrna survivors began raising vegetables on the outskirts of St. Augustine. By the time of Zéspedes' arrival in the province, those most skilled in agriculture, fishing and general craftsmanship had managed to accumulate a little capital. Their gardens were supplemented by vineyards, groves of fruit, and pastures for dairy cattle, while a few had built sloops to engage in coastal trade. Part of the former New Smyrna residents left the province during the British evacuation, but the majority looked to the incoming Spanish governor as a deliverer. On July 12, 1784, when first the Spanish flag flew over the Castillo, Father Campos' parishioners presented petitions to Zéspedes, asking acceptance as natural vassals of the Spanish crown because of their religion and also because Minorca was returned to Spain by the second Treaty of Paris in 1783. Until he received instructions for official land surveys, the governor advised them to continue occupancy of their homes and the free use of their accustomed garden plots. Knowing that Father Campos had complete information about his parishioners, Father Hassett concentrated on the remaining population segments.

The other elements of St. Augustine's population remaining from the British era had not experienced misfortunes as great as the former New Smyrna residents. They stayed in Florida for religious reasons, or because they hesitated to abandon their recently-established shops and agricultural enterprises. Whether original British colonists in Florida or recent refugees from the American Revolution, they preferred to accept Spanish political control rather than

---

[2] Michael J. Curley, *Church and State in the Spanish Floridas, 1783-1821.* (Washington, D. C., 1940), pp. 25-44.

face the unknown hazards of beginning life again in unknown surroundings. Furthermore, frightening tales of social resentment
and physical suffering had drifted back from Providence island,
dumping point for the last impecunious groups of evacuees from
East Florida.

In Father Hassett's census taken in December, 1786, these former British subjects came under the heading of "foreigners." The
classification included twenty-three families totaling eighty-six
persons with one hundred twenty-seven Negro servants, some of
whom were free Negroes. The birthplaces of the eighty-six "foreigners" listed the American colonies of Georgia, the Carolinas,
New York and Pennsylvania; and the foreign areas of Scotland,
Ireland, Italy, Switzerland and parts of Germany. How a Benga-
lese merchant with a Hindu slave turned up in eighteenth century
St. Augustine is still a matter of conjecture. The foreigners also
indicated religious diversity, with representation of Calvinists,
Methodists, Lutherans, Quakers and Catholics.

Spanish families living in St. Augustine in December, 1786,
slightly outnumbered the so-called "foreigners," and were equally
diverse in origin. The total of thirty families included fourteen who
had lived in Florida before 1763, five recently-immigrated Canary
island households, and eleven representatives of peninsular Spain.
In addition, there was a family of Mexican Indians who does not
appear on the census list but is nevertheless recorded in the baptismal
register.

Of all the families representing various parts of the Spanish
empire, the greatest unity prevailed among the former Florida residents, whose presence supplied the slender thread connecting the
first and second Spanish régimes in St. Augustine. These *Floridanos*
were the remainder of a group of 343 families whose experience
after leaving St. Augustine in 1764 paralleled the plight of the
British Loyalists in 1784. After they evacuated Florida, the
Spanish government tried to resettle them in a pioneer community
at Matanzas, Cuba, but they were town-dwellers without the
training to convert tropical forest into cultivated land. A few
were murdered by slaves donated to them by the government to
assist in the strenuous task. A few families went to Campeche,
in New Spain, but the majority of the *Floridanos* stayed in Havana,
hoping for jobs in the royal service or land grants in the suburb of
San Antonio. The able-bodied men meantime earned only a
pittance rowing *guadaño* boats, the small skiffs with awnings used
for harbor communication. The term *guadaño*, literally meaning

"scythe," denotes the slender, curved shape of the boats. Former leading citizens of St. Augustine, representing 166 families, drew up a memorial in 1766, two years after their arrival in Havana, mentioning that some of the more unfortunate were reduced to begging, sleeping in doorways, selling their clothes, and even prostitution. The men petitioned to receive their back pay, which had been sent from New Spain but never distributed, and for repayment of loans to the presidio in Florida.

In the course of the next twenty years following the memorial, the *Floridanos* in Havana naturally decreased in number and lost their unity. An unknown percentage was incorporated into the staff and troops of Zéspedes' occupation force. Father Hassett's census listed fifty persons with ten Negro slaves as the number of civilians returning from Cuba. They were sailors or small tradesmen, making shoes or selling tobacco. On returning to St. Augustine, Francisco Joseph Huet brought with him his father, aged seventy-eight, a native of Spain and a brother of the Third Order of St. Francis. Although Father Hassett classified Francisco Sánchez as a *Floridano*, his inclusion in the rest of the group would distort the total picture. Furthermore, he never left the province. Sánchez and his Negro Catholic consort had eight baptised children living in St. Augustine, while the thirty-nine slaves at his ranch had fourteen children. A year after Father Hassett's census, Sánchez married the seventeen year old daughter of a North Carolina planter, Theophilus Hill, and established a new household at his ranch north of town. He also began developing a new plantation near his father-in-law's property on the St. John's river.

The most recent arrivals in St. Augustine were the five Canary island families, part of a group of 129 former Pensacola colonists whom the government intended to transfer from Havana to St. Augustine. Three families were passengers on the vessel wrecked near Cape Canaveral on November 4, 1786. On reaching St. Augustine November 18, they became an immediate problem for Governor Zéspedes, who lodged them in vacant houses and supplied them with food and clothing until some means for their subsistence could be arranged. These five families represented the first implementation of the May 8 order concerning population development for East Florida. In the broader colonial picture, they were indications of the home government's program to improve colonial agriculture through the migration of Canary Islanders, a significant population movement in the empire during the eighteenth century.

One hundred twenty Canary island families came to St. Augustine at the very end of the first Spanish period.

According to Father Hassett's census, the remaining eleven Spaniards were five wine shop keepers, a carpenter, tailor, two sailors and two merchants, one of whom was born in Ceuta, Spanish fortress on the North African coast opposite Gibraltar. These families for a variety of reasons had become established in St. Augustine during the two years since the colony was returned to Spain. A rough summary of the civilian groups in Father Hassett's census taken in St. Augustine in December of 1786 indicates: 86 of American or north European descent, 97 of Spanish descent, 469 former New Smyrna residents, and 291 Negroes, or a total of 943 residents. The civilian population was markedly overbalanced by the 1800 dependents of the garrison, who formed an integral part of the community. But the military force also evidenced an interesting diversity, with detachments from the Cuban based Havana Regiment, the Irish-born Hibernia Regiment, and the Inmemorial del Rey Regiment which included soldiers from Spain and the Spanish Kingdom of Naples. The Irish contingent left this small international settlement in 1788 when the entire regiment returned to Spain, and the effective strength of the St. Augustine garrison decreased from 500 to 400 men.

Governor Zéspedes postponed his survey of the rural inhabitants until he settled matters pertaining to the garrison. This was the difficult period in the early winter of 1786 when shipwrecks in November and December delayed the arrival of new troops and the replacement of weapons and ammunition given to the Indians in the spring. The governor also had to send to Georgia for emergency flour supplies because the ship from New York expected in November was still missing at Christmas time. With reasonable supplies of food and ammunition on hand, the troop rotation completed, and warfare between the Creek Indians and Georgians temporarily suspended, the governor felt safe in commencing a tour of backwoods Florida late in January, 1787. Zéspedes' expedition, spurred by José de Gálvez' interest in developing the province, was not an unusual undertaking. A Spanish colonial official customarily toured his area of jurisdiction soon after assuming office, just as a newly-crowned king journeyed through his realm.

The governor's party included his son, Lieutenant Vicente Domingo de Zéspedes, Captain Carlos Howard, Father Miguel O'Reilly, Chief Engineer Mariano LaRocque, and a group of soldiers and sailors. The touring party first ascended the North river, a twenty mile long stream flowing parallel to the coast and entering the harbor just north of the Castillo. They passed by vineyards, peach orchards, small fields ready for spring planting, former British rice plantations, and James Hume's "Oak Forest" estate, which had become the King's woodcutting preserve to furnish firewood for the barracks' bake ovens and cook houses. Along the river Father O'Reilly counted thirteen British and Minorcan families, totaling forty-six Europeans and fifty-six Negroes.

Near the head of the river, Francisco Sánchez' cattle grazed on the Diego plains that had been his family's ranchland since early in the century. From the North river, the governor's party hiked overland to north-flowing Pablo creek, a smaller stream entering the St. John's river about six miles from the ocean. Zéspedes wanted to inspect the swampy intermediate area before recommending a connecting canal to provide continuous inland navigation from the St. John's river to St. Augustine. He knew that former Spanish governor Manuel de Montiano had recommended such a canal before the middle of the century. The British were on the verge of putting the plan into operation when the American Revolution broke out, but the idea did not become a reality until the American government dug the canal as part of the Atlantic inter-coastal waterway. In Zéspedes' era, canoe travel from one stream to the other was often possible after heavy rains. At the mouth of the St. John's river, the governor walked along the hard white-sand beach, noting the high sand dunes, fresh water springs, and the leaping surf where the incoming waves meet the outflowing river current. In former years, the bar at the entrance to the St. John's river had been an unimportant obstacle to navigation, but recent storms almost closed the channel.

A dozen miles upstream on the St. John's river, Governor Zéspedes made the first important stop on his itinerary. The location was San Vincente Ferrer, a military outpost located on the high ground on the south bank of the river that the British had called St. John's bluff. As soon as he assumed office, Zéspedes sent fifteen men to replace the British detachment stationed at this important point commanding the inland navigation route between the St. John's and St. Mary's rivers. Ascending the river bank in January, 1787, Zéspedes could see the shingled roofs and brick chimneys of the taller buildings projecting above the surrounding wooden palisade. Once inside the enclosure, he noted that the

outpost was composed of five separate buildings. The main barracks, with a fireplace for warmth and shutters to keep out the
winter wind, offered welcome shelter for the travelers. This
building, measuring about twenty-four by thirty-six feet, was
two stories high, with a cellar below and a garret above. There
were three large rooms on the first floor, and a stairway to five
rooms on the second floor where a ladder provided access to the
two tiny cubby holes under the roof. Additional housing was
available in a smaller structure, only about twelve by fifteen feet
in size, also boasting a fireplace. At a distance from the two
dwellings were a storehouse with an outside staircase to the
attic area, a thirty foot long stable, and a small cook house. All the
buildings were made of pine board on cedar post foundations. In
1782, the bluff had been the site of a British refugee town of 300
houses, but the inhabitants had evacuated, most of them reducing
their homes to planks in order to take them along. House frames
too large to be accommodated in the holds of vessels were cast aside
at St. Mary's harbor. All trace of this settlement, like the town
of Hillsborough on the St. Mary's river, fast disappeared.[3]

Directly opposite San Vicente Ferrer, on the north bank of the
St. John's river, a small creek led to the mouth of the Nassau river
where a second creek continued to St. Mary's harbor by way of
"The Narrows" behind Amelia island. The fifteen mile area between the St. John's and St. Mary's rivers was intersected by
numerous creeks and swamps, cutting off six areas near the seacoast
designated as islands. Between the two larger rivers, the Nassau
river followed a short and tortuous course. All along these waterways, the British had continued logging operations up to the final
evacuation of the province, and abandoned logs of oak, cedar and
red bay still lay along the shores. Governor Zéspedes inspected the
entire route, pausing to check the population of the islands lying
between the waterway and the open ocean. On Talbot island he
found five American families, a total of twenty-eight people, engaged in farming with the aid of twenty-two slaves. A single
family of six people lived on Fort George island.

By January 29, the governor's party was encamped at the crude
border fort on the north end of Amelia island, where the mile wide
entrance to St. Mary's river separated Spanish territory from Cumberland island in Georgia. Until illness forced the resignation of

---

[3] Charles Loch Mowat, *East Florida as a British Province, 1763-1784*,
(Berkeley, 1943), p. 138. Also, Wilbur Henry Siebert, *Loyalists in East Florida,
1774-1785* (2 vols., Deland, 1929), I, p. 177.

Captain Manuel de los Reyes in September of 1786, he had been in charge of the Amelia island post, acting as lieutenant governor of the northern section of the province. Since Zéspedes did not have a similarly capable officer, he maintained only a detachment of twenty-five soldiers at this location, rotating the comand among the officers of the St. Augustine garrison. During the brief stopover at Amelia island, Father O'Reilly held mass, using the portable altar he had brought along for the benefit of troops who seldom had the opportunity to attend church in St. Augustine.

From the island outpost, the governor sailed sixty miles up the St. Mary's river to the fording point on the main road to Georgia before retracing his route back to San Vicente Ferrer. The road from the ford on the St. Mary's river to St. Augustine, usually called the King's Road, had been built by British engineers and still was the only road in the province. It originally extended south to New Smyrna, but after the settlement there was abandoned, the roadway became obliterated by underbrush. In the course of his excursion along the northern frontier of Florida, Zéspedes located on the Spanish side of the river twenty-two British Loyalist families, 123 people with twenty-six Negroes. For Father O'Reilly the tour also served as a missionary journey, and his interviews with the isolated inhabitants included queries concerning their religious principles. Many of the backwoods families had never seen a preacher or priest of any faith. They received Governor Zéspedes and Father O'Reilly with curiosity as well as courtesy, many agreeing to provisional baptism of their children although they were reticent concerning their own conversion. Far up the river, Father O'Reilly baptized six-year-old Elizabeth Kean, the little girl who had survived being scalped by Indians the previous year.

The second portion of the governor's tour followed the St. John's river over a hundred miles upstream to the Indian store maintained by Panton, Leslie and Company near present day Astor. The St. John's river, originating almost two hundred miles south of St. Augustine, flows north through many channels and lakes up to Lake George, maintaining its general course about twenty-five miles from the ocean. The channels unite north of Lake George as the river broadens to a width of one to three miles, turning east at Cowford, modern Jacksonville, to enter the ocean thirty-five miles north of St. Augustine. Careful check of the habitations along the fertile St. John's river, for the most part clustered near the bend at Cowford, revealed twenty-eight families, comprising 126 persons.

The majority of the 240 slaves in the St. John's section belonged to the plantations of Francisco Fatio, Theophilos Hill, Francisco Sánchez, and William Pengree who had startled the governor by boldly returning to Florida in December, 1786. William Pengree had left his plantation, "Laurel Grove," during the period of the British evacuation and settled in Camden County, Georgia just across the border. But the terrors of the Creek-Georgian hostilities in 1786 persuaded him to return to the relatively greater security of his plantation in Spanish Florida. With his wife, child and forty-eight slaves, he moved into his former residence, before riding to St. Augustine to announce his change of plans.

In the course of the seventy mile journey beyond New Switzerland, Francisco Fatio's plantation almost due west of St. Augustine, the touring party encountered very few human beings. Twelve miles from New Switzerland, Governor Zéspedes inspected the abandoned Spanish fort at Picolata, built of stone brought by barge from Anastasia island. Picolata was the site of the Indian congress held by the British in 1765 to determine the boundaries for European settlements in East Florida. Not far from Picolata, he found Job Wiggens, son of a free Negress, who cultivated several hundred acres of land with the aid of seventeen slaves, to provide a living for his wife and four children. A former Indian trader and interpreter, he also operated a ferry service for Indians crossing the river on their trips to St. Augustine. Zéspedes made a mental note of this public service, and included an annual stipend for Wiggens in his future budget recommendations.

A mile from modern San Mateo, the touring party viewed the high bluff marking the site of the Rollestown settlement, founded by Denys Rolles, who brought forty-nine prospective settlers to Florida from London slums in 1764. The deep, narrow channel at this point afforded anchorage for vessels loading indigo sold to bidders in London coffee houses. In 1782, Rollestown had encompassed eighty thousand acres, with a town and central square laid out, and a road cut through the forest in the direction of St. Augustine. Fearing that Indians might attack his colony after the British departed, Denys Rolles removed his settlers in 1783 and even took away the handsome sash windows, the principal ornament of his own home.[4]

4 Carita Doggett Corse, "Denys Rolle of Rollestown, A Pioneer for Utopia," *Florida Historical Quarterly*, VII, (1928), pp. 115-131.

The weeks spent in the interior wilderness of Florida were a revelation to Governor Zéspedes. He had observed many kinds of scenery in his life, the dry plains of La Mancha, rocky precipice of Morocco, the contrasting mountains and tropical jungles of Cuba. None of these experiences stimulated his imagination to the extent of the river excursion with alternating views of cultivated crop land, mysterious forests of live oak festooned with Spanish moss, and limitless swamps and savannas. During the winter season when Zéspedes made his tour, the woodlands offered an unusually deep vista. In February, the oak, maple and cypress stood gaunt and leafless, although the pines, cedars and broad-leafed evergreens retained their year-round density. Here and there the roving eye was arrested by the deep red of an early-flowering maple, the subdued cerise of a redbud, feathery wild plum, or opaque white of the dogwood, the trees whose bloom precedes the formation of leaves.

Florida offers a variety of strange natural phenomena. Stopping to explore the creeks entering the river, Zéspedes noted the warm, sulphur-smelling springs as well as the sweet, cool springs from which they filled their drinking jugs. All along the St. John's river, they observed the vacant and tumbled down dwellings formerly inhabited by British colonists. Saplings, underbrush and tangles of vines were already growing up in abandoned rice, indigo and cotton plantations in the process of being reclaimed by nature, a discouraging sight adjacent to an abundance of natural resources.

For the first time, Zéspedes saw the magnificent trees described to him by residents of the British era. The tall pines the governor had admired on the shores of the Nassau river were slender reeds compared with the stately cypress of the St. John's river swampland. Around the base of the tree, the cypress "knees" projected several inches above the water, their two foot breadth growing from the serpentine under-water roots. The impressive central shaft, often ten feet in diameter, rose eighty feet in the air with a flat umbrella of foilage at the top, trailing long streamers of moss. Such trees were felled by eight or ten men, standing on a stage built above the surrounding "knees." The hollowed trunk of the cypress formed the canoe used by the Indians to travel from Florida to Cuba or the Bahama islands. Cypress shingles and boards provided the most durable materials for frame buildings in Florida.

With the abundance of natural game, the travelers scarcely needed their supplies of ground corn, dried beans and rice. The marshes were thick with ducks and wild pigeon about to begin their annual northward migration. Wild turkey and white-tailed deer were other forest delicacies. A few white hairs from the deer's tail, ravelings of red ribbon, and mottled turkey feathers made a lure to attract a ten or twenty pound trout hiding beneath a patch of floating plants eddying near the river bank. Fish boiled with rice in sour orange juice, and meat barbecued over open coals were excellent fare for woodsmen.

The occasional high banks along the river provided the most suitable places for members of the touring party to eat or stop overnight. These select locations were invariably crowned with broad-branching oak, tall magnolias with shiny green leaves, and orange trees heavily laden with fruit. The orange trees originally planted by early missionaries now grew wild throughout the forest, although some of the groves had been cleared by English settlers in order to cultivate plantation crops. Before nightfall each evening, the sailors pulled on shore the open launch and large canoe, which the touring party used for transportation. Tents were pitched and bearskins spread on the ground to protect the governor and his companions from the damp chill of mid-winter.

The travelers occupied the short evening hours with smoking and conversation over an occasional jug of *aguardiente,* while the alligators roared along the river banks close by and a distant loon shattered the silence with a demoniacal cry. Soldiers maintained the bright fires throughout the night to ward off predatory wild cats and alligators. The sounds at nightfall subsided, replaced by the nocturnal noise of rustling wood rats and racoons, and owls hooting in the tree tops, for the populous wilderness was never quiet. In stormy weather they tried to sleep in spite of rattling dry leaves, crackling branches and moaning pine trees. During the final day's journey before reaching the Indian trading house, the travelers sailed fifteen miles across Lake George, passing three romantic forested islands that added much to its natural beauty. Four miles further upstream from the south shore of the lake, they reached Panton's store, a pine board and shingle building situated back from the river near a grove of orange trees.

Zéspedes' river journey to the Indian store duplicated the route followed by one of the eighteenth century's most famous travelers, botanist William Bartram. After accompanying his father, John Bartram, to Florida in 1765, William Bartram returned in April and May of 1774. He navigated the St. Mary's river to its fording point, then followed the inland passage to the St. John's river and sailed alone to the Indian store, at that time called Spalding's

Upper Store. In 1774, the lower trading post was in charge of Charles McLatchy, who in 1783 opened Panton's store at Apalache. Charles McLatchy and Job Wiggens, whom Bartram mentioned as his guides in 1774, supplied much of the Indian lore that enlivened his minute account of Florida's natural scenery. Job Wiggens, of course, was the man whom Zéspedes found operating the Indian ferry service near Picolata. Although Bartram made his pioneer botanical expedition to Florida before the American Revolution, the first edition of his bestselling "Travels" did not appear in Philadelphia until 1791.[5]

The Indian store that Zéspedes' touring party visited was a more elaborate establishment than the trading post Bartram saw in 1774. Under Panton, Leslie and Company's management, the place had become a packing house for hides, and an agricultural and stock-raising enterprise. Fifty or sixty Negroes worked here in the vegetable gardens and corn fields, and took care of several hundred head of cattle providing the St. Augustine garrison with fresh meat. In the nearby forest, gangs of laborers felled timber to make a leather-tanning substance from the bark. To protect the trading post, the most remote habitation in the province, Zéspedes stationed there a contingent of eight soldiers well-supplied with firearms and ammunition. Storekeeper John Hambly and his wife, Maria, were honored to receive the illustrious delegation of government officials who reached their home during the second week of February, 1787. Winter was their busy season, and Indians were still hunting and bringing in skins to be packed in barrels and shipped down the St. John's river for exportation to England. Here on the fringe of the Indian hunting grounds, Father O'Reilly held mass for the second time during the tour. At the conclusion of the service on February 14, 1787, he baptised Hambly's seven months old son, youngest of their four children, with Lieutenant Vincent Domingo de Zéspedes as godfather.

The return trip down the St. John's river was more rapid. By two o'clock on the afternoon of February 17, Governor Zéspedes was enjoying the civilized atmosphere of Fatio's New Switzerland estate. He sent the launch and canoe with their respective crews back to Amelia island, and wrote their commanding officer a letter praising their fine service during the course of a placid trip. The

---

[5] William Bartram, *Travels through North and South Carolina, Georgia, East and West Florida*, (Philadelphi, 1791). See chapters 3 and 4. The route is easier to visualize in reading the new annotated edition by Francis Harper; *Travels of William Bartram, Naturalist's edition* (New Haven, 1958).

governor intended to proceed directly to St. Augustine the next morning, but heavy rain set in during the night and continued throughout the following day. Weary of outdoor life by this time, the governor's party was grateful to rest a few days and enjoy the hospitality of Florida's finest plantation.

Francisco Philipe Fatio took advantage of the delay to discuss with Zéspedes the need for developing the local naval stores industry, a favorite theme he had already proposed to officials in Spain. In the British era, his three plantations along the St. John's river had exported pitch, tar and turpentine, but in 1787 the only forest products were cured lumber and cypress shingles. Because he had served on the arbitration board, Fatio assumed a quasi-governmental status, which he tended to exploit. Although the governor found Fatio's air of superior knowledge about provincial affairs a little trying, he nevertheless listened attentively to the exposition of economic problems. A master of five languages, Fatio was the only educated European in the province equipped to discuss this vital subject in Zéspedes' native tongue.

The Fatios were a singularly international family, and change of sovereignty in the province was not as significant for them as for the average British family. Fatio himself had been born in Switzerland. In 1771, he had followed his brother's lead and taken his family to England, where he chartered a vessel in 1776 to move his household to East Florida. Although trade was not financially profitable during the war years, he kept one of his two vessels in European trade in order to supply his large establishments in Florida. New Switzerland, his largest plantation, had a twelve mile river frontage. Fatio had five children; the eldest, Luis, was thirty-five years old in 1787. Although Fatio was not of the Catholic faith, his wife was a Catholic, originally from Italy. For her benefit, Father O'Reilly celebrated mass before the governor's party left New Switzerland.

The governor and his companions covered the final thirty miles overland to St. Augustine on horseback, reaching the city gate on February 20 after twenty-eight days of travel. According to Engineer Mariano LaRocque, they had traversed 450 miles by land and water, a strenuous trip for the sixty-seven year old governor. After counting the Anglo-American inhabitants of the northern section of the province, he added 283 whites and 388 Negroes to the population statistics. Zéspedes reported the total civilian population as 1,390.

Stating East Florida's population with precision is impossible,

since the rural inhabitants tended to avoid authorities in moving
about, and there was a small interchange between St. Augustine
and Havana. It is difficult to reconcile Father Hassett's St. Augustine census of 1786 and the number of rural inhabitants that
Zéspedes counted on his tour, with the totals announced in May
of 1787 and a later reckoning in September of 1788. Father
Hassett's census of the St. Augustine neighborhood listed 943 persons within a fifteen mile radius of town, probably including those
living along the North river and south of town along the Matanzas river. Zéspedes counted an additional 571 along the St.
John's and St. Mary's rivers. Although the sum of these two
figures is 1514, Zéspedes' report in April, 1787 gave the provincial total as only 1390, divided into 900 whites and 490 Negroes.
The April report to José de Gálvez restricted the St. Augustine
population to 578 Europeans and 179 Negroes. In the fall of
1788, Father Hassett figured that East Florida's population, ex-
clusive of the garrison, was made up of 1,078 whites, 284 Negroes in St. Augustine and 367 more Negroes in the country making
a grand total of 1729.[6]   At that time, Governor Zéspedes informed
the captain general of Cuba that he felt responsible for 200 families, and an additional 450 slaves. Probably the governor was
fairly close in estimating the civilian population at 2000 in April,
1789.

Florida's population in Zéspedes' era may seem very small, but
it was not ridiculously low when considered in relation to previous
populations. After two hundred years of occupancy, the Spanish
population in 1764 numbered 3,096 including the garrison. Even

[6] Census of Inhabitants of East Florida given to the visiting Auxiliary Bishop
Fray Cyril de Barcelona in September, 1788.

Ages	Single		Married		Widowed		Total
16 - 25	40	14	13	46		2	124
	M	F	M	F	M	F	
Up to 7	160	189					349
7 - 16	81	69		9			159
16 - 25	49	14	13	46		2	124
25 - 40	42	23	96	87	2	6	256
40 - 50	25	11	48	21	4	8	117
Over 50	14	12	19	10	6	12	73
	371	318	176	173	12	28	1078

The population of East Florida consisted of 1078 white inhabitants, 284
Negroes in St. Augustine and 367 slaves in the country, making a total of 1729,
excluding the garrison. Michael J. Curley, *Church and State in Spanish Florida,
1783-1822* (Washington, 1940), p. 117.

with generous land grants, private investment, and government subsidies for plantation crops, the pre-revolutionary population of British East Florida was only 1,000 whites and 3,000 Negroes, plus a garrison of one or two hundred soldiers.[7] Adding Zéspedes' statement of the civilian population in East Florida in 1787, which he gave as 1,390, to his estimate of the garrison dependents, 1,800, makes a total of 3,190. In all its colonial history, peninsular Florida contained few people, except for the brief boom when over 13,000 Loyalist refugees swarmed into the province between 1778 and 1782. The signs of desolation and disintegration that Zéspedes found on his tour were evidence of the hasty exodus of 13,000 transients. The important factor in the provincial population during Zéspedes' régime was its distribution. Spanish East Florida was characterized by a Minorcan capital, and a British population located in the northern section near the Georgia border and the Indian hunting grounds.

---

[7] Mowat, *op. cit.*, p. 137.

St. George Street West

IX

Future Florida: A Vision

THE VISION of a glorious future for East Florida was forming in Governor Zéspedes' mind throughout the course of his journey in the interior of the province during January and February of 1787. With the excitement over the return of his son-in-law, Lieutenant Juan O'Donovan, from his imprisonment in Havana— a happy event occurring in March, 1787—the governor did not put his thoughts on paper until April. His ideas for the future development of East Florida clearly reflected late eighteenth century Spanish interest in population growth, land improvement and conservation. In Spain, Charles III actively promoted agricultural production and stock raising, and the program for internal colonization of the sparsely populated Spanish peninsula. During his reign, six thousand German and Flemish immigrants and many Spanish workers were settled in fifteen new towns in the Sierra Morena district. With concern for preserving natural resources, the Spanish government also ordered town councils to plant a certain number of trees annually in their respective areas. From this regulation, originated the custom of Arbor Day, a celebration since adopted in many countries of both hemispheres.[1]

In addition to his knowledge of currrent thinking in Spain,

---

[1] Rafael Altamira, *A History of Spain* (Princeton, 1949), p. 457.

Zéspedes indicated a familiarity with arrangements for aiding new settlers in Louisiana and West Florida. The provision of livestock, farm implements and daily flour rations, one of the details of his own plan, almost duplicates a similar provision of the program that Bernardo de Gálvez instituted in 1778 for settling Canary island families along the Mississippi river.[2] In the post-Revolutionary War period, Zéspedes' attitude differed from that of the Louisiana and West Florida governors in one important respect. Although they permitted the immigration of former British Loyalists and Americans, a form of laxity criticized by Alexander McGillivray, Zéspedes adamantly refused to accept Anglo-Saxon Protestants in his own province. The plan that he sent to José de Gálvez revealed his own determination to implant Spanish Catholic tradition in East Florida. In the course of fifty pages, including a description of his tour, Governor Zéspedes outlined in detail a program for developing the population and resources of East Florida.

Obviously, the country required additional people, who should be European Catholics rather than American Protestants from the adjoining states. He decided that land should be apportioned on the basis of twenty acres for each head of a family, plus ten acres for each additional member of the family. To avoid speculative gain, he specified that land could not be sold during the lifetime of the original settler. After ten years of tax-free occupancy, settlers should pay for a land survey and accept the responsibility of tax payment assessed according to productivity of the land.

The governor also had ideas for spending the fifty thousand pesos a year allotted by the royal order of May 8, 1786. Although he expected settlers to build their own homes, he believed impecunious families should be provided with homes at the king's expense. The royal bounty should also provide basic capital items: a cow and a sow, pregnant if possible, a cock and two hens, agricultural implements, cooking utensils, table and benches. The first year, or until he harvested his first crop, a colonist could be subsidized with a pound and a half of flour a day and one *real* (approximately twenty-five cents) in cash. Given this auspicious start, Zéspedes believed a colonist should prove his worth in the first ten years. At the conclusion of this interval, the industrious colonists would be rewarded with additional land, while the unsuccessful would find their acreage curtailed.

---

2 John Walton Caughey, *Bernardo de Gálvez in Louisiana* (Berkeley, 1934), p. 79.

In the overall program for land usage, Zéspedes made a few special provisions. He expected settlers to clear a quarter of their land by the end of the ten year trial period, or have adequate numbers of animals at pasture on lands suitable only for grazing. Conscious of the importance of conservation, he demanded that settlers plant new trees each year to replace those cut in logging operations or tapped to produce turpentine. The governor also kept in mind the ancient privileges of the king, reserving for the crown all gold, silver or copper mines that might be found in Florida. Also reserved to the king was the right to resume control of land necessary for fortification or national defense. All these stipulations were included in sixteen rules listed by the governor in his report to José de Gálvez.

A plan for granting land to future settlers had to be worked out in harmony with a system for providing land and valid titles for the existing residents of the province. To put in operation any form of land distribution, the province needed a surveyor. Zéspedes' original candidate for this position, former British Loyalist William Maxwell, unfortunately died soon after joining Mariano La-Rocque's engineering staff. Before the new settlers received land grants, the governor believed allotments should be made to the Minorcans and *Floridanos*. Many of these families, and the new Canary Islanders, were living in buildings that reverted to the king's possession when the British departed. While waiting for the government to clarify land and property ownership, the inhabitants took little interest in fencing and improving land or repairing homes. Furthermore, buildings belonging to the king could not be renovated without royal permission.

By means of carefully devised land laws, Zéspedes believed he could incorporate the Anglo-American population into orthodox Spanish Catholic society. In all justice, land titles of the British residents should be confirmed, but in his system only Roman Catholic residents of East Florida could inherit land, houses or city lots. In Zéspedes list of rules, all new settlers had to be Roman Catholic, and all British residents had to accept instruction with reverence and agree to raise their children in accordance with the Catholic faith. The governor was confidant that under Father Hassett's energetic direction, the missionary effort would be successful. As in earlier correspondence, he recommended establishing three additional parishes in East Florida, for the St. John's river, Amelia island, and the suburban area along the North river. Supervising the work of the new parishes required five additional Irish

Catholic priests, two assigned to each of the outlying parishes and one for the North river community. Anticipating the approval of the new parishes, Father Hassett requested 200 catechisms and 500 other devotional books for instruction of new converts. He later arranged through Gardoqui's chaplain to have English prayer books printed in New York for use in East Florida missionary work.

The plan Zéspedes worked out for East Florida was paternalistic almost to the point of being ultra modern even in the era of the eighteenth century "enlightenment." In addition to providing for the economic and spiritual welfare of the colonists, Zéspedes believed the king should assume responsibility for their medical care. He requested the appointment of an English speaking doctor to be stationed with the detachment at Amelia island, a base for attending colonists in the northern section. Zéspedes advocated free medical care for all needy inhabitants through increased salaries to the government physician, the surgeon and apothecary in St. Augustine. Facilities of the royal hospital should also be available to needy inhabitants. For the sake of the other residents, the apothecary should dispense medicine at reasonable prices under some form of government license. Developing good, healthy Catholic families appreciative of the royal bounty was the goal of Zéspedes' population plan. In his extreme emphasis on family life, the governor preferred to prohibit immigration of single men unless they were proficient in some desirable trade.

Governor Zéspedes' imagination spun dreams of future glory, based on the signs of agricultural potential observed along the St. John's river, and the reports of British production. If he had enough industrious families, he was certain the productivity of East Florida would surpass the hey-day reached in the last years of British occupancy. In 1776, the colony exported 65,000 oranges and small quantities of lemons and limes, 860 barrels of rice, and 58,295 pounds of indigo; while in 1781 and 1782 tar and turpentine production rose to 50,000 barrels. In the future, the governor visualized extensive rice plantations along the marshy shores of the Nassau and St. John's rivers, and well-organized production of naval stores in the pine forests further from the banks. From gashes in the trees flowed the resinous substance which was the basis of turpentine. Burning cones and dead wood produced tars and resins which the governor thought the Spanish navy could use in preference to similar products imported from the Baltic seacoast. The river land of the central parts of the peninsula already pro-

duced cotton for home consumption, and many acres of similar
land could be brought into cultivation. The area along the Mosquito lagoon, where the New Smyrna colony grew sugar and
indigo, would support a new settlement also raising silk worms
fed by the mulberry trees native to the country. Cochineal insects,
source of red dye, flourished on the type of cactus known locally
as prickly pear.

Hard-working settlers were assured ample supplies of delicious
food. Corn, beans, potatoes, melons and a variety of fruit grew in
the kitchen gardens of St. Augustine where the soil, the poorest in
the province, was refertilized each year with ground shells. Further
south, below the frost line, year-round production would be more
profitable. Cattle and hogs thrived on land too poor for cultivation. In addition to the imported stock, the province still abounded
in deer, wild turkey, water fowl, fish and oysters.

Zéspedes knew East Florida would derive no profit from the
increased production unless the colonists secured a market outside
the province. While the economy was still in its infancy, he recommended permitting the colonists to export fruit and orange juice
to ports in the American states, and wood products to the West
Indies islands. St. Mary's harbor was best adapted to promote a
flourishing trade, since at was the only port deep enough to admit
the large vessels needed for loading heavy lumber and for trans-
atlantic commerce. Of course, using St. Mary's harbor required
special permission from superior officials in Spain, since existing
regulations recognized St. Augustine as the only port for legal
shipping in East Florida. To acquire the necessary European manu-
factured goods, Zéspedes advocated direct trade with Spain in preference to continuing the hazardous shipping connections with
Havana.

Industrious colonists, vigorous missionary effort, and relatively
unrestricted trade were the keys to the future of Spanish Florida, in
Zéspedes' opinion. He knew the healthful climate already exerted
a powerful attraction, drawing visitors from icy northern cities and
baking southern islands. If the province fulfilled his dreams, he
envisioned a future population of a million people utilizing two
million *caballerias* of land from the St. Mary's river to Cape Sable,
the southern tip of the Peninsula.[3]

Zéspedes' optimistic portrait of future Florida never reached

---

[3] A *caballeria* in Florida and Cuba is equivalent to 33 acres.

José de Gálvez, the man whom the governor expected to take over
the guardianship of the infant colony after the death of his illustrious nephew. The letter dated May 12, 1787, enclosing Zéspedes'
carefully designed plans for Florida's development, arrived in
Madrid after the death of the famous colonial secretary on June 20,
1787. News of this tragedy did not reach St. Augustine until fall.
Throughout the spring and summer of 1787, the governor im-
patiently awaited some instructions to follow up the royal order
of May 8, 1786 which would enable him to administer oaths of
allegiance and parcel out land to the present inhabitants. His only
indication of any further interest in East Florida on the part of
the home government came as an exasperating surprise in April.
Dispatches from Captain General Ezpeleta informed him that a
navy lieutenant was about to leave Havana to search for islands
near Florida still in the hands of the British, and on arrival in St.
Augustine he would investigate Florida's forest products.

According to Ezpeleta, Lieutenant José del Rio Cossa left Madrid with a commisison from the secretary of the navy, Antonio
Valdez, to inspect East Florida's resources of wood, tar and turpentine, a job Zéspedes had just completed as part of his tour of the
province. Del Rio was carrying out a court order of June 8, 1786,
the result of a memorial sent direct to Madrid by Francisco Fatio,
who used every possible avenue to promote the local naval stores
industry. It profoundly irked Zéspedes to learn that Fatio had
achieved results from his direct contact with the court. Like any
other government official, he resented Fatio's reluctance to present
his appeal "through proper channels."

At the time Lieutenant del Rio presented himself in Havana in
March, 1787, Ezpeleta was trying to figure out some means for
carrying out a puzzling order from José de Gálvez to locate two
islands near the Florida keys which the British had reportedly failed
to release in 1784. Evidently, the attention of the foreign office
had been called to a global map noting near the tip of Florida two
islands marked "B. Spiritu," belonging to England. This alarming discovery prompted a royal order in October, 1786 directing
a search for the islands, and their immediate seizure. Spanish court
officials invariably were hazy regarding Caribbean geography, a
vagueness further confused by inaccurate and conflicting maps. The
relation between the Florida keys, the mainland, Cuba and the
Bahamas had aroused controversy in 1763 when Florida was ceded

to the English. Official concern in 1786 undoubtedly arose from reconsidering matters under discussion twenty years earlier.[4]

The fuss appeared ridiculous to Governor Zéspedes. With obvious asperity, he notified his superiors that any useful or useless islands, reefs, bays or cays along the Florida coast were undoubtedly included in the cession made by the Treaty of Paris in 1783. When there were so many vital problems in East Florida needing the consideration of the ministry, he was particularly irritated to learn the two objectives that were bringing a navy lieutenant all the way from Spain.

Although Zéspedes was scarcely inclined to offer either welcome or assistance to Lieutenant del Rio, his attitude changed completely when the young man reached St. Augustine. This officer, who instantly established his personal popularity, was obviously working to acquire additional merit and win promotion. Since he was also a personal protegé of Antonio Valdez, secretary of the navy, the governor and his staff combined efforts to assure his enhanced reputation on his first special task. Lieutenant del Rio received expert guidance to St. Mary's harbor, mapped by Mariano LaRocque in 1785 and rechecked in 1787. He viewed the tallest pines on the Nassau river and questioned Theophilos Hill and Francisco Fatio at their plantations concerning prospective production of turpentine and allied products. In a few weeks, he completed his report as well as an enormous map transported to the Ministry of Marine in a large wooden tube. With deference to his superior officers, the lieutenant changed the name of Lake George to "Laguna Valdéz," and designated another large inland lake as "Laguna Morales," honoring the Cuban navy commander, Francisco Xavier Morales. The report pointed out that the Spanish navy could secure turpentine, tar and resin from East Florida rather than the Baltic area, reiterating an opinion both Fatio and Zéspedes had previously tried to impress on the home government. He added that the exportation of naval stores from Florida to Spain might curtail the province's illicit commerce with Americans. Having such brief contact with Florida, Lieutenant del Rio naturally made mistakes. His most sensational error was the statement that twelve thousand British refugees had been engaged in turpentine production.

Lieutenant del Rio left Florida on July 18, 1787, bearing Zéspedes' recommendations to the navy commander in Cuba, with

---

[4] Charles W. Arnade, "Florida Keys: English or Spanish in 1763?," *Tequesta*, XV (1955), pp. 41-53.

the added suggestion that he have the privilege of presenting his
report personally to the ministry in Madrid. Commander Morales
was amazed and impressed by the speed with which the lieutenant
returned with his map and report. Three years later, his report
was brought up for consideration by the merchant marine.[5]

Zéspedes hoped that as a result of the lieutenant's visit the few
local plantations producing naval stores might find an export market in Spain. But he became discouraged when he considered the
more general problem of how to get additional qualified residents
in East Florida and how those people could make a living, in view
of the marketing restrictions imposed by Spain's mercantilistic
commercial system. In midsummer of 1787, he received another
stern reminder from José de Gálvez that Florida colonists were expected to avoid American markets and limit their trade to Havana.
This particular admonition came in answer to Zéspedes' letter of
August, 1786 written when he was grasping at straws to find
justification for Florida's vital trade with the American states. At
that time he came across a two year old copy of the *Mercurio,*
a Madrid newspaper, in which he found reference to two royal
orders for January 22, 1782 and November 24, 1783 concerning
trade concessions for Trinidad and the Windward islands. Thinking they might be construed to apply in his own province, he consulted José de Gálvez, and also wrote the governor of West Florida and the intendant in New Orleans to secure copies of the orders.
Martin Navarro, intendant for Louisiana and West Florida, sent
back a copy of the 1782 order, but said he had not received a copy
of the latter regulation. The reply from José de Gálvez, written
in March of 1787, merely said that the orders mentioned were not
adaptable to Louisiana or the Floridas, but added the assurance that
the king would provide for the commerce of Florida. From this
letter, the governor deduced that the suspense of waiting for instructions would be further prolonged.

In the meantime, his people had to sell produce and buy clothing
in nearby American markets, where such goods were much cheaper
than in Havana. When the intendant in Havana criticized Zéspedes
for permitting this meager trade, he received a scathing reply.
Zéspedes insisted that prevention of this commerce would cut off
the income of his small population, who deserved leniency since

---

[5] José del Rio Cossa, "Descripción de la Florida Oriental Hecha en 1787 por
Teniente de Navio D. José del Rio Cossa, publicada ahora por vez primera con
algunas notas por le P. Agustin Barreiro." Madrid: *Sociedad Geografica Nacional*
(1935) Serie B, Numero. 61.

they were not accustomed to Spanish law. Strict enforcement would force people to leave the province or become dependent upon the government for susbistence. Since the Cuban intendancy was unable to provide food for the garrison, the officials certainly could not manage to feed the civilian population. The governor stoutly upheld his own opinion of what policies were advantageous to the royal service. Feeling that the remnants of two previous political régimes required tender care, he often used the term for a horticultural nursery in referring to the civilian inhabitants of East Florida. Unless he had a bluntly stated royal order direct from the king, he refused to adhere to regulations that definitely would blight his "nursery" population.

The delay in making definite decisions about Florida's commerce and immigration also embarrassed Zéspedes' relations with Gardoqui in New York as well as with the intendant in Havana. The Spanish representative in New York already had been placed in a difficult position by Zéspedes' requests provisions, and now he became uncomfortably involved in the confused immigration problem. In conjunction with the royal order of May 8, José de Gálvez recommended that Gardoqui help to locate foreign Catholic families who would make desirable immigrants for East Florida. Knowing the home government's interest in this matter, Gardoqui sent an Irishman named David Carroll Franks to talk with Zéspedes in July of 1787. Franks was anxious to find a new world home for seventy tenant farmer families from his relatives' estates in Ireland. They originally intended to settle in the American Confederation, but Franks found conditions too unsettled in the new republic and turned to Gardoqui to see if land were available in the Spanish possessions. Zéspedes reacted favorably to the statement of the case to this point. But when Franks said that the prospective immigrants needed their passage paid, and assurance of land grants, he knew his hands were tied. Somewhat regretfully, he told David Carroll Franks to return to New York to await the determination of the king. Gardoqui later sent individual families, men bearing his strong personal recommendations as well as ornate official passports, but in each case Zéspedes turned them away. Until he had explicit instructions, and more money, the governor was unwilling to increase the number of families in the province whom he considered his personal responsibility.

The stalemate continued throughout Zéspedes' régime, with scant evidence of ministerial interest in Florida's population or economy. In January of 1790, a request arrived for samples of the various kinds of wood native to the province. Eventually, direct trade with Spain began on an experimental basis, but the first shipload of tar and barrel staves did not leave until May, 1791. In the meantime, local commerce continued along customary routes. For example, during the month of January, 1790, Francisco Fatio brought the only merchandise from Havana. Other imports were flour, salt, cheese, saddles and nails from New York, butter and cheese from Wilmington, and potatoes from Charleston. Zéspedes remained keenly disappointed that St. Mary's harbor never received official approval as a commercial port for East Florida.

No further action was taken during his governorship concerning immigration following the arrival of the five Canary island families in the fall of 1786. From the subsequent behavior of the Canary Islanders, Zéspedes concluded that they were more likely to become perpetual public charges than successful farmers. He begged Captain General Ezpeleta to postpone sending the rest of the Islanders until some adequate provision was made for handling the first group. As a matter of actual fact, the five families represented the total results of the government program for populating East Florida enunciated in the royal order of May 8, 1786. If the home government's lack of sustained effort to rehabilitate East Florida could be attributed to one factor, that factor would be the death of José de Gálvez in June, 1787. Certainly there was a complete change of political climate in court between the time that Gálvez requested Zéspedes' recommendations and the time that the governor's lengthy reply reached Spain.

Under Gálvez' energetic direction, East Florida problems frequently came before the royal council during the spring of 1786, as soon as word arrived that the British definitely had left the province. Actually, the royal order of May 8 was the climax of a series of measures approved during the spring of 1786 to reconstruct East Florida. In this period, the major correspondence from Zéspedes and other East Florida officials for the years 1784 and 1785 received the royal council's consideration. In January, the council permitted the establishment of a school, requested by Father Hassett in October, 1784. After examining the map of St. Augustine indicating the run-down state of buildings and fortifications, the council approved temporary repairs for the Castillo, troop barracks and officers' quarters. In February, 1786, the government could not spare additional funds to repair any of the one hundred houses virtually uninhabitable as a result of neglect since the departure of the British occupants. On April 5, the king settled the status of the Anglo-American Protestants remaining in East Florida with two royal orders. The first granted permission for the former Loyalists to continue living in the province under Spanish protection. The same day, the king ordered the Bishop of Salamanca to search for traditional Irish priests to convert the non-Catholics in Florida. Panton, Leslie and Company received official permission to handle the Indian trade of East Florida, using British merchandise, on May 6. Two days later, the king authorized the annual expenditure of fifty thousand pesos to finance immigrant families and other new residents of East Florida. On June 10, the royal order was issued sending Lieutenant José del Rio Cossa on his voyage to inspect East Florida's forest products.

Though constructive, these royal orders had the defects of piece-meal legislation. The real need was for a set of permanent regulations establishing the civilian government and ending the transitional period of military occupation. The regulations, budget and situado were all closely related. In a small province like East Florida, the annual budget practically defined the structure of government, since it listed the officials, their duties, and the sum of money prescribing their activities. The royal orders issued in the spring of 1786 could supplement, but not substitute for, a coherent plan of provincial administration. José de Gálvez obviously though his nephew was arranging for East Florida's civilian government, but before this oversight could be corrected, both men were dead.

A less sympathetic atmosphere prevailed in the colonial office when Zéspedes' report reached Madrid in the summer of 1787. In the first place, confusion existed immediately following the death of José de Gálvez because the numerous matters that he had managed singlehanded were divided into two separate categories and placed under different ministers. The two colonial secretaries succeeding Gálvez in July, 1787 were: Antonio Valdez, formerly secretary of the navy, who assumed responsibility for military, financial and commercial affairs in the colonies; and Antonio Porlier, who supervised religious matters, and the administration of justice. Delays naturally occurred in the assignment and handling of borderline subjects, such as Zéspedes' report dealing with both commerce and religion. In the second place, not all personnel of the colonial office shared the conviction of the Gálvez family concerning the importance of the American border provinces.

After the death of José de Gálvez, several members of the court circle openly questioned the advisability of retaining East Florida, a subject raised at intervals during the previous two centuries.

José Salcedo, head of the Louisiana Bureau, formulated the case
opposing the retention of the province. In the course of a highly
derogatory memorandum, Salcedo contended that Florida's maintenance expense exceeded its usefulness. He suggested returning the
peninsula to England as a gift, and if the British seemed reluctant,
he advocated offering a million pesos to get rid of the territory.
Salcedo's discussion contained a certain amount of misinformation,
such as the statement that it was necessary to sail out into the
Atlantic and circle the Bahama islands in order to reach Cuba from
St. Augustine. In assuming that 230,000 pesos would be an annual
demand for East Florida, he misinterpreted Zéspedes' budget of
December, 1786. He failed to note that only 120,000 pesos was
requested for current expenses, while 110,000 was needed to cover
accumulated indebtedness. Salcedo leveled specific criticism at
Zéspedes' ambitious plans for the future development of the province. Viewed from distant Spain, these projects appeared as
quixotic as might be expected of a *caballero* from La Mancha.

Salcedo's memorandum circulated government offices for over
a year. In January of 1790, the critical report and selections from
Zéspedes' most eloquent descriptions of Florida's potentialities
were submitted to Luis de Las Casas just before he left Spain to
become the new captain general of Cuba. Las Casas postponed
his decision until he reached Havana, where he became convinced
of the peninsula's usefulness. Zéspedes, who was well-informed
concerning events in America and nearby islands, knew very little
about politics in Spain. In 1787, he did hear a rumor that Spain
might turn Florida over to her ally, France, but he was unaware
of the serious proposal in 1788 to return Florida to England.
During his governorship, Zéspedes struggled valiantly to make a
flourishing colony out of the most expendable province in the
Spanish empire.

St. George Street to City Gates

X

Threats From the Turbulent Frontier

GOVERNOR Zéspedes never became completely engulfed by East Florida's internal problems because his attention constantly was drawn beyond the confines of his own province to events of importance in the American states and the trans-Appalachian wilderness. Although his personal contacts were limited to entertaining a few distinguished visitors, his horizon of interest included the opposing Indian and American frontier settlements, and British activities in the "Old Northwest" where England did not surrender the border forts to American officers until 1796. After the arrival of Diego de Gardoqui in July, 1785, Zéspedes also followed the trends on the diplomatic front in New York and Madrid, as well as the struggles of the nascent American government.

Perhaps Governor Zéspedes overdramatized the importance of his own responsibility on the southern frontier of the new American republic. Certainly he was acutely conscious of his position, commanding the most impressive Spanish fortification on the North American mainland, a presidio at the eastern end of a chain of fifteen smaller outposts extending along a thousand mile frontier to St. Louis and the Illinois country. Everything along the frontier vitally interested Zéspedes, who served in the two-fold capacity as an instrument for carrying out Spanish policy and as a listen-

149

ing post to receive information for modifying Spanish policy, particularly with reference to the American states and the Indian nations. As part of his responsibility, he wrote voluminous reports, trying to separate fact from rumor, and analyzing current events for the benefit of the Spanish foreign office and for Gardoqui, who was trying to arrange a treaty in New York. The Treaty of Paris in 1783 had postponed adjustment of American-Spanish differences for future bilateral negotiation.

The Spanish governor had several sources of information on American affairs. Colonel Thomas Brown, former British Indian superintendent, provided detailed accounts of activities in the Georgia Assembly and the American Congress, in both of which he had intimate friends. Zéspedes' other principle sources were Alexander McGillivray, William Panton and John Leslie, and the leading newspapers of the southern states. William Panton relayed news from England, and on trips to the Island of Providence brought back the confidential letters of Colonel Brown. Personal letters of McGillivray to both members of the firm were shared with Zéspedes and the Spanish governors in Pensacola and New Orleans. McGillivray sent Panton copies or summaries of his correspondence with American officials, and with land hungry frontier leaders promoting schemes opposing American official policy. As a result of these cross currents of correspondence, the court in Madrid was well-informed concerning the internal affairs of the American States. The port of St. Augustine functioned as a convenient intermediary point for forwarding mail between Gardoqui and Havana, connecting there with the monthly mail to the mother country. When the general tenor of information became more alarming, Zéspedes and Gardoqui received instructions not to send any letters overland, but to entrust their mail only to reliable sea captains.

The general mood of the Spanish court had altered since the days when Gardoqui's firm surreptitiously supplied the American Revolutionists, when the Viceroyalty of New Spain raised 887,000 pesos to finance the British colonies' struggle for independence, and Yankee shippers swarmed into Havana harbor. Even during the war, authorities in Havana, alarmed by the activities of foreign merchants, became anxious to suppress the popular enthusiasm awakened by participation in the American Revolution. As the war drew to a close, Spain began to sever connections with the new independent nation, now viewed as a potential menace. In 1782, permission to supply food to Cuba was revoked and the following

The city gates, looking south on St. George Street. This view is similar to a drawing dated 1869

View of the Governor's House in East Florida. Watercolor sketch, dated November, 1764. Original in the British Museum, Kings Maps, cxxii862a.

Aerial view of the Castillo de San Marcos, Matanzas Bay and Anastasia Island, with the new lighthouse in the distance. Probably taken in early Twentieth Century.

Old Charlotte Street, looking south toward the plaza. All these houses were destroyed by fire in 1911.

Anastasia Island watchtower, from the 7th Regiment: New Hampshire Volunteers in the War of Rebellion, by Henry F. W. Little (Lt.) Concord, N.H. 1896.

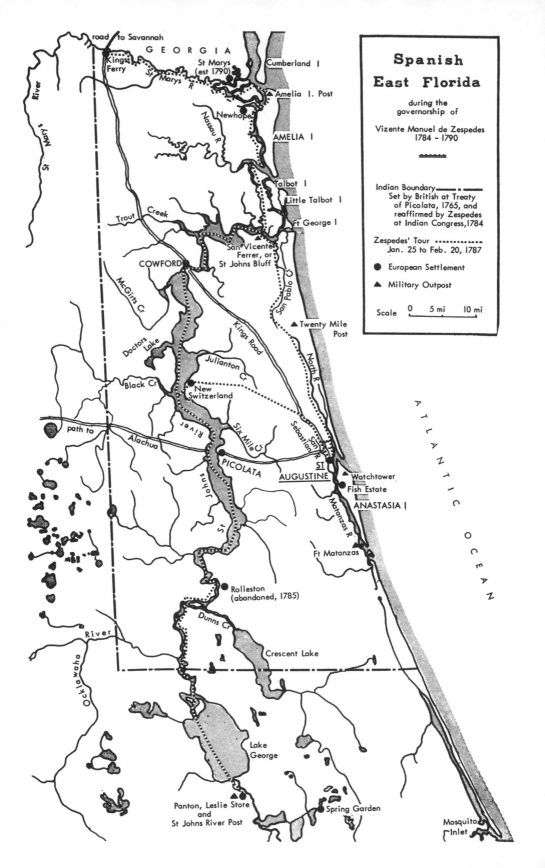

Spanish East Florida during the governorship of Vizente Manuel de Zespedes 1784 – 1790

road to Savannah

GEORGIA

Kings Ferry

St Marys (est 1790)

Cumberland I

Amelia I. Post

Newhope

AMELIA I

Nassau R.

Talbot I

Little Talbot I

Ft George I

Trout Creek

San Vicente Ferrer, or St Johns Bluff

COWFORD

San Pablo Cr.

Twenty Mile Post

McGirts Cr.

Doctors Lake

Kings Road

Julianton Cr.

Black Cr.

New Switzerland

North R.

path to

Alachua

River

Six Mile Cr.

Sebastian

San ... R.

PICOLATA

St Johns River

ST AUGUSTINE

Watchtower
Fish Estate

ANASTASIA I

Matanzas R.

Ft Matanzas

ATLANTIC OCEAN

Rolleston (abandoned, 1785)

Dunns Cr.

Crescent Lake

River

Ocklawaha

Lake George

Panton, Leslie Store and St Johns River Post

Spring Garden

Mosquito Inlet

Indian Boundary
Set by British at Treaty of Picolata, 1765, and reaffirmed by Zespedes at Indian Congress, 1784

Zespedes' Tour
Jan. 25 to Feb. 20, 1787

● European Settlement

▲ Military Outpost

Scale   0   5 mi   10 mi

View of St. Johns River.

year Spain declared American commerce illegal, at the same time closing the Mississippi river to American shipping. The trend continued with the specific prohibition of American trade with Cuba in 1784 and the ouster of all American merchants from Havana in 1785[1]. Furthermore, after viewing the revolutionary leadership exhibited by Boston lawyers, Spain forbade the study for law degrees in the universities at Havana, Santo Domingo, Mexico and Lima.[2]

By the time Gardoqui reached New York in 1785, Spain had developed a frosty reaction to the new republic, but American diplomats countered the chilly Spanish attitude with a series of aggressive demands. Eastern merchants wanted provision made for trade with Spain. Western frontier leaders expected to regain legal use of the Mississippi river trade route. Expansionists insisted on maximum land acquisition, marking the north border of West Florida at the thirty-first parallel of latitude rather than thirty-two degrees, eight minutes. Zéspedes followed the course of the various proposals made by representatives of both countries in New York, occasionally fearful of a complete break between Spain and America. After common agreement between the two countries seemed impossible, Gardoqui returned to Spain in 1789. But during the course of his fruitless negotiations, he received some very interesting information from Governor Zéspedes.

One of the first frontier developments that Zéspedes reported was the State of Georgia's audacious attempt in the spring of 1785 to establish a new political division called "Bourbon County" in territory claimed by Spain along the Mississippi river. The projected western county, extending from the Yazoo river south to the thirty-first parallel of latitude, included the Natchez district conquered by Bernardo de Gálvez and currently garrisoned by Spanish troops. First news of Bourbon County came to Zéspedes and other Spanish officials from their reliable informant, Alexander McGillivray. In June of 1785, Zéspedes secured a printed copy of the legislative act creating Bourbon County to send to José de Gálvez and other officials. Georgia's attempt to establish Bourbon County in the disputed area was successfully foiled by Spanish officials in Natchez, British Loyalist emigrés settled in the district, and the militant opposition of the Indians. But for the Georgians,

---

[1] Harry Bernstein, *Origins of Inter-American Interest, 1700-1812* (Philadelphia, 1945), pp. 26, 35.

[2] Ramon Guerra y Sánchez, José M. Pérez Cabrera, Juan J. Remos, Emeterio Santovenia, *Historia de la Nación Cubana* (4 vols., Havana, 1952), II, p. 133.

the defeat was only the first rebuff in their repeated efforts to gain
land on the Mississippi river, and allied privileges of river navigation and Indian trade in adjacent territory.

Additional information verifying Georgia's objectives reached
Governor Zéspedes in August of 1785 from Colonel Brown, who
was about to depart for New Providence with the last contingent
of British Loyalists. While on shipboard in St. Mary's harbor,
Colonel Brown received a candid letter from a friend in Savannah
containing some paragraphs he knew would be of interest to Zéspedes. He intended to send extracts when Antonio de Zéspedes
returned to St. Augustine at the conclusion of his unauthorized
jaunt to St. Mary's, but lively young Antonio departed on too
short notice. The writer in Savannah asserted that frontiersmen
moving westward into Spanish territory would receive indirect aid
from Congress, although the legislative body would represent to
Spain that the frontier people were beyond control. The final paragraph of the letter gave a clear picture of goals shared by ambitious
Georgians.

> At all events we are determined to possess ourselves of
> the territory and privilege of navigation agreeable to the
> treaty of peace — and 'tis an object richly worth con-
> tending for — The Spanish & Indian commerce of the
> Eastern & Western branches of the [Mississippi] river
> will amply repay the loss of blood or toil in the conquest
> & a prospect that would satiate ambition or avarice.

The letter with the insight into Georgia politics arrived in
Zéspedes' hands at an appropriate time. A special courier was in
St. Augustine taking papers from Bernardo de Gálvez, Viceroy of
New Spain in Mexico City since May of 1785, to Diego de Gardoqui who had just arrived in New York. The courier, Enrique
White, was a person already marked for his unusual ability. The
following year, 1786, Governor Miró selected White to act as host
for Alexander McGillivray when the Creek chief visited New Orleans. A close friend of Captain Howard and a fellow officer of
the Hibernia Regiment, Captain White became governor of West
Florida in 1793, serving until he transferred to the governorship
of East Florida in 1796, where he continued in office until shortly
before his death in 1811. While Captain White was in St. Augustine in August, 1785, Governor Zéspedes provided him with a copy
of the information received from Colonel Brown to add to the
other confidential messages directed to Gardoqui. Additional copies

were sent to the captain general of Cuba, to Bernardo de Gálvez in Mexico City, and to José de Gálvez in Madrid.

In the following years, evidence from other sources repeatedly reinforced Zéspedes' impression of malevolent American designs on the bordering Spanish territory. In May of 1786, Carlos Howard translated for him an editorial from an unidentified American newspaper providing a naked revelation of the extent of American ambition. The article entitled "Punic Faith," signed by Fabius, boldly prophesied the doom of the Spanish border provinces:

> Spain foresaw that America must be its natural enemy, an enemy so formidable that it would shake the foundation of the Spanish Empire in the Indies . . . Both the Floridas and Louisiana because of their situation and small population and agricultural deficiencies must in time fall under the dominion of the American States.

Fabius went on to state that Spain would hesitate to risk open war for two reasons: First, a war would imperil the opulent Mexican empire; and second, the natives of South America would find it a favorable occasion to gain independence. In conclusion, Fabius urged his fellow-Americans to aim toward the conquest of Mexico, claiming that two thousand valiant soldiers under the command of experienced leaders could complete the conquest of the richest country in the world in a few weeks. Furthermore, the gold and silver of Mexico would provision the army, so that the campaign would cost the invaders nothing.

The inflammatory articles in the American press did not alarm Zéspedes as much as the more secret activities in frontier territory. In 1786 and 1787, rumors from the wilderness were unusually prolific and always included at least a grain of truth. Governor Zéspedes found indications that England was trying to gain control of all the Indian fur trade from the Straits of Mackinac to the Gulf of Mexico, excluding both Spanish and American interests. This new element in the picture was most disquieting, because Spain counted heavily on the friendship of the southern Indians. British agents definitely were at work in the trans-Appalachian region. Entering by way of the Great Lakes, they were at least sowing the seeds of rebellion against the young American republic, possibly with the view of establishing another political entity under British protection. By 1786, John Connolly had returned to his old haunts around Fort Pitt, where formerly he had spread disaffection harming the Continental army's war efforts. He soon moved into Kentucky. In 1782, Connolly had been released from his second term in an American prison only on condition that he leave immediately for England.[3]

A new rash of plots and intrigues developed after the American Congress in August of 1786 considered a measure postponing demands for Mississippi river navigation for thirty years, in favor of promoting a commercial treaty with Spain. Although Gardoqui had been instructed to refuse any trade agreement, this indication of Congress's intent to sacrifice the demands of frontier settlers to the more powerful seaboard interests caused a violent reaction. Impatient frontier leaders soon tried every possible stratagem to secure land and trade on the Mississippi river, despite lack of congressional support. They connived to form new political units, to infiltrate Spanish territory, to secure Indian land from Alexander McGillivray, and to ingratiate themselves with Spanish officials. Conspirators and informers contacted Spanish representatives from New Orleans to New York, in Havana, France, and in Spain itself.[4]. Clues to one of the most farfetched schemes were revealed exclusively to Governor Zéspedes in September of 1787, when he received a mysterious letter from a Thomas Powell of Charleston. Zéspedes at first dismissed the letter as the work of an impostor.

Even without the addition of American frontier plots, the fall of 1787 was an abnormally tense period in Zéspedes career as governor of East Florida. He had discounted American threats as long as the republic was weakened by dissension. He really expected a separate republic to form west of the Appalachian mountains. But in the fall of 1787, the states held a constitutional convention and devised a stronger system of government which he realized would diminish their preoccupation with internal problems. A second factor temporarily unnerving to Governor Zéspedes at this time was an erroneous report of Alexander McGillivray's death. It was true that an agent of the Georgia Assembly had offered four horseloads of ammunition to anyone who could kill McGillivray, but the canny chief managed to foil the attempted murder plot. The fall of 1787 was also the critical juncture when Zéspedes feared that raging war between the Creeks and Georgians might involve his province. After he received the first clues to a widesperad American conspiracy from Thomas Powell, he began to wonder if Georgia's menacing behavior were connected with

---

[3] Carl Van Doren, *Secret History of the American Revolution* (New York, 1941), p. 415.

[4] For complete discussion of these conspiracies, see Arthur Preston Whitaker, *The Spanish-American Frontier* (Boston and New York, 1927).

some more extensive range of hostile activities in the American states.

All these factors combined to produce an unusually tense atmosphere by November of 1787 , when Zéspedes learned more about the large scale plot against the Spanish colonies. In a second letter, Thomas Powell offered to supply information of importance to the Spanish nation about projects originating in Kentucky. Zéspedes still remained skeptical. Almost immediately, however, Carlos Howard heard from Enrique White in New Orleans that a stranger named James Wilkinson had just arrived in town from Kentucky. He was reported to be a brigadier in the American army, although he claimed to be a doctor by profession. According to Captain White's letter, Wilkinson seemed to be an affable fellow, who allegedly planned to settle among the Spaniards, but who probably had other motives. A letter from Gardoqui in November of 1787 also mentioned strong indications that men were gathering on the Ohio river in Kentucky to start downstream and attack Spanish posts along the Mississippi river.

In view of this vague, but corroborating evidence of suspicious activities originating in Kentucky, Governor Zéspedes hurriedly arranged late in November for Thomas Powell to come to Florida for a personal conference. He sent a sloop to Charleston, with a trustworthy Minorcan captain, to take him a passport for the voyage. The captain found Powell suffering from a severe throat infection, but brought word that he expected to be able to travel within ten days. By this time, Zéspedes' numerous problems were further confounded. When he desperately needed the linguistic and diplomatic skill of Captain Howard to interview anticipated representatives of the Georgia Assembly, as well as his Charleston informer, the governor was also forestalling army demands that Howard rejoin his regiment in Cuba and return to Spain. It may be of incidental importance to add that at this point Zéspedes was at least casually involved in preparations for the wedding of his youngest daughter, which took place on December 6, 1787.

Thomas Powell finally arrived in St. Augustine about the middle of December, shortly after James Seagrove returned to Georgia in a pacified mood. Captain Howard queried Powell at length, and secured ten pages of signed testimony regarding his personal history and the conspiracy he was so anxious to reveal to Spanish authorities. According to Powell, leaders in Kentucky were infiltrating Spanish settlements to organize a general uprising in the Mississippi valley, to be coordinated with the arrival of an army of 5000 men descending the Ohio river to seize Natchez and New Orleans. All supplies were being furnished in Kentucky, except for nails and salt which were to come from London. There was evidence that a load of indigo had already left Charleston for London to pay for the latter two items.

As another branch of the same ambitious plot, a young New Englander named Thomas Brown and a partner had already been accepted as Spanish subjects and established a lodging house on the Island of Trinidad, a base for carrying the campaign to South America. There, as in the Mississippi valley, the objective was to encourage the colonists to "throw off the Spanish yoke" and follow the example of the British colonists in North America in proclaiming independence. Financial backing for the combined schemes came from "gentlemen of property" in the Carolinas and Virginia, and Powell could supply about a half dozen names. Much to Zéspedes' surprise, the conspiracy included no representation from Georgia.

Thomas Powell also willingly told his own rather exciting personal history and explained the way he became involved in a plot of such amazing proportions. After surviving combat, capture and prison escape in the early part of the American Revolution, he lived inconspicuously in New Jersey until 1781 when he went south to join General Nathanael Greene's army marching on Charleston, a city evacuated by the British in December, 1782. While the siege was in progress, Thomas Powell met a former acquaintance, Colonel "Light Horse Harry" Lee, who recommended him for the difficult job of exchanging supplies through battle lines. With the consent of the commanding generals of both armies, Thomas Powell took rice and other provisions into Charleston for the British army and returned with clothing for the ragged Continental army and liquor for its officers. The exchange was carried out on the basis of credit supplied by John McQueen, on whose plantation Colonel Lee's troop was quartered. The John McQueen mentioned by Thomas Powell was the same gentleman who visited Zéspedes in December, 1784. After Powell was detected secretly removing gunpowder and salt from Charleston, he was apprehended by the British for the second time and sent to New York as a prisoner, but he promptly escaped.

When the war was over, Thomas Powell returned to Charleston to secure the money that the State of South Carolina owed him for his supply services, a sum he claimed was over three thousand pounds. Because of the currency shortage, he accepted payment in drygoods and groceries, disposed of through a partner who shared in the profits. The partner, Captain George Farragut of Orange County, South Carolina, introduced Powell to the conspiracy in June of 1786, when plans were still in the formative stage. Powell agreed to contribute to the venture the funds owed him by the State of South Carolina. He was further encouraged to participate on discovering that his former schoolmate, Thomas Brown, was also involved in the plot. He knew Brown had sailed to the Caribbean islands, but had not learned earlier of the reason. A long and severe attack of fever, beginning in July of 1786, prevented Powell from attending the first two meetings of the conspirators in North Carolina. He knew, however, that he was chosen to accompany Farragut and Brown in promoting the revolution in South America. Farragut notified him in June of 1787 to be ready for action by January of 1788.

In some solitary summer walks, Thomas Powell came to the conclusion that he did not want to embroil himself or humanity in a second war for independence that could conceivably lead to international hostilities. Yet he was at a loss to decide how to halt the progress of the plot without danger to himself or his friend Farragut. Coming from a Welsh Catholic background, he finally hit upon the idea of sending a message to Governor Zéspedes by an Irish priest who had just arrived in Charleston. Powell's allusion to a Catholic priest in Charleston is worthy of note because it is the earliest record of a priest in South Carolina after the American Revolution. Official history mentions a shadowy figure, a Reverend Mr. Ryan, under whose guidance Catholic religion was first exercised in Charleston in 1788.[5]

Shortly after signing his testimony on December 21, 1787, Thomas Powell returned to Charleston. Before leaving, the governor insisted that he accept a gratification of one hundred pesos to cover his travel expenses, and promised that his friend Farragut would never suffer corporal punishment if caught, and that he himself could always seek asylum in the Spanish dominions. Zéspedes arranged for Powell to correspond in cipher with Captain Howard, and urged him to write as soon as he attended the next meeting of the conspirators. Zéspedes particularly wanted definite information as to the time of Farragut's planned departure from America, his destination, and prospective time of arrival in the

---

[5] John Gilmary Shea, *Life and Times of the Most Reverend John Carroll, embracing the History of the Catholic Church in the United States, 1763-1815* (New York, 1888, pp. 316-317.

Spanish Indies. Although the plot seemed fantastic to the governor, he believed his informant was completely sincere. Weak and trembling from recurrent attacks of fever, appearing older than his twenty-eight years, Thomas Powell left the impression of a man whose mental and physical strength had been severely taxed. But he was no impostor.

A curious coincidence, recorded in Zéspedes' official papers but never mentioned in letters to the foreign office, concerns the Thomas Brown of Trinidad, whom Powell describes as an old schoolfellow. In June of 1787, Gardoqui in New York gave permission to a Thomas Brown, who had arrived with a valid passport from the governor of Trinidad, to return to Trinidad by way of St. Augustine. Brown stopped briefly in St. Augustine in August of 1787, shortly before Zéspedes received his first letter from Thomas Powell. The only important point in Powell's testimony that appears erroneous upon investigation is his statement regarding the three thousand pounds owed him by the State of South Carolina. On the other hand, this is the approximate sum of a debt arising out of wartime services that the state paid to Captain George Farragut.[6]

After Thomas Powell departed, Zéspedes decided that there was enough evidence lending credibility to the startling revelation to warrant further precautions along the Georgia frontier. He believed that any uprising in the Mississippi valley would create a break between the United States and Spain, certain to precipitate military aggression along the Georgia border. Furthermore, under cover of international hostilities, renegades on both sides of the border could murder and plunder indiscriminately in raids more destructive than open warfare. To keep track of the border situation, he arranged for his son Antonio to take over the next three months' assignment at Amelia island, beginning in January of 1788. Antonio had calmed down considerably in the three years since he ran away to the St. Mary's harbor, and the governor always preferred to entrust special tasks in the province to members of his family. The month of January passed without overt action on the part of the conspirators, however, or news of further significant developments.

---

6 South Carolina, State Auditor, *Copy of the Original Index Book Showing the Revolutionary Claims filed in South Carolina between August 20, 1783 and August 31, 1786, kept by James McCall, Auditor General* (Columbia, Janie Revill, 1941). George Farragut was a captain in the South Carolina navy from May 12, 1780 to March 10, 1783. His claim is in the South Carolina Archives, Document No. AA 2309, Account 7 F.

If Thomas Powell's conspiracy seemed to fade out, he at least introduced Zéspedes to another frontier character, Dr. James O'Fallon. After Powell returned to Charleston in December, 1787, Dr. O'Fallon inquired about his trip to St. Augustine and Powell remarked that he was considering settling in Florida. The idea appealed to O'Fallon, who was momentarily discouraged because his party had lost out in a municipal election. Powell arranged for O'Fallon to correspond with Captain Howard, sending a warning that O'Fallon probably was associated with suspicious western projects.

Dr. O'Fallon tried to interest Zéspedes in a gigantic scheme for populating the northern section of East Florida by bringing from Ireland or France five thousand families, each to receive eight hundred acre grants of land. He offered to take over responsibility for all territory between the St. John's and St. Mary's rivers, from the Atlantic coast to the Gulf of Mexico. In a most ingratiating manner, O'Fallon avowed a deep loyalty to Spain and cited as evidence the services that his Irish relative had performed in the Spanish army. On the other hand, Zéspedes received private information that this man, who purported to be a physician, was probably an apostate priest and therefore a reprehensible character. Zéspedes nevertheless felt obliged to keep in contact with Dr. O'Fallon, whose letters pestered Howard and Zéspedes for almost three years.

The rapid succession of disturbing events during the fall of 1787 convinced Governor Zéspedes that East Florida's defenses needed a thorough overhauling. He hoped that something could be accomplished before another Georgia border crisis arose, before any frontier conspiracies matured, and before the avid interest in north Florida land was backed by force. Taking all these possibilities into consideration, he formulated a new defense plan for his province in January, 1788. In the new plan, he combined military reform with his ideas for establishing a reliable Spanish population in East Florida. The new recommendations were submitted to Antonio Valdez, who was promoted from secretary of the navy to the foreign office in July, 1787 after José de Gálvez' death. In writing to Valdez, Zéspedes also tied in the development of the naval stores industry with his military proposals, reminding Valdez of the recent mission José del Rio Cossa organized when Valdez had been navy secretary.

Key to the successful defense program was the creation of a permanent army force in the province, a recommendation he had mentioned frequently since he first sketched the military needs for

Bernardo de Gálvez in April, 1786. The tragic loss of life accompanying the exchange of troops again impressed the governor in August, 1787, when the schooner *San Josef* disappeared while returning to Havana with the loss of three officers and forty men in the Inmemorial del Rey Regiment. The *San Josef* vanished eight months after the wreck of the third vessel meeting disaster during the fall of 1786. Zéspedes believed that the current assignment of only four hundred men for East Florida was insufficient to staff the local garrison and outposts so vital in the event of frontier turbulence. In the first Spanish régime, and at the beginning of his own governorship, five hundred men were stationed in St. Augustine. In anticipation of a population expanding in numbers and area of settlement, he now requested a fixed battalion of eight hundred men.

Zéspedes wanted a fixed battalion for reasons other than the prevention of losses sending troops to and from Havana. To counterbalance the foreign element in the existing population, he suggested recruiting the new battalion in Spain, preferably in Catalonia or Galicia. He wanted married men of robust health, who would be given land and financial aid from the fund for population development established by José de Gálvez. He also preferred veteran Spanish soldiers to form a nucleus for the new battalion thus inculcating a tradition of discipline and loyalty. To protect the frontier, Zéspedes planned a series of rural settlements around defense posts. The citizen soldiery of the new outposts would be available for active duty, but the rest of the time would be occupied producing log wood or turpentine for export, and cotton and agricultural products for their own subsistence. The governor understood that an army trained in battle maneuvers was useless in the swamps and forests. Florida could be defended only by men who had the Indian's knowledge of the forest, and the Georgian's familiarity with its creeks and inlets. Zéspedes' ideal citizen-soldier was a man equally adept in using gun, hoe and paddle to protect his own hearth and home.

In distributing the additional military personnel around the province, the governor first of all wanted to double the size of the Amelia island post, increasing the strength to fifty men. He also favored increasing the size of the detachment at San Vicente Ferrer, where he proposed establishing a customs house, hoping the home government would soon grant permission for ships to use St. Mary's harbor in preference to St. Augustine. Next on the governor's list of recommendations were two additional posts for the St. John's river, the first at the river mouth and a second sixty miles upstream where a boat was kept for the convenience of Indians crossing the river to reach St. Augustine. The two new posts, in combination with those existing at San Vicente Ferrer and Panton's Indian store near Lake George, would form a chain of four military settlements along the St. John's river. Southward on the Atlantic coast, Zéspedes selected two more locations of military importance. He wanted a detachment on Mosquito inlet to prevent illicit wood cutting by men from Providence island, to aid voyagers wrecked off Cape Canaveral, and to protect settlers that Zéspedes hoped would move to this previously productive region. Looking to the future, the governor planned to station soldiers at Cape Florida to keep track of English sailors from the Bahamas who frequented the Florida keys.

Although he clearly pointed out the military significance of the outlying districts, Zéspedes did not intend to diminish the importance of the staunch old Castillo whose military strength was already firmly established. In case of extreme emergency, the entire population of St. Augustine could probably take refuge within its walls. The Castillo de San Marcos was the principal protection for the provincial capital, with three outposts on the perimeter of the town. On the mainland opposite the southern tip of Anastasia island, stood Fort Matanzas, a round tower surrounded by the sea at high tide. Small vessels could ascend the Matanzas river at this point to St. Augustine, or gain access to the San Sebastian river flowing behind the town. This entry point had always been guarded by eight men serving in rotation as a detachment of the main garrison. At the north end of Anastasia island, another small force maintained constant vigil at the watchtower and guarded the nearby storehouse for gunpowder. North of the city, a dozen men were stationed at the outer defense line, the earthworks extending from the North river to the San Sebastian river.

In addition to the strategically distributed defense posts, the governor stressed the importance of mobile military forces. He strongly advocated a cavalry unit for East Florida, and a light artillery unit that could operate from gun boats along the rivers. From first hand observation he knew the effectiveness of General Tonyn's light horse troop. With these additions, Zéspedes felt that the province would be equipped to meet future emergencies, although he doubted if his recommendations would soon receive approval. The ministry in Madrid was very slow in acting on his first request to Bernardo de Gálvez for stronger defenses on the

St. Mary's border. In April of 1788, shortly after sending the
elaborate defense plan to Antonio Valdez, Zéspedes received permission to erect a stone tower on Amelia island with a guard of
a corporal and four soldiers. The letter was scarcely worth acknowledging, except to mention that if the money were provided
to quarry the stone and transport it to the island, the tower might
be built.

After Zéspedes submitted his new defense plan and sent Antonio
to observe border developments in January of 1788, the possibility
of immediate action appeared remote. The rumored Kentucky
conspiracy, like the Georgia border crisis, caused only brief excitement in the governor's office. Zéspedes followed Powell and O'Fallon as long as contact with them seemed profitable. After his interview in St. Augustine in December of 1787, Powell provided no
further concrete information about the conspiracy. By May of
1788, Zéspedes finally decided that Powell's rumored plot was outside his jurisdiction, since it did not directly concern the internal
affairs of East Florida. He suggested that Gardoqui follow up the
matter, and sent Thomas Powell a letter of recommendation for
that purpose. At this point, Powell vanished from the official
scene. The governor also tried to divert O'Fallon's stream of
correspondence to Gardoqui, supplying a letter of recommendation
similar to the one he gave Powell, but the device was useless. At
last Zéspedes learned in April of 1790 that O'Fallon was moving
westward, and immediately he warned Governor Miró to be on
the lookout for the arrival of a potential troublemaker.

Zéspedes was well aware that conspiracies in the back country,
particularly in Kentucky, were as characteristic a feature of the
American frontier as warfare between Indians and pioneers. They
continued until Spain signed the Treaty of San Lorenzo in 1795,
finally acceding to American demands for Mississippi river navigation and for the international boundary at the thirty-first parallel
of latitude. This treaty placed the coveted Natchez district within
American territory. Dr. O'Fallon was just at the beginning of his
career when Thomas Powell introduced him by letter to Carlos
Howard. In a later intrigue, he became the agent of the South
Carolina Yazoo Land Company and managed to pervert the company's colonizing plan, which had some Spanish sanction, into a
projected attack on Louisiana in 1793. He was exposed by James
Wilkinson, whose suspicious arrival in New Orleans impressed Governor Zéspedes in November, 1787. Wilkinson, after a vacillating
career as a Spanish agent to separate Kentucky from the union, was

the American general who received the Spanish post at Natchez when it was evacuated in 1798, in compliance with the Treaty of San Lorenzo.[7]

Concerning Powell's conspiracy, Zéspedes finally concluded that it was just another plot that fizzled out in the back country where it had originated. The governor completely ignored the reference to a projected independence movement for South America. In his mind, independence was synonymous with lawlessness, the chief defect of the American republic. The idea that this notion could take root in the Spanish empire was too wild to merit serious consideration. Both the governor and Gardoqui marveled at the peculiar type of personality generated in the frontier atmosphere. Gardoqui commented that these bedazzled Americans seemed to think that gold and silver grew on trees in Spanish lands. Zéspedes described the conspirators as avaricious adventurers, who ignorantly believed that in the Spanish colonies they had only to scratch the earth like barnyard fowl to find wealth, and thus fulfill their foolish dreams. The governor agreed that these intrigues could not easily be prevented, and certainly bore close observation. He became inured to perennial rumors that Americans were gathering at the falls of the Ohio river to descend on Spanish posts on the Mississippi, as the first step toward the conquest of Mexico.

---

[7] Whitaker, *op. cit.,* pp. 141, 221.

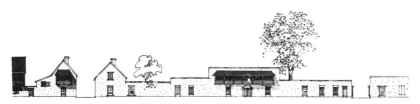

Charlotte Street—East Side

XI

Fray Cyril de Barcelona's Visit

THE ONLY higher official who visited East Florida during Zéspedes' governorship was Fray Cyril de Barcelona, who arrived in July, 1788 to investigate the religious life of the province and remained in St. Augustine until June 12, 1789. His formal inquiry occupied only six weeks, from the middle of September until the end of October, 1788, but his presence added dignity and color to religious ceremonies for almost a full calendar year.[1] Fray Cyril came to East Florida at the insistence of Father Luis Peñalver y Cardenas, Bishop of Havana, whose responsibilities included the periodic survey of communities within his diocese. When this territory suddenly increased at the end of the American Revolution with the addition of the Floridas, Fray Cyril de Barcelona, then vicar of Louisiana, was elevated to the position of auxiliary bishop in charge of parish visits in the new provinces on the mainland.

A year prior to Fray Cyril's visit to St. Augustine, the Bishop of Havana had evidence that the provincial capital needed investigation by a higher religious authority. In July, 1787, a young woman named Antonia Garriga complained that Governor Zéspedes and Father Hassett had conspired to force her departure from East Florida and separate her from her daughter. The bishop naturally

---

[1] Michael J. Curley, *Church and State in the Spanish Floridas,* 1783-1821 (Washington, 1940). The visitation is discussed in pages 100-118.

164

believed such serious charges deserved checking. He was aghast when he finally learned the complete story of Antonia Garriga's bout with the authorities in East Florida, during which she defied both priest and governor. Zéspedes was still trying to settle the uproar she had created when Fray Cyril de Barcelona came to East Florida.

Antonia Garriga, sometimes called Antonia Selorte, had at least two husbands, but her broad range of activities bordered on nymphomania. She had been a problem to authorities since the period of the British evacuation in the summer of 1785. After living six weeks as an evacuée on a transport vessel in St. Mary's harbor, she fled to the Spanish brigantine, the *San Matias*, in July, claiming she wanted to return to her native Minorca by way of Havana. Always capable of arousing male sympathy, Antonia easily won the protection of Captain Pedro Vásquez, but he became suspicious when her story appeared to vary so widely from that of the husband who came to reclaim her. She quickly became friendly with the crew of the *San Matias*, and received gifts of money and clothing. General Tonyn charged that Antonia had been seduced by a Spanish officer, and demanded that she be forced to return to the *Cyrus*. Captain Vásquez speedily decided that Antonia was too disruptive an influence to keep on shipboard, and sent her to the governor's custody in St. Augustine. She made no effort to leave the province, however, but soon achieved a notorious reputation. The husband whom she supported followed her back to town.

Father Hassett first tried counseling her with firm admonitions, then secured Governor Zéspedes' aid in having her locked up briefly to reflect on her sins. The parish priest finally decided that Antonia was a hopeless case, but he was determined to save her fourteen year old Mulatto companion. The girl was the illegitimate daughter of Antonia's first husband, an Englishman who had lived in St. Augustine until his death. Antonia shamelessly used the girl to carry messages arranging for illicit meetings, as she used her second husband as a shield for her extramarital ventures. Antonia was strong-minded, and her husband sufficiently weak-willed, so that she was able virtually to force him to act as procurer. He finally escaped this ignominious role by taking a job on a government gun boat patroling the St. Mary's river.

Father Hassett became enraged when he discovered that Antonia had tried to steal the papers proving the free status of her Mulatto stepdaughter in order to sell her in Charleston. He decided that the woman had passed the limits of toleration in trying to sell the girl into slavery in a heretical environment, without even the protection of baptism. Taking matters into his own hands, Father Hassett had the girl baptised and placed in the protection of a respectable Spanish family where she received the necessary instruction in honest living and in the Catholic faith. But he had to call on the governor again for a few strong soldiers to force Antonia on shipboard when she was finally evicted from the province in July, 1787.

Governor Zéspedes and Father Hassett thought they were rid of Antonia when they shipped her to Havana, but she used her earnings and her talent for misrepresentation to create trouble for them in Cuba. She protested to the captain general that her husband had unjustly sent her away, with the connivance of Governor Zéspedes. She informed the Cuban bishop that East Florida authorities had refused to allow her "daughter" to accompany her to Cuba, and that the girl's moral life was endangered by the presence of the second husband. Finally, the Havana prelate became convinced that this was a sad case of a broken home, where a child might suffer unless the parents were reconciled. He appealed to Father Hassett to have Antonia's husband bring the Mulatto girl to her "mother" in Havana, and thus reunite the family.

Both Father Hassett and Governor Zéspedes were incensed to learn the extent to which the truth had been warped by Antonia's dishonesty. Furthermore, she continued to cause discord in St. Augustine by writing her former neighbors letters describing the excitement and luxury of life in Havana, in comparison with the drab existence in East Florida. In response to virtual orders from the captain general to send the Mulatto girl to Havana, Zéspedes postponed her departure by explaining that he would send her with the first respectable woman going to Cuba. Since passenger traffic between Florida and Cuba was almost solely sailors and soldiers, he felt the girl could be kept in her present good surroundings for several months at least. Certainly she did not want to join Antonia, nor did Antonia's husband. In one candid and carefully phrased sentence, Zéspedes finally communicated to the captain general the lack of wisdom in ordering Antonia's husband to bring the girl to Havana. Since she was not bad looking, and though born innocent was unfortunately sophisticated in certain ways, the governor feared her virtue might be endangered on a voyage in close proximity to sailors, chaperoned only by a man who had served as his wife's pimp.

Antonia Garriga was an isolated case, not a typical female representative of the community, for most women in St. Augustine were pious members of Father Hassett's congregation. Yet it was clear that an atmosphere of discouragement and disillusion prevailed in the town and seemed to engender a corresponding wave of dissolute living. Everyone suffered in the summer of 1788, when most of the government employees had been without salary since December of 1786. The decay in the local economy seemed to precipitate a similar decadence in the moral fibre of the military and civilian population.

The key to the basic social problem is in one simple statistical comparison for the year 1788. While the garrison maintained about four hundred soldiers, for the most part unmarried, there were in the entire province only fifty-five unmarried women between the ages of sixteen and forty. The large proportion of the military spent their time exclusively in masculine society, drinking, carousing and gambling illegally in St. Augustine wineshops catering to their trade. Those who found favor with the limited feminine element naturally made the most of their good fortune, often creating problems for Father Hassett. The parish priest did his best to assure the future of illegitimate children by securing reliable godparents, usually leading members of the community. Governor Zéspedes was not surprised when Distinguished Sargeant Juan Sively added the name of an illegitimate daughter to the parish register. On the other hand, he was disappointed when Dimas Cortes, a treasury official second in importance to Gonzalo Zamorano, was caught in the same fashion.

Governor Zéspedes was unpleasantly aware of the growing sexual irregularity in the small community, and attempted in several ways to correct the situation during Fray Cyril de Barcelona's lengthy stay in St. Augustine. When the rising incidence of homosexuality among the soldiers included little boys, offenders were prosecuted and sent to Havana for trial. Zéspedes was still waiting for the arrival of a legal official to handle infractions of the law in East Florida. Until he had this assistance, he adopted the policy of taking testimony and sending the prisoners and indictments to Havana to await the decision of the *auditor de guerra* in Cuba. The boys, sons of Spanish, Minorcan and English parents, were remanded to the corrective attention of their families with the exception of one unfortunate orphan who was sent away because there was no one responsible for him in St. Augustine. Perhaps the town became a better community without him, but it is doubtful if he found a therapeutic environment in Havana.

The governor and parish priest tried to maintain some semblance of standards among the higher ranks of the governmental staff, but were not always successful. The official whose behavior was most offensive to Governor Zéspedes was the notary, Domingo Rodríguez de Leon. The governor found reason to question his professional integrity in taking testimony of a Negro woman who was seeking to prove the free status of herself and her daughters. He also knew the notary was an outrageous libertine, responsible for the separation of more than one married couple in St. Augustine. Nevertheless the government could not operate without an official notary. Until the captain general of Cuba provided a substitute, or the court in Madrid managed to get an assessor to St. Augustine, Domingo Rodríguez de Leon was indispensable to the legal machinery of the province. The governor requested his replacement, but the slowness of official red tape kept him on duty, attesting to official documents to the end of Zéspedes' regime.

If the notary stayed on, one of Captain Carlos Howard's assistants had to leave the province abruptly during the period of Fray Cyril de Barcelona's official visit. The assistant was discovered in his shirttails one evening in the bedroom of one of St. Augustine's better homes. With the vehement protests of an aggrieved husband and incriminating testimony of observant neighbors ringing in his ears, Zéspedes hastily dispatched the young man to Havana on a conveniently departing schooner. Sending him to Havana for reassignment avoided the need for formal proceedings and a public scandal. The governor was inclined to protect the young secretary, since he at least had served capably in his official duties. The captain general in Cuba praised the governor for his prudence.

Father O'Reilly as well as Father Hassett fought vigorously to save souls in St. Augustine. One of his most stubborn opponents was a Mulatto named Samuel Rumford with a long record of misdeeds dating from the British era when he had been sentenced to forced labor. Father O'Reilly admonished Samuel Rumford to abandon his vices, but the culprit resented this interference to the extent that he finally threatened to kill the priest. For two years, Father O'Reilly lived in periodic terror, until Zéspedes decided early in 1789 that he had sufficient grounds to expel Rumford from the province. When the governor and the clergy decided to cast out evil, they literally threw the offender out of East Florida. Rumford drew this punishment for sending a "gift" of salt meat to an acknowledged enemy, whose dog died after eating the fish. Circumstantial evidence seemed sufficient to arrest Rumford and send him to Havana for trial. In the confusion of official correspondence, Zéspedes later received an order to release Rumford, but not until the Mulatto had already departed. The governor was anxious for an excuse to send along Rumford's wife, as well.

The independent crusade conducted by the governor, priests and new military commandant relieved Fray Cyril of the need for initiating any action while he was in St. Augustine. Prior to the bishop's arrival, however, Zéspedes had hoped that the mere presence of the ecclesiastical dignitary would curb violations of the Christian moral code. The governor looked forward to Fray Cyril de Barcelona's visit to the province. On the other hand, before reaching East Florida, the auxiliary bishop dreaded the thought of inspecting the religious life of a community including a percentage of English Protestants. He postponed carrying out his instructions as long as possible, hiring a Madrid lawyer to represent to the court the impossibility of fulfilling this assignment. Fray Cyril had discovered some very unsavory situations in Louisiana on an earlier parish visit, and disliked being compelled to face similarly disagreeable experiences in East Florida. He tarried thirty months in Havana during a period of ecclesiastical reorganization, hoping for promotion to a Cuban bishopric, thus avoiding the unpleasant task in East Florida altogether. But Fray Cyril's ambitious persistence annoyed Cuban clerics and resulted in two royal orders for him to continue his mission on the mainland. With a seventeen-page letter of minute instructions, and orders never to return to Cuba without special permission, Fray Cyril disconsolately sailed for St. Augustine on July 8, 1788.

During his prolonged stay in Havana, between religious inspections in Louisiana and East Florida, he had at least acquired a congenial companion for the trip he feared would be unpleasant. Quite by chance he had met a Capuchin priest, Fray Ignacio Olot, returning to Spain from missionary service in the Orinoco valley of eastern South America. Although he had no salary available for an assistant, Fray Cyril had an expense account to provide food and lodging. Fray Olot came to St. Augustine as secretary to the auxiliary bishop, whose retinue included two pages. On arriving in St. Augustine on July 18, they were welcomed with a formal religious procession and escorted to one of the king's unoccupied houses, where they established temporary residence. The heat and lethargy of St. Augustine in late summer contributed to delaying

Fray Cyril's initiation of formal inquiries. He hoped he could carry out the dreaded task of reading the "Edict of Public Sins" with more aplomb after becoming oriented in an unfamiliar environment. His first public participation in the life of the town occurred in the annual celebration of the Feast of St. Augustine, patron saint of the town, on August 28. On this occasion the ceremonies were more elaborate than usual because they served the added purpose of giving thanks for the birth on the previous March 29 of the Infante Don Carlos Maria Ysidro, son of the Prince and Princess of Asturias.

Finally, in the middle of September, Fray Cyril de Barcelona buckled down to his assigned task. He understood his obligation to impart sound doctrine, promote wholesome customs, correct abuses and counsel the faithful of the province to lead good lives. On September 14, he called together the people of St. Augustine to hear the "Edict of Public Sins" in preparation for giving testimony concerning the moral condition of the parish. They were instructed to report if the priests left their dwellings incognito, danced at weddings, engaged in private business, or failed to give attention to last wills and testaments. If they knew of instances when the sexton was late in opening the church, ringing the bells, these should be told to the *visitador*. Finally, the parishioners were admonished to give information about any persons who lived in concubinage, caused broken homes, failed to make their Easter duty, married clandestinely, or gave bad examples to children.

The following day, Fray Cyril administered the sacrament of confirmation to a large number of inhabitants and arranged for similar services on subsequent Sunday mornings following High Mass. But he waited in vain for any revelations of the moral condition of the parish. There were a few complaints about the high fees for ecclesiastical services, but these were set by the bishop in Cuba. One citizen objected to the fact that Father Hassett refused to hold a rogation procession to ask God's blessing on the crops during a severe drought. The people of St. Augustine exhibited the characteristic pride of a small community, unwilling to confess local sins to an outsider. Fray Cyril de Barcelona appreciated the reason for the silence of the parishioners. In a way he was relieved, but he also had nothing to report to his superiors.

In an effort to gain some candid testimony, he called in two lay witnesses for further inquiry. The first was Captain Miguel Iznardy, on whose vessel Father Hassett had been shipwrecked en route from Philadelphia to Havana when the priest was on his way to join the occupation force in St. Augustine. Captain Iznardy admired the fortitude with which the priest faced the disaster, and found nothing to diminish his good opinion after he became a merchant residing in St. Augustine. He had few observations to make, his reticence probably increased because of his recent arrival in the province. Bernardo de Madrid, official physician, was the second witness whom Fray Cyril privately questioned. The old doctor had a distinguished record of recent public service. For an undisclosed number of years after receiving the degree of bachelor of medicine, he engaged in private practice. In 1782, he briefly occupied the chair of medicine at the University of Havana before receiving an appointment to attend the expeditionary force organized by Bernardo de Gálvez to capture New Providence island. When illness disabled many of the soldiers, he purchased a schooner to take those in his care back to Havana. In St. Augustine, Bernardo de Madrid's patients included soldiers, officials, and colonists whom he often supplied with free medicine if they had no money. He was the one who gave provisional baptism to babies with questionable chances of survival, and attended elders up to the moment when a priest was summoned to administer the last rites of the church. The two witnesses had little reason to criticize the local priests, and no comment to make about other members of the community. Father Hassett and Father O'Reilly certainly led exemplary lives. They both had difficulty in preaching in fluent Spanish, however, and Father Hassett often used a book. In their final moments of life on earth, the townspeople seldom sought the Irish priests, usually preferring the solace of their compatriots, Father Campos and Father Traconis, the hospital chaplain.

Once his parish inspection was launched, Fray Cyril de Barcelona carried out his instructions with commendable thoroughness. He visited the school and the cemetery, checked parish records, and looked over the limited facilities for public worship. He was very favorably impressed by the school, which had been in operation since the summer of 1785 with Father Traconis in charge of primary instruction. Over a year after primary classes began, intermediate instruction was added under the direction of José Antonio Iguiñez, who had come to St. Augustine as assistant keeper of artillery stores. The school house visited by the auxiliary bishop was an old building renovated in 1787 and furnished with new desks and benches. Fray Cyril carefully read the regulations governing the operation of the school, a set of rules that Father Hassett had written and read aloud to his teachers at the opening of the new school year in September, 1787.

If the boys followed the regulations devised by Father Hassett, they attended school from seven o'clock in the morning until noon, and from two o'clock until sundown throughout the winter season. During the summer months, school closed an hour and a half before sunset. On entering the schoolroom, a student was expected to curtsey, hang up his hat, bless himself in the name of the Blessed Trinity, and sit down quietly to begin his work. If he needed to leave the room, he took a special ruler from the teacher's desk, set in motion a swinging pendulum, and made haste to return the ruler before the pendulum stopped. With this device, only one pupil could be absent at a time. Clean feet, when it was warm enough to go barefooted, as well as clean faces and hands were school requirements. Once a week the students cleaned the school. Father Hassett cautioned the boys not to loiter after school nor commit mischievous pranks. In regard to discipline, the priest enjoined the teachers to be moderate and to avoid corporal punishment.

Intellectual goals for the school were simple. The primary class concentrated on reading and writing, while intermediate pupils learned arithmetic, including the multiplication tables. All instruction was given in the Spanish language, although Minorcan continued to be common speech in St. Augustine. General examinations before the parish priest took place at the beginning of each month and the boys were seated according to their performance. The highest ranking student literally sat at the head of his class, but might be displaced in the next month's examination.

Religious instruction formed an integral part of the teaching day. Father Traconis taught the primary class how to recite the rosary and hear mass properly. The advanced class memorized the catechism as well as the multiplication table. The older pupils learned to assist at mass, helping the sexton two at a time. Four times a year, all pupils over seven attended confession accompanied by their teachers. Each boy was notified two days in advance, in order to have time to examine his conscience. In small groups, they were dismissed from school to go to the church for confessional. Boys old enough to receive the Holy Sacrament of Eucharist were instructed in the need for repentance in order to make the sacrament valid. Teachers and pupils continued their joint religious activities outside the school. On Saturday evening, they attended the *Salve*, a low mass featuring the singing of the "Salve, Regina," universally popular anthem in honor of the Blessed Virgin Mary. They also were present on Sunday vespers, services on special religious holidays, and all services including the preaching of the Gospel.

Fray Cyril de Barcelona was understandably surprised to find a primary school of creditable quality operating in St. Augustine. No similar educational endeavor existed in Louisiana or West Florida. Since government supported elementary education was unusual in the Spanish empire, the school represented a major achievement for the young province of East Florida. Opening the school was the idea of Father Hassett, who had established a school of mathematics and navigation as well as a primary school in Philadelphia near the end of the American Revolution. The rules he devised for the Philadelphia schools, probably similar to the regulations used in St. Augustine, had received the commendation of Charles III. One phase of the eighteenth century enlightenment in Spain included an interest in primary education, usually under private sponsorship, however. For example, José de Gálvez and his brothers established a school for boys and a school for girls in their home village.[2] The primary school operating in Santiago de Cuba during Zéspedes' interim governorship was established by a private benefactor in 1754.[3] As soon as Father Hassett made the suggestion, Zéspedes became an enthusiastic supporter of a Spanish language school for St. Augustine. It was an excellent method to Hispanicize the polyglot population of the provincial capital. Without the benefits of modern psychology or sociology, both men instinctively realized the value of imprinting Spanish cultural tradition on the minds of the younger generation. There is no indication of school enrollment, but a reasonable guess would be fifty pupils. The only statistical guide is the census of 1788 stating that there were 240 boys under sixteen years of age in the province. The St. Augustine school was limited to boys, but the instruction program included Negroes and Mulattoes, seated in a separate section of the room.

Although the school was beginning its second year in a remodeled building when Fray Cyril de Barcelona visited St. Augustine, he found that religious services were conducted in temporary quarters on the second floor of a house on the south side of the plaza. The parish church used during the first Spanish régime was in very shaky condition when Zéspedes arrived in the province, and col-

[2] Herbert Ingram Priestly, *José de Gálvez, Visitor General of New Spain* (Berkeley, 1916), p. 6.

[3] Ramon Guerra y Sánchez. José M. Pérez Cabrera, Juan J. Remos. and Emeterio S. Santovenia, *Historia de la Nación Cubana* (10 vols., Havana, 1962), II, p. 301.

lapsed completely during the course of the next few years. The
current church location was awkward, presenting difficulties for
elderly people who had to climb the steep stairs in order to attend
service. Furthermore, the laughter of soldiers on the nearby square
often intruded upon the quiet and reverent intervals of the mass.
Nevertheless, the well-furnished interior invoked the proper atmosphere for divine worship.

As soon as he reached East Florida, Father Hassett made an inventory of the few items that Father Campos had brought from
the church of San Pedro at New Smyrna. Finding these inadequate,
he promptly wrote the bishop in Havana to secure additional supplies. The bishop was unable to find the furnishings brought back
in 1763, except for a baldaquin, an ornate silver decorated canopy
usually placed above a saint's image, the sole religious object remaining from the old parish church which was the center of worship during the first Spanish period. The baldaquin arrived with
a generous consignment of religious goods sent by the bishop in
July, 1786 in the care of an infantry captain returning to East
Florida at that time. Additional church property acquired in 1786
included many silver objects: a lamp for the Holy Sacrament,
covered chalices for sacred wafers, communion cups, a candelabrum
for the governor's candle, crosses for burial service, an incense
vessel and a shell for baptismal water. The bishop also supplied
a missal stand for the use of the choir, wooden crosses and cruci-
fixes, and two altars with new linen altar cloths and frontal
hangings. For the priests conducting services, he provided complete
vestments, including white linen robes, corded girdles, hooded
capes, surplices and various accessories of the proper colors to denote
the different seasons of the ecclesiastical year.

The need for a new church building in St. Augustine was already
recognized, and a site reserved on the north side of the plaza. The
first plans drawn by Chief Engineer Mariano LaRocque were re-
jected as too expensive, and returned to the governor while the
auxiliary bishop was still in the province. Adding his advice and
support to the project of a new church, Fray Cyril de Barcelona
approved the cost-reducing measure of using stone from the old
parish church and from *Nuestra Señora de la Leche*, a chapel north
of the city. The modified plans submitted in September of 1789
were approved, a piece of good news reaching Florida late the
following June just before Zespedes' departure from the province.
Since financing was assured from the proceeds of the sale and rental

of church property, work soon commenced, and the cornerstone of the new church was laid in February, 1793.

In going through the parish records, Fray Cyril felt that he had to comment on the fact that no financial accounts existed for the years 1784 and 1785. Aside from this one omission, all seemed perfectly in order. He encountered considerable difficulty in reading the Latin entries in the marriage and baptismal records, however. In the future, he recommended entries in Spanish and he provided a form for this purpose. On October 6, 1788, he personally performed the first marriage ceremony recorded in the new manner, easily the most important wedding of the year. The bride was Francisco Fatio's daughter, Sophia, and the groom was George Fleming, a Dublin-born Irishman who had lived in South Carolina before he became a resident in the Fatio household sometime during the British period. In formal official style, the record listed the three Sundays on which the marriage bans had been published, and stated that this particular ceremony took place in the reception room of the "bishop's palace" in St. Augustine. The witnesses were the three local parish priests, Thomas Hassett, Miguel O'Reilly and Pedro Campos.

No detail of religious life in the province escaped the visiting bishop's notice. Fray Cyril insisted that in the future chaplains must always wear the clerical soutane. He also asked Father Hassett to preach every Sunday, and see that vespers were held every evening. Although he recognized the substantial number of conversions among the Anglo-American Protestant population, he felt the Negro element had been neglected. One important diocesan statute stated that owners of Negroes must have them baptized within a six months interval, or be liable to excommunication and fine by civil authorities. Fray Cyril advised Father Hassett to ring the church bell each Sunday to summon slaves for instruction in preparation for their baptism and confirmation.

The missionary endeavors of the two Irish priests merited Fray Cyril's honest praise. In presenting a comprehensive set of population statistics for the province, Father Hassett pointed out that 80 of the 295 former British Protestants had already been converted to Catholicism, and twelve more were receiving instruction. Perhaps this was a conservative accomplishment, but the vicar had been warned by José de Gálvez not to accept converts without thorough instruction and careful examination. By 1789, the list of converts numbered 98, about evenly divided between the Europeans and Negroes. But in May, 1790, Father Hassett laid the basis for en-

larging the Catholic population of the province, when he baptized
78 children and 51 slaves during a 600 mile missionary journey
in the northern section of the province. Fray Cyril de Barcelona
concluded his formal visitation with a militant appeal for continuation of the missionary work, preaching from the Old Testament
text of Kings III 20: 39, "Keep this man, and if he slip away, thy
life shall be for his life."

After surviving the initial ordeal of preaching the "Edict of
Public Sins," Fray Cyril de Barcelona began to enjoy living in St.
Augustine. Originally he had intended to return to New Orleans
soon after Christmas. But he postponed leaving on reflecting that
during the season of prevailing northern winds it would be almost
impossible to sail from Havana to New Orleans, and he knew it
would be impolitic to remain long in Cuba. As a result of his in-
decision, the auxiliary bishop and his entourage remained in East
Florida until the following June. The extended stay of the visiting
clergy gave the provincial priests several months of exceptional
sociability. For Fray Cyril de Barcelona, the interval in St. Augustine was a pleasant relief after his previous years of friction with
French priests in Louisiana as well as with the bishop of Cuba.

The six priests associated together in St. Augustine during the
winter of 1788-1789 represented a variety of backgrounds and
experience, each one supplying anecdotes from a different part of
the world. Fray Cyril de Barcelona and Fray Ignacio Olot both
appear to have come from Catalonia, where the Capuchin order
maintained a center for missionary training. Fray Cyril entered the
mission field in Louisiana in 1772, four years after the province
was transferred from France to Spain. He found life difficult in
the midst of a predominantly French population, and first of all
had to master a new language. Moreover, he soon was at odds with
the French Capuchins already established in the province. Some of
their number seemed too worldly and pleasure seeking, and even
suspect from the political point of view. After he was given control
of Louisiana, Fray Cyril evicted one priest from the province and
eventually replaced all the French missionaries with Spaniards of
the same order.

When Bernardo de Gálvez began the conquest of West Florida,
Fray Cyril was vicar of Louisiana and consequently responsible
for sending additional priests into the newly conquered territory.
He was appointed auxiliary bishop in 1782, in view of the enlarged
area coming under the jurisdiction of the Cuban diocese. Early in
1785, while in Havana for his formal ordination, Fray Cyril

participated in numerous public functions and confirmed nine thousand persons in the course of a few months. Reluctantly, he left the ceremonious routine of the island capital to undertake his first parish inspection in New Orleans in July, 1785, but he returned to Havana in December as soon as he learned the bishop was ill.

Fray Cyril's attentive presence annoyed the biship, who reminded him that his primary responsibility was the inspection of ecclesiastical affairs in Louisiana and the Floridas, the mainland territories too extensive for the bishop to cover in person. Furthermore, Fray Cyril had already incurred the bishop's disfavor by complaining to the colonial minister. Fray Cyril had informed José de Gálvez that his three thousand peso salary was too small to pay the travel expense required by the inspection without an additional allowance from the bishopric of Havana, which he implied was a wealthy and close-fisted organization. In an effort to dislodge Fray Cyril from Havana the second time, the bishop canceled the powers previously granted him for Cuba, removed him from his New Orleans pastorate, and finally cut off his salary completely until he embarked on his trip to East Florida. After all these distressing events, Fray Cyril found St. Augustine a pleasant haven. During the winter, he concentrated on improving his knowledge of the English language, with Father Hassett's help, so that he could hear confession when he went to West Florida.

Father Olot, the second visitor in St. Augustine that winter, brought tales from southeast Venezuela, a mission field vastly different from French populated Louisiana. In the late eighteenth century, the Orinoco valley of South America became an area of Spanish frontier expansion similar to Texas and California in North America. Angostura, [modern Ciudad Bolívar], the focal point of valley life located four hundred miles upstream on the Orinoco river, was not founded until 1764, although Spanish settlements were established on the Caribbean coast of Venezuela in the early sixteenth century. The area south of the river where the Catalonian Capuchins had their mission district is a hilly wilderness of forest and swamp, in sharp contrast to the grassy *llanos* stretching away from the northern bank where the Franciscans were predominant. When Father Olo was in Venezuela, the Capuchins operated a series of Indian missions east of Angostura along the Rio Caroni, which descends from the Guiana Highlands and enters the Orinoco from the south at San Felix, about one hundred fifty miles downstream from Angostura. The indefatigable traveler

Alexander von Humboldt reported that in 1797 the Capuchin order supervised thirty mission stations in "Carony," with an aboriginal population of sixteen thousand souls.[4] The villages of primitive people, subsisting mainly on cassava and plantain, were located on river banks surrounded by the immense tropical forests that later inspired the literary descriptions of W. H. Hudson's "Green Mansions."

In St. Augustine, Father Olot undoubtedly remarked on the flies, the chief scourge of the Orinoco valley, and possible he bore the spotted scars of their noxious sting. They contributed to the spread of tropical disease, which in some form attacked the missionary and necessitated his departure. In order to reach the outside world again, he had to follow a three hundred mile course through waters harboring the deadly electric eel and schools of carniverous *caribe* fish, which attacking in unison can strip the flesh from a man's bones, before reaching the crocodile infested delta of the Orinoco and the sea route to Havana. Evidently his health was not so greatly impaired as to prevent a side trip to St. Augustine, a city whose climate was often praised, before completing his homeward journey. Fanning away the Florida mosquitos blown into town by an occasional westward land breeze was only a mild discomfort compared to the insect and animal life he had battled in South America.

Of all the local priests, Father Campos was the one who most appreciated the extended visit of the auxiliary bishop and his assistant, because they spoke his native language. The Minorcan dialect, a variant of Catalan, is a language quite different from Castilian, the form of speech that the court tried to impose on the rest of the Spanish provinces. It was a rare privilege for Father Campos to converse freely with the visiting Capuchins, the only priests understanding Minorcan who came to Florida after the deportation of his assistant in 1774. The elderly priest was growing increasingly frail. As recently as January of 1788, Governor Zéspedes had sent another request for a Minorcan-speaking replacement so that he could return to Minorca. Fray Cyril was deeply moved by Father Campos' tales of suffering in New Smyrna, and singled him out for special merit in making a report to his superiors.

Father Hassett, vicar and ecclesiastical judge of East Florida, was a youthful host to his distinguished older guests. In 1788, Father

---

[4] Alexander von Humboldt and Aimé Bonpland, *Personal Narrative of Travels to the Equinoctial Regions of the New Continent during the Year 1799-1804* (9 vols., London, 1821), VI, p. 351; and V, pt. 1, pp. 76-87.

Hassett was only thirty-seven years old, while Father O'Reilly was a year younger. No one knows what observations Father Hassett made to his associates on the basis of his two years in the cultural capital of the new republic, a city with a strong Quaker influence. But he could recount the dramatic tale of his experience after leaving Philadelphia for St. Augustine in June, 1784. Father O'Reilly, who remained in Cuba to serve as a troop chaplain during the American Revolution, was the only priest spending the winter in St. Augustine with experience in military service. These two priests were the vanguard of twenty Irish clerics who served in Louisiana and the Floridas during the last years of Spanish domination.

Father Francisco Traconis, the hospital chaplain, was the member of the group with the most limited experience, having lived exclusively in Havana prior to his journey to East Florida. By the time of Fray Cyril's visit, he was heartily sick of his job teaching the primary school and wished he had never volunteered to give the instruction. In 1788, he received two months emergency leave after his father died leaving him with the responsibility for the family property and two orphan sisters. He hoped the auxiliary bishop would arrange his return to Cuba, but Governor Zéspedes steadily refused to release him from his important educational work. Zéspedes knew the task assigned to young Father Traconis was difficult. He also knew the chaplain had accepted an appointment in Florida mainly to win promotion to the cathedral in Havana, a reward he would richly deserve if he spent five years teaching the alphabet and the recitation of the Rosary to young Floridians. Father Traconis was finally granted a benefice in Havana in 1791.

After actually observing the situation in the East Florida parish during the course of the winter, Fray Cyril de Barcelona made some very sensible suggestions which unfortunately were ignored by his ecclesiastical superiors. To relieve Father Campos and Father Traconis, he recommended that Father Olot take over the duties of the Minorcan pastorate and teach the primary class in school. In his talks with Father Hassett, Fray Cyril came to appreciate the importance of establishing new parishes among the English residents of the St. John's and St. Mary's rivers. He suggested that Father Hassett and Father O'Reilly undertake this assignment themselves, and secure a Spanish priest to reside in St. Augustine.

But the clear statements of Fray Cyril to the Bishop of Cuba were no more influential than the eloquent pleas of Zéspedes and Father Hassett to Madrid. Father Hassett's original request in 1784 for additional Irish clergy reached the attention of Charles III at a time when the king was under pressure from the Franciscan order for the reactivation of their former mission territory in Florida. Governor Zéspedes, informed of the Franciscan's request, did his best to clarify the changes that had taken place among the Southern Indians during the past quarter of a century, changes that made a resumption of missionary work impossible. Nevertheless, it was sometimes difficult in Madrid to correlate all pertinent information at the time crucial decisions were made with reference to overseas possessions. Rather unaccountably, two perplexed Franciscan fathers arrived in St. Augustine in November, 1789, six months after Fray Cyril's departure. Since they comprehended neither Minorcan nor English, they had little to contribute to the provincial religious life. Zéspedes' successor requested their recall soon after he assumed the governorship. The arrival of the two Franciscans was a bitter dissappointment to Father Campos, who died on May 19, 1790 after waiting eight years for a Minorcan priest so that he could spend his last days on his native island.

Governor Zéspedes took advantage of the presence of distinguished ecclesiastical guests in planning the funeral obsequies honoring the illustrious monarch, Charles III, who died December 14, 1788. News of this tragedy did not reach Cuba until February, 1789 to be forwarded to St. Augustine. The royal order announcing the death of the king, prescribed six months of mourning. On March 11, Governor Zéspedes announced arrangements for proper observance in the provincial capital. To the roll of muffled drums, a military detachment marched from the Castillo to the city gate, around the parade, and down to the barracks entrance, posting notices of public mourning to begin on March 22. According to the governor's decree, full mourning was to be worn by all royal officials, staff members of the treasury department, the controller of the royal hospital, and every head of a family. In the temporary church quarters on the plaza, funeral obsequies for the soul of the departed king were held for nine consecutive days, with Fray Cyril de Barcelona chanting the mass. At the first service, Fray Ignacio Olot preached an impressive funeral oration, extolling the virtues and accomplishments of Charles III. For the whole community, the king's death increased the solemnity of the Lenten season preceding Easter services on April 12, 1789, in which all the clergy played important roles.

With the next ships from Havana bringing troops for the annual rotation, word came that a new bishop from Puerto Rico had been installed in office in the Cuban capital on March 30, replacing

Father Luis Peñalver y Cardenas who had transferred to Mexico City. If Fray Cyril de Barcelona had been waiting for some last minute chance for a position on the island, his hopes now were destroyed. He knew he had to leave St. Augustine soon in order to avoid the season of predominantly southerly winds making it difficult to sail to Havana during the summer. After packing rather deliberately, he left St. Augustine with his entourage on June 12, confident that he had counseled the settlers to lead good lives and sufficiently strengthened to face the inspection of religious life in West Florida.

Charlotte Street—East Side

XII

Military Reform and Intruders

THE rotation of troops in the spring of 1788 involved not just
the usual partial replacement of military personnel, but a complete
change of command, since Lieutenant Colonel Guillermo O'Kelly
had to rejoin the Hibernia Regiment in Havana and return to Spain.
The new commandant, Lieutenant Colonel Ignacio Peñalver y
Calvo of the Havana Regiment, was a stern disciplinarian who
attempted to reform the casual and often slipshod habits of the
frontier garrison. His arrival marked the beginning of a vexatious
period of adjustment for his subordinates. On several occasions
during that interval, Governor Zéspedes felt obliged to modify the
new commandant's decisions, in order to maintain peace between
the different army units in the presidio and to conform with his
own humanitarian interpretation of military discipline.

The incidents creating friction among the soldiers and officers of
the local garrison began in June of 1788 with a hassle over the
dragoon's responsibilities for guard duty. When he assumed command in St. Augustine, Colonel Peñalver decreed that the dragoons
share with the infantry the duty of maintaining order in the barracks, as well as the more honorary assignment of standing guard
at the fort. Although both the dragoons and the infantry were
housed in the same quarters, the dragoons customarily had enjoyed

a privileged status, and alternated with infantry only in guard duty at the Castillo de San Marcos. The new commandant also requested that the dragoon's head officer be mounted on horseback while on duty at the fort. Lieutenant Andres de Alvear, new officer in charge of the dragoons, protested against the addition of barracks duty for his men and mounted duty for himself.

Colonel Peñalver countered with a most effective weapon in military administration; he called an impromptu inspection of the dragoons' horses and accoutrements. Only ten of the fifteen horses belonging to the contingent of dragoons were at hand, since five were being used for reconnaissance and courier service at San Vicente Ferrer and Amelia island. Early in June, Colonel Peñalver rode five miles north of town to the vicinity of old Fort Mosa where the horses were pastured. Glancing from one to another of the ten decrepit animals grazing in the field, he immediately understood Lieutenant Alvear's reluctance to accept mounted guard duty. The lieutenant had been embarrassed to admit that he had no horse of his own, although this possession might be expected of the head of a mounted army unit, and those belonging to the detachment were obviously a sorry lot. Closer inspection revealed that eight were of advanced age, three suffered from saddle sores, and among them was a pregnant mare and a colt. The leather was mildewed on the badly worn saddles and halters, and buckles and stirrups were rusty and corroded.

Colonel Peñalver sharply criticized Lieutenant Alvear for not mentioning this disgraceful situation, and promptly wrote Alvear's superior officer in Havana. In short order, the little tiff among local officers mushroomed and involved a hierarchy of officers in both Florida and Cuba. Lieutenant Alvear blamed his predecessor, who had returned to Havana, for concealing the state of the unit from superior officers. The colonel of dragoons in Havana tried to prevent further circulation of Peñalver's damaging report. The captain general in Cuba reprimanded the dragoon officers for interfering with the internal government of East Florida. The squabble began when Zéspedes was engrossed in preparations for the arrival of Fray Cyril de Barcelona, and for this reason the governor postponed thorough investigation of the case until September after the bishop commenced his formal parish inspection.

In November, Zéspedes thought he solved the problem by transferring the dragoons from the troop barracks to an empty building in the center of the plaza, where they enjoyed a somewhat separate position. He nevertheless insisted that Lieutenant Alvear report to the commandant, and share in both types of guard duty, although mounted duty was not required. The dispute had survived for five months, creating enmities not easily dispelled. The status of the dragoons in East Florida was still under discussion in Cuba in December of 1788. Hoping to end the tiresome wrangle, Governor Zéspedes summarized the matter as a general misunderstanding, which he himself should have settled more promptly. He utilized the occasion to plead for funds for new horses and a stable to house them, and explained to the captain general that Colonel Peñalver's primary objective was to call attention to the delapidated state of the East Florida "cavalry."

Before the altercation between the infantry and dragoons had developed to major proportions, the entire garrison was shocked by the severity of the punishment that Colonel Peñalver decreed at the opening of his campaign to prevent the decay of discipline in East Florida. The first serious offenders were two common soldiers who imbibed too much wine in a local tavern on the afternoon of June 2, 1788. Emerging unsteadily into the sunny streets, they jostled against each other, shouted insults, and one finally wounded the other in an inaccurate exchange of gunfire. News of the original incident spread rapidly through the town without causing undue excitement. But the feeling of resentment was universal when both soldiers were arrested as soon as the wounded infantryman was discharged from the hospital two weeks later. At the conclusion of a brief council of war, the commandant sentenced the offenders to the gallows for dueling, an act forbidden in a regulation of January 16, 1716 and included in the army ordinances revised in 1765. Colonel Peñalver always justified his actions by citing the specific article and paragraph of the royal ordinances which he believed applied to the case at hand.

In this particular case, Governor Zéspedes prevented enforcement of the council of war's verdict and sent the indictment to Captain General Ezpeleta to be reviewed, including eyewitness descriptions of the clumsy encounter that Colonel Peñalver termed a duel. The captain general's legal adviser decided that the incident could not be termed a duel, since no formal arrangements were made concerning a precise time and place for meeting. He also was inclined to be lenient, since the evidence clearly indicated that the soldiers were ignorant of the fine points of the regulation forbidding dueling. Each blamed the other for initiating the combat, a futile defense since the law prescribed equal punishment for the contestants no matter which one issued the challenge. On July 12, 1788, the legal officer in Havana suspended the sentence handed down in St. Augustine, and recommended milder punishment in passing the case to the Supreme Council of War in Madrid for final judgment.

Throughout the fall of 1788, Colonel Peñalver continued his determined efforts to bring the standard of behavior in St. Augustine up to the letter of the printed regulations. One general reaction to his disciplinary campaign was a sudden development of the problem of desertion, which may have had roots in long-standing dissatisfaction, but more likely was an indication that the soldiers did not relish being reformed. Most deserters were apprehended, but a few stationed at Amelia island fled into Georgia.

Governor Zéspedes interfered with discipline on one further occasion, when whipping was the punishment imposed. The culprit in this case was a soldier who had slipped out of the barracks at night and unfortunately attracted attention to his unauthorized presence in the town by getting into a fight. Governor Zéspedes soon learned that the subalterns had decided to inflict twenty-five lashes on the soldier. Furthermore, the soldier's company captain did not intend to be present to supervise the punishment. Strongly disapproving the entire procedure, he reprimanded the subalterns, ordered the arrest of the neglectful captain, and advised the commandant that such punishment could not be approved. The governor did not care what was the penalty prescribed in the ordinances, although he recognized that whipping was common in some army regiments. Still, he would not admit that this was a proper punishment for soldiers caught outside the barracks in St. Augustine. It was too easy to get out, and infractions of the general rule were too common suddenly to demand severe corporal punishment for this offense.

The governor realized that something had to be done to curtail the nocturnal activities of the soldiers. Formerly, the barracks had been surrounded by a strong board fence, now fallen to pieces, and the building itself was in such bad condition that it could not be locked at night. There had been frequent incidents of pilfering and vandalism, when fences and courtyard walls were damaged, and fruits and vegetables taken from kitchen gardens. To curb these excesses, Zéspedes decreed that, in the future, any soldier found outside the quarters after retreat without justification would have to work for a month cleaning the barracks, wearing shackles on his legs.

Colonel Peñalver was not wholly a martinet, interested only in the punctilious observance of rules and regulations. He also showed genuine concern for the physical and moral well-being of the garrison. He could see the connection between the delapidated state of the public buildings and poor physical surroundings for the troops, and the consequent slackness of personal standards and military discipline. As the new commanding officer, he felt obliged to correct conditions tolerated by officials who had gradually become accustomed to the situation and felt that improvement was hopeless.

Housing accommodations in the two barracks were scarcely adequate. The larger barracks, dating from the British period, had a ground floor of brick, masonry second story, and a third floor, garret and tower of wood. By the fall of 1788, the wooden portions of the building were about to collapse and the engineer believed these upper portions should be torn down for safety. The second barracks, built of coquina, had been the Franciscan convent in the first Spanish period. Including an addition constructed by the British, it could house seven or eight hundred men. In both structures, windows and doors had long ago disappeared, and now the door frames, roofs and floors were beginning to rot away.

Plans for repairing the barracks first were submitted to Bernardo de Gálvez in May of 1785, and partially approved by the court in February of 1786, although no funds were provided for materials and labor. To secure funds for this purpose, Zéspedes sent a special request to Gálvez in August of 1786, but the message did not reach Mexico until after the viceroy's death. Items for repairs were always included in the budgets submitted to the colonial office, and the universally bad condition of the presidio was reported to Valdez as recently as January of 1788.

By securing material and labor on credit, Mariano LaRocque nevertheless had completed several thousand pesos worth of repairs vitally needed to prevent buildings from sagging. Urged to action again by the new commandant, Governor Zéspedes and Engineer LaRocque submitted estimates for repairs in December of 1788. They recommended using the solid portions of the larger barracks for a storehouse, quarters for presidiarios and lodging for officers, as soon as the smaller stone barracks was in shape for the troops. With the size of the St. Augustine garrison reduced to three hundred and sixty men, both barracks were unnecessary. Not all measures to improve the physical environment of the troops required major expense. Cognizant of the lewd and rowdy behavior in the barracks and jail, Colonel Peñalver begged the governor to supply better lamps and illumination for both quarters. He rightly sensed that the dingy glow of a candle stuck in an empty wine bottle fostered disorder in the barracks, and no light at all was provided in the jails.

In October of 1788, Zéspedes was also grateful to the commandant for calling his attention to the lack of blankets which would be needed before the chill winter weather settled along the north Florida coast. Zéspedes had secured blankets and coarse straw mattresses from Charleston, through an English contractor, when he first arrived in St. Augustine. After four year's use, the blankets were worn out and the straw mattresses unusable. Now the soldiers were sleeping on the floor, often trying vainly to keep their knapsacks and weapons dry as the fall rains leaked through the rotten shingles of the roofs and broken windows of the barracks. To save money, Zéspedes asked the intendancy in Havana to supply heavy Spanish linen ticking so that mattresses could be made locally. He was dissatisfied with the coarse and expensive cotton nankeen available in Florida. After repeating his request for blankets in December, the governor again secured blankets in Charleston, in spite of the home government's instructions in abjure trade with American firms. Unfortunately, the worst of the winter was over before the soldiers were able to sleep with a little more warmth at night.

Colonel Peñalver showed particular solicitude for individual soldiers with serious or chronic disorders. Early in August of 1788, he arranged to transfer to Havana three incapacitated infantrymen who needed more extensive treatment than was available in the local hospital. In October, he sent to Cuba four more soldiers, probably with respiratory ailments, whom he felt should avoid the winter season in St. Augustine. When the commandant returned to Havana in the spring of 1789, he took along a second lieutenant recommended for early retirement because he suffered from cancer.

On the whole, Governor Zéspedes was sympathetic toward Colonel Peñalver's many efforts to reform the St. Augustine garrison. He interposed his own higher authority only when the new commandant's methods seemed unduely harsh. The governor knew that troops serving in East Florida did not adhere closely to military regulations. On the basis of evidence collected during the Delany murder in November of 1785, Zéspedes declared that, if he punished every infraction of the rules coming to light in the testimony, he would be left with a skeleton staff, and he would have to begin by punishing the commandant himself.

Zéspedes never criticized Colonel Guillermo O'Kelly in his correspondence with superior officials. As commandant, Colonel O'Kelly did not appear to take a very active part in garrison matters. His presence was noticeable only when he took over the governor's job for four weeks in 1787 when Zéspedes was touring the province. Zéspedes usually dealt with the adjutant, Captain Eduardo Nugent or the captains of the various units on duty in St. Augustine. Service records are not particularly helpful in evaluating officers of the Hibernia Regiment, because there were so many duplicate names. Since the regiment was shifted as a unit, the men all served in the same campaigns and their records are confusingly similar. In the post-revolutionary period, for example, the regiment included at least two officers named Guillermo O'Kelly, Eduardo Nugent and Juan O'Donovan. A Captain Guillermo O'Kelly, who participated in the siege of Pensacola with Eduardo Nugent, was promoted to a colonelcy in 1789. But the only Guillermo O'Kelly with the rank of lieutenant colonel in 1784 was an officer who by 1789 was broken in health and so paralyzed that he had to be retired from the service. This fact may explain the lack of vigor in the military command at St. Augustine prior to the arrival of Colonel Peñalver.

Good reasons other than an inclination to improve discipline existed to justify Colonel Peñalver's reform program, instituted so promptly on his arrival in St. Augustine. Certain ominous signs in evidence when he assumed command made it reasonable to try to put troops in shape for active duty. By the first of May, 1788, Zéspedes was just beginning to believe that Thomas Powell's conspiracy would never materialize, but he knew also that other plots of a similar nature were being generated perpetually on the American frontier. More disquieting was a series of recent events within East Florida, on the St. Mary's river and along the south Atlantic coast.

To maintain public tranquility in the St. Mary's area, Zéspedes relied on Henry O'Neill, the former British officer whom he appointed border agent at the beginning of his régime. During the period of the British evacuation, O'Neill's authority was backed by the presence of the Spanish military force on the *San Matias* in the harbor. The departure of the vessel early in 1786 weakened his position. Henry O'Neill was honest and loyal, but since he tried to prevent illegal trading across the border, he naturally made enemies. He also was subject to dizzy spells that temporarily confused his mind and prevented him from being alert at all times. In

December of 1787, eighteen men from the St. Mary's section submitted a petition requesting that O'Neill be replaced by a man named Captain Richard Lang. O'Neill later claimed that some of the names were forgeries. Zéspedes was not favorably impressed by the petition with half of the "signers" identified only by crude check marks, their names written in by friends. The petition was the governor's first specific indication of new trouble from the restless and uncontrollable inhabitants of the St. Mary's area.

The second bad sign was the reappearance of Daniel McGirt, who brazenly arrived on a vessel from Providence about the middle of March, 1788. McGirt's passport from the governor of the Bahamas was dated in December, 1787, and Zéspedes wondered where he had been since the passport was issued. Zéspedes permitted McGirt only a brief interview with Francisco Sánchez, his attorney, in the presence of Lieutenant Remigio O'Hara and Thomas Tonno, the British merchant in whom he had particular confidence. The governor did not learn until early April that McGirt did not return immediately to Providence as ordered, but spent a week in the St. Mary's area after entering the harbor on March 27. He was arrested by Henry O'Neill, but later released on condition that he stay off the south bank of the river.

The third misfortune in the troubled border region was the murder of Henry O'Neill early in May, 1788. No one could prove that either Lang's partisans or McGirt's friends were responsible for the crime, but the sequence of events could not be ignored. When Henry O'Neill was killed, it was generally agreed that the act was perpetrated by a Georgia trader seeking revenge. Zéspedes left the apprehension and punishment of the suspect in the hands of the governor of Georgia. He shortly requested a pension for O'Neill's widow and nine children. O'Neill had served the Spanish government faithfully for four years without pay, trusting Zéspedes' word that he would receive a government appointment when the permanent staff was organized. Selecting a successor for O'Neill was a delicate problem. Zéspedes knew he had to rely on some man who held status among his neighbors. Choosing a man whom Lang opposed undoubtedly would cause trouble. With considerable uneasiness, he appointed Captain Lang in June, 1788 to preserve order in the St. Mary's district, hoping that official responsibility would keep him in line and place him more directly under administrative control.

In April, 1788, shortly after Zéspedes learned of McGirt's unwelcome presence on the St. Mary's border, he also received dis-

tressing intelligence from south of St. Augustine. Indians who had
visited the Bahamas reported that a party of men from Providence
had landed at Indian River inlet, about one hundred and sixty miles
down the coast. The rumor soon was substantiated by two British
captains from the Bahamas and a St. Augustine ship owner. The
governor knew that people from Providence were in the habit of
hunting turtles, cutting wood and collecting salvage along the
south Florida coast, but he could not assume that the recent arrivals
had the same harmless motives. By some inferences in the testimony,
Zéspedes decided that this might be a project to be quashed without
delay.

The governor immediately organized a small expedition in
charge of Lieutenant Juan O'Donovan, his son-in-law, and O'Donovan's close friend, Lieutenant Remigio O'Hara, to investigate the
bays and inlets south of Cape Canaveral. Other members of the
military force were a sergeant, two corporals and ten infantrymen.
Captain Lorenzo Rodriguez and his son, who both possessed a
minute knowledge of the shoreline, served as guides for the reconnaissance mission, which sailed on May 1 aboard an armed
launch accompanied by a smaller boat.

The governor gave explicit directions about procedure. If the
expedition sighted a settlement, the military force should remain
under cover but send representatives ashore in the small boat to
ask for water or make some excuse to observe the size of the group.
If the settlement boasted superior strength, the expedition should
proceed to Havana and make a report. But if the intruders could
be overpowered without bloodshed, the soldiers should take them
as prisoners on board the launch then burn their shelters to dis-
courage future interlopers. Any ship from the settlement should be
captured and sent to St. Augustine under the command of Captain
Rodriguez, with Spanish crew and guards, while young Rodriguez
continued the investigation of the shoreline. Prisoners should be
treated with humanity and women with particular decorum.

The governor sent along rum and tobacco to be used as Indian
presents. He knew the Indian river lay within the boundaries of the
hunting lands, and wanted the natives to understand that the expedition aimed only to prevent encroachment on their territory.
If the investigation revealed nothing, the two lieutenants and their
force should continue to Havana and report to the captain general
of Cuba.

The departure of the reconnaissance mission to the Indian river
district took place three days after Colonel Peñalver's arrival in St.

Augustine. The murder of Henry O'Neill, the border agent, occurred a few weeks later. These disturbing events at the beginning
of his tour of duty in Florida could easily convince the new commandant that the garrison should be prepared to undertake military
action and needed stronger discipline. Six months later, in November of 1788, the Castillo housed twenty-six foreign prisoners,
whose presence in St. Augustine was a direct consequence of the
mysterious party arriving from Providence in April, 1788. Unable
to locate any of the British intruders, the small Spanish force
searched the coast for many miles before sailing to Cuba to report
their uneventful investigation. Lieutenants O'Donovan and O'Hara
presumably departed directly to Spain in July with the rest of the
Hibernia Regiment. Other members of the reconnaissance mission
prepared to return to St. Augustine in late August.

The elusive intruders from Providence were actually a group
under the leadership of William Augustus Bowles, a flamboyant
adventurer with British support, who made his first preliminary
incursion into Florida in the spring of 1788. Bowles' future ap-
pearances created difficulties for Alexander McGillivray, the Panton
firm, Spanish governors and American officials until he died in
Morro Castle in 1806. Bowles was only fifteen years old when he
first arrived in Florida in 1781 as an ensign in the Maryland loyalist regiment, one of the units defending Pensacola from Spanish
attack during the American Revolution. After the city surrendered,
he went to live among the Creek and Seminole Indians, learning
their language and customs.[4] Before leaving the nation, he married
in Indian fashion a daughter of Perryman, the Lower Creek leader
who later acted as McGillivray's special deputy to carry messages
and confer with Zéspedes. By 1785, Bowles was in the Bahama
islands, his previous experience already enlarged by such varied
pursuits as acting, gambling and portrait painting.

Bowles' project in 1788 was organized by a trading firm, Miller,
Bonamy and Company, with the secret support of Lord Dunmore,
last royal governor of Virginia who served as governor of the
Bahama islands from 1787 to 1796. Members of the firm had
grievances against Spain dating from the investiture of the Bahamas
by Spanish troops in 1782, and a separate grudge against William
Panton, whose mercantile empire included a warehouse at New
Providence. Miller and Bonamy aspired to take over the Indian
commerce in Florida monopolized by Panton, Leslie and Company.
After Bowles unobtrusively landed in Florida in April of 1788, he
made his way overland to the Lower Creek towns. In June, while

the Irish lieutenants were searching the Atlantic shoreline, Alexander McGillivray went to meet the "stranger" whose presence in the nation had recently been reported. McGillivray was very surprised to find that the new arrival was an acquaintance he had known in Pensacola during the American Revolution. In talking with McGillivray, Bowles refused to reveal his contacts, but gave assurance that British friends wanted to supply the Creeks with ammunition for their war with Georgia. Since McGillivray was worried because Miró and O'Neill hesitated to continue military aid to the Creeks, he readily accepted Bowles' offer to bring presents and ammunition to Apalache in the fall. Bowles soon returned to Providence, taking with him two Creek chiefs.

Zéspedes did not learn Bowles' identity or purpose until he received a long letter from Colonel Thomas Brown in September, 1788, explaining Bowles' real objectives and his sources of support in the Bahama islands. To make clear his disapproval of the project, Colonel Brown refused to receive the Indians accompanying Bowles to Providence. In September, additional evidence came from John Hambly, Panton's storekeeper on the St. John's river, who relayed Chief Payne's report that Bowles expected to bring presents to the Indians by way of the St. Mary's river before Christmas. Outside interference with the Indians was one thing that Zéspedes would not tolerate. He immediately sent an express messenger to Alexander McGillivray, warning him of Bowles' dangerous objectives. He also wrote Governor George Handley of Georgia that Bowles might endeavor to prevent peace between the Creeks and Georgians by plundering in Georgia, and blaming depredations on the Indians. Privately, Governor Zéspedes believed it perfectly possible for Bowles to use Georgia traders jealous of William Panton in order to establish himself in the Indian trade. Any attempt to upset the Indian trade would cause trouble for Spain.

Reports of Bowles' connections in New Providence were followed by news of his return to the Indian river section of East Florida. Although Bowles' party of thirty actually landed in October, factual evidence did not reach Governor Zéspedes until deserters began to straggle into St. Augustine in November. The odd assortment of ship deserters, recently jailed criminals and drifters drummed up in Bahama bar rooms, testified that they had enlisted originally in the belief that the Creek Indians would grant them lands. To further their ambitions for a life of ease and plenty, they expected to plunder Negroes from Georgia and retire to the Indian country. Sitting around the fire with their pipes, having set aside their red silk regimental standard and drum bearing the British coat of arms, they learned that a primary objective was to seize the Panton store near Lake George and kill John Hambly, the storekeeper.

East Florida gave a poor reception to William Augustus Bowles and his associates. During an exceptionally wet fall season, the men pushed north along the St. John's river, discouraged by cold weather and a shortage of food. After Indians told them that Spanish soldiers were out on a search, they by-passed the Indian store and headed for the Alachua villages. Here they learned that the rumor of reconnoitering Spanish troops was false, but the majority of men from Providence has lost their spirit and sneaked away to the Spanish outpost on the St. John's river to give themselves up to the authorities. By November 19, twenty-six deserters were securely locked in the Castillo de San Marcos. Carlos Howard took down their declarations, which could not be proved but seemed to concur with the reports from Colonel Thomas Brown. A few deserters stated that a schooner bringing part of the group to the Indian river had returned to the Bahamas to collect a second party to attack the Panton store at St. Marks.

An attack on the St. Marks store, the most improbable goal associated with Bowles' activities in 1788, was accomplished in 1792. After the seizure of the Panton store at St. Marks in 1792, Spanish authorities apprehended Bowles and imprisoned him in Havana, Madrid and Manila. En route back to Spain in 1797, he escaped at Sierre Leone and secured renewed support in England for his activities in Florida, which continued until he was arrested a second time, with American aid, in 1803.[1]

The mere suggestion of an attack on the St. Marks store in 1788 convinced Zéspedes that Bowles deserved to forfeit his life. Bowles was the only man for whom Zéspedes recommended capital punishment during his career as governor of East Florida, aside from the pirate who died in the St. Augustine in January, 1785. In regard to Bowles, his instinct was sound, if lacking in his usual humanitarian quality. As soon as Carlos Howard copied the declarations of the deserters, Zéspedes informed Alexander McGillivray of a possible attack on the Indian store at St. Marks. The governor hoped McGillivray would arrange to have Bowles sent in chains to Pensacola, or even killed.

McGillivray used his own methods to check the incredible reports sent from St. Augustine by John Leslie and Governor Zéspedes.

[1] Lyle N. McAlister, "William Augustus Bowles and the State of Muskogee," *Florida Historical Quarterly* XXXX (1962), p. 317-328.

He delegated his brother-in-law, Luis Milfort, to ferret out information from Bowles' small remaining band. Milfort was a French adventurer who came to America just before the American Revolution and lived for twenty years in the Creek nation before returning to Europe. Late in December, 1788, Milfort accompanied Bowles' party from Perryman's home to the coast of the Gulf, where they waited for the schooner from the Bahamas bringing gifts for the Indians. After several weeks passed without sign of a sail on the horizon, Bowles returned to Perryman's home. Left behind to continue the vigil were two Indians, Milfort, and a treasure of Miller, Bonamy and Company who had accompanied the Bowles expedition from Nassau. Milfort gained the treasurer's confidence, and learned that Bowles was allied with a firm anxious to destroy Panton's business. Through this information channel, McGillivray's suspicions received confirmation. He assured the Spanish governors that he would divide the long-advertised boatload of presents among deserving chiefs and send Bowles out of the country. McGillivray's confidence recently had been restored by news that the Spanish government would resume aid to the Creek Indians. Powder, shot and small arms were already on order for the spring season.

The tardy schooner finally appeared near the Flint river in early February with a disappointing array of merchandise, very unimpressive to the delegation waiting for great gifts. Under these circumstances, McGillivray had no difficulty in convincing Bowles to leave the nation. McGillivray discounted the tales of the deserters in St. Augustine and decided that banishment was sufficient punishment for an Englishman guilty of deception, particularly when the Englishman was the son-in-law of an important Creek chief. If McGillivray felt he had effectively disposed of the adventurer Bowles, he still had to dispel the fears that Bowles' presence stirred up in the mind of Arturo O'Neill, governor of West Florida.

Rumors of the wildest nature circulated through the Floridas following the original appearance of Bowles, to the detriment of relations between McGillivray and Spanish officials in Pensacola, Mobile and New Orleans. The most apprehensive and thoroughly misinformed individual was Governor O'Neill, whose private sources of intelligence were Timothy Lane, a trader expelled from Creek country by McGillivray; Carlos Weatherford, estranged husband of one of McGillivray's sisters; and John Linder, Jr., former associate of Daniel McGirt who was rapidly becoming the leading troublemaker in Tensaw, a new English settlement north of Mobile. This nefarious trio managed to convince Governor O'Neill that McGillivray and Panton were secretly securing British support from New Providence to organize an attack on Pensacola. O'Neill also received the impression that Perryman's daughter was Colonel Thomas Brown's concubine, and the colonel himself was a party to the plot. Since O'Neill reported these grave misconceptions to the captain general of Cuba, McGillivray again sought Zéspedes' aid. He relied on Zéspedes' candor and clarity of expression to convey a more accurate version of the Bowles incident to higher authorities.

Bowles' incursion was an expensive and troublesome emergency for the governor and for the commandant, charged with the responsibility for the twenty-six foreigners imprisoned in the Castillo. Having lost their leadership, the deserters no longer were dangerous, but getting rid of them was a problem. The governor dispatched the two Americans and three Germans in the band to Georgia, but no American port would accept the twenty-one Englishmen. Zéspedes finally decided to send the remaining Englishmen in small groups to Havana, to await the disposition of Captain General Ezpeleta. Bowles' followers were just a portion of the undesirables leaving St. Augustine during the early spring of 1789. Along with the chastened adventurers, the ships sailing southward carried the half dozen soldiers convicted of homosexual practices, the orphan boy similarly sentenced, the Mulatto suspected of attempted poisoning, and the indiscreet clerk from Carlos Howard's office. Among the last to leave East Florida that spring were two worthier men, Colonel Peñalver and Fray Cyril de Barcelona, both well aware that during their concurrent residence the province was relieved of a sampling of offenders against the laws of God and the king.

Treasury Street—South Side

XIII

Fiesta In St. Augustine

IN Spanish society, the antidote for all the world's sorrows, disappointments and perplexities is a fiesta. St. Augustine badly needed such a tonic by the summer of 1789, when Governor Zéspedes initiated plans for a gala celebration honoring the new monarchs, King Charles IV and Queen Maria Louisa. He first scheduled the celebration in St. Augustine to take place at the conclusion of the six months' official mourning for the death of Charles III, a period which began on March 22, 1789. If the original plans had been carried out, the observance in the provincial capital of East Florida would have occurred close to the date of Charles IV's formal coronation in Madrid on September 23, 1789. Because the royal standard and portraits of the new sovereigns did not arrive until late November, the fiesta in St. Augustine was delayed until December 2, 3, and 4, 1789. In the meantime, however, local morale was bolstered by anticipation of the event.

The celebration honoring Charles IV was an exciting novelty in the lives of soldiers and townspeople who under ordinary circumstances had little variety in their social life. They welcomed the prospect of relief from the monotony of existence in East Florida. Preparations for the fiesta provided occupation for a community otherwise faced with an enervating absence of activity in the summer of 1789. For most of the inhabitants of St. Augustine, there was nothing to do but wait. With varying degrees of resignation and impatience, they were waiting for the arrival of a permanent garrison, for regulations granting land and establishing the civil government of the province, and for an officer from the Captaincy General of Guatemala appointed in 1789 to succeed Zésperdes as governor of East Florida.

In the summer of 1789, military affairs in St. Augustine were in a state of transition. Zéspedes learned in April that a third battalion of the new Infantry Regiment of Cuba would be permanently assigned to St. Augustine. He was gratified that this recommendation would become a reality during his term of office, although the exact date remained uncertain. The Infantry Regiment of Cuba was formed in June, 1788 when the Inmemorial del Rey and Hibernia Regiments returned to Spain. In the beginning, only two battalions were organized.[1] The royal order of December 13, 1788 directing formation of the third battalion, to be stationed at St. Augustine, was one of the last measures signed by Charles III before his death on December 23. The royal order announcing the third battalion specified that soldiers and officers currently on duty in St. Augustine could transfer to the unit with promotion. Carrying out these provisions, Governor Zéspedes accepted a number of applications during the spring of 1789 from men who wished to remain in Florida.

Responsibility for organizing and training the third battalion rested with Captain General Ezpeleta, according to the royal order of December 13, 1788. Ezpeleta had little time to carry out these instructions because late in March, 1789, he received orders to leave as soon as possible for Santa Fe de Bogota to become viceroy of New Granada. After Ezpeleta's departure from Havana in May, 1789, responsibility for the third battalion devolved upon the *teniente del rey*, Domingo Cabello, head of the Cuban government pending the appointment of a new captain general. These new developments in Cuba came at the time of the annual spring rotation of troops assigned to the St. Augustine garrison. Since the third battalion was not yet organized, soldiers from the Infantry Regiment of Zamora temporarily filled the vacancies in the Florida garrison created by the return of troops to Havana in May and

---

[1] Serafín María ae Soto y Abbach, Conde de Clonard, *Historia Orgánica de las Armas de Infantería y Caballería Españolas desde la Creación del Ejercito Permanente hasta el Día* (14 vols., Madrid, 1851-1859), XII, p. 41.

June of 1789. But in July, 1789, officers of the Zamora Regiment were recalled to Havana to return to Spain, leaving the St. Augustine garrison below its quota with only a contingent from the Havana Regiment remaining in the province.

Zéspedes felt fortunate to have Captain Howard still on his staff to supervise military affairs during the transitional period of regimental reorganization. Since November of 1787, the two men had parried successive demands for Captain Howard to rejoin the Hibernia Regiment in Havana, prior to embarkation for Spain. Zéspedes first postponed compliance with the order for Howard's return by explaining the captain's importance in Florida diplomatic affairs during the Georgia border crisis and the Thomas Powell incident. The governor later insisted that Howard's health would fail if he returned to Havana, and medical reasons required his living in Florida. Writing the colonel of the Hibernia Regiment, Captain Howard carefully explained that he could not return to Havana without the permission of Governor Zéspedes, currently his commanding officer. Zéspedes very early requested Howard's transfer to the permanent garrison for East Florida, when one was formed, but he was satisfied to have his able secretary transferred to the Havana Regiment, a military order which finally reached St. Augustine in January of 1789.

When Colonel Peñalver returned to Havana, the temporary command at St. Augustine became the responsibility of the highest ranking captain in the garrison. In this situation, strict adherence to army instructions was unsatisfactory to Zéspedes. Since Carlos Howard had held a captain's commission longer than any officers assigned to the garrison staff, the governor managed to place temporary command of local troops in the safe hands of his secretary of government. Aside from general reliability, Captain Howard's qualifications included past experience in military administration. For three years, he was in charge of cadet training for the Hibernia Regiment. Zéspedes was confident that Howard could administer military affairs capably until the arrival of the third battalion.

During the summer of 1789, soldiers of the garrison were making elaborate preparations for the fiesta honoring the new Spanish monarchs. As their contribution to the celebration, they were casting and rehearsing a play entitled *Amigo, Amante y Leal* (Loving and Loyal Friend), written one hundred and fifty years earlier by a leading representative of the Golden Age of Spanish drama, Don Pedro Calderón de la Barca (1600-1681). This play was published first in 1653 in a collection of contemporary Spanish comedies, although it probably was written about 1630.[2] The comedies by Calderón were favorite theatrical entertainment in the Spanish colonies throughout the eighteenth century, and in the 1760's enjoyed a brief vogue with audiences in London and Philadelphia. Calderón's continuing popularity in the Caribbean area is attested by the fact that a collection of his comedies was published in Cuba in 1839.[3] The play *Amigo, Amante y Leal* was sufficiently familiar so that the official report of the festivities honoring Charles IV in St. Augustine did not even mention Calderón, but followed the practice common in the colonial theatre of including only the title of the play.

Comedies staged in the town plaza were a favorite form of recreation for Spanish soldiers, although this type of entertainment temporarily lost popularity in St. Augustine after hooded or costumed assailants stabbed Lieutenant Delany following a play rehearsal in November, 1785. By the summer of 1789, the unpleasantness surrounding the murder was far in the past, and the entire community was looking forward to the drama scheduled for production by the Havana Regiment.

Governor Zéspedes' special personal plans for the celebration began in the spring of 1789. The mail packet bringing news of the death of Charles III included a letter from Antonio Valdez notifying the governor that some large salary deductions made during the previous five years would be returned. In a prosperous and grateful mood, Zéspedes ordered a quantity of silver medals for distribution during the fiesta celebrating the coronation of Charles IV. In March of 1788, he had appealed to the colonial secretary for a salary increase, citing the fact that previous Spanish governors of Florida were paid 5,000 pesos while his current salary was only 4,000 pesos. He also mentioned the heavy expense entailed by his recent positions in the royal service, traveling between Havana and Santiago de Cuba and more recently entertaining General Nathanael Greene and other prominent American guests.

Zéspedes particularly protested against the largest deductions from his modest salary. Although he willingly contributed twelve pesos a year to the fund for invalid soldiers and eleven pesos to the

---

[2] Harry Warren Hilborn, *A Chronology of the Plays of D. Pedro Calderon de la Barca* (Toronto, 1938), pp. 13-15.

[3] Cayetano Alberto de la Barrera y Leirado, *Catálogo Bibliográfico y Biográfico de Teatro Antiguo Español, desde sus Orígines hasta Mediados del Siglo XVIII* (Madrid, 1860), pp. 52-54.

widows and orphans fund, he objected to the 1192 pesos for the
media anata, a tax levied on nobility for defense purposes but from
which military men were usually excused. Zéspedes' salary was not
altered in response to his pleas, but a royal order decreed that the
annual payment would be exempt from the *media anata* in the
future, and provided for reimbursement of taxes already collected.
The prospective refund from the Havana treasury came close to
6,000 pesos. All this figuring was purely bookkeeping procedure.
He had never claimed any of the pesos delivered to the St. Augustine treasury. His entire salary was still a debit item in the provincial accounts. Nevertheless he had a feeling of improved financial
status when he ordered medals commemorating the celebration of
Charles IV's coronation in St. Augustine.

Governor Zéspedes personally designed the silver medals, weigh-
ing about a half peso, which were probably cast in Mexico.[4] In
selecting appropriate symbols for his commemorative medal, he
sincerely regretted that St. Augustine lacked a municipal coat of
arms, although the city was one of the oldest in the Spanish Indies.
One face of the coin naturally featured a profile of Charles IV,
with his name and the year 1789 inscribed around the border.
On the reverse side, the center was occupied by a large floral representation of a jasmine blossom, chosen by the governor as the
emblem of Florida. Above and below were a lion and a castle, the
traditional emblems of Castile, the single Spanish kingdom to
whom the overseas possessions belonged and the region Zéspedes
was proud to claim as his native land. Zéspedes' selection of jasmine
to symbolize Florida is interesting, since it was not a native plant.
Varieties of jasmine brought from Spain and the Canary islands
were generally five-petaled, scarcely resembling the stylized floral
design shown on the coin.

For Governor Zéspedes, the importance of the coronation celebration increased when he received word on June 3, 1789 that his
successor had been appointed on March 24. Since he expected
the new governor, Juan Nepomuceno Quesada, to arrive from
Guatemala within a few months, he now viewed the forthcoming
fiesta as a climax to his own régime. Plans were expanded in order
to make sure that the celebration would be a memorable event in
local history. The entire population soon became involved in
arrangements for a three day program of parades, religious services,

---

[4] One of these medals is in the possession of Mr. Harley Freeman of Ormond
Beach, Florida. Medals commemorating special events were fairly common, but
this is the only medal struck for Florida of which there is authentic proof.

theatrical performances, dances, dinners and other events. With preparations completed by September, it was a distinct disappointment to have to wait for the portraits and royal standard. On October 2, Governor Zéspedes issued a proclamation formally postponing the coronation festival until these essential items arrived.

When ships from Cuba finally reached St. Augustine on November 23, 1789, they brought not only the long-awaited official portraits, but also the new commandant and several other additions to the governmental staff as well as the entire third battalion of the Cuban Regiment. The new military unit had been formed in Havana on October 1, 1789 with Barolomé Morales as colonel and new commandant for the St. Augustine garrison. The third battalion of the Cuban Regiment was permanently stationed in East Florida until 1815. Governor Zéspedes enthusiastically greeted Colonel Morales, who was one of his closest friends in the Havana Regiment. When Zéspedes left Cuba, Morales held a captain's rank and both men had sons who were young cadets in the regiment. Since the beginning of his governorship, Zéspedes frequently had sent confidential messages to Morales concerning such problems as Lieutenant O'Donovan's arrest and financial relief for the St. Augustine garrison.

Zéspedes was not as happy about the arrival of some other passengers on the troop transports. He was particularly annoyed to have Bartolomé Benítez, a new treasurer for the garrison, reach St. Augustine. One of the losing battles that Zéspedes fought with the Cuban intendancy concerned the appointment of a new treasurer for St. Augustine. The first treasurer, though appointed in 1785, did not arrive until July, 1788 and his health was so poor that he survived only three months. In the meantime, overworked Gonzalo Zamorano performed a treasurer's function, without title or addition to his 1200 peso salary. Zéspedes urged the appointment of a worthy member of the local hospital staff to the treasury post, but the Cuban intendant insisted on the right to choose a successor. As it happened, Antonio Valdez took the matter out of their hands. The colonial secretary gave the job to Bartolomé Benítez, a provincial intendant in the Philippines. When Benítez arrived in St. Augustine on November 23, 1789, he brought a royal commission granting him an annual salary of 3,000 pesos, although the former treasurer received only 800 pesos a year.

Father Hassett was more disconcerted than the governor in meeting the two priests who disembarked from the transports bringing the permanent military force to St. Augustine. Two members of the Franciscan order had been sent from Spain to assist Father Hassett with missionary work in Florida. Clearly unsuited to serve in the province because they spoke neither English nor Minorcan, the Franciscans nevertheless remained in Florida until Quesada sent them back shortly after he became governor. A more interesting clerical visitor arriving in St. Augustine at the time of the coronation celebration was Father William O'Brian, pastor of St. Peter's church in New York City. Father O'Brian's parish lost its principal source of financial support when Diego Gardoqu returned to Spain in the summer of 1789. During the first week in December, Father O'Brian was in St. Augustine on his way to Cuba to seek funds from the Bishop of Havana.

With all the new arrivals, the festival honoring Charles IV also became a celebration welcoming the permanent garrison, a grand send-off for the Havana Regiment, and a joyous reunion for the families of the governor and new commandant. Knowing that vessels were waiting in the harbor to take the retiring Havana Regiment back to Cuba, Governor Zéspedes hastily completed final arrangements for the celebration. He had to reorganize plans slightly in order to include the important officials who had recently arrived in the province. The formal ceremonies called for two honorary titles, the *reyes de armas,* a term surviving from medieval times to signify the officials in charge of public ceremonies, who actual function might be classified as parade marshals. These honors were granted to Colonel Morales and Captain Joseph de Saavedra of the Cuban Regiment. The governor reserved the principal honor, that of royal standard bearer for his son, Lieutenant Vicente Domingo de Zéspedes of the Havana Regiment. Vincente had proved his ability in 1787 during the long tour of the back country along the St. John's and St. Mary's river. Zéspedes assigned him a prominent role in the celebration, understanding that official reports would bring his name to the attention of superior officers.

The general pattern for a coronation festival was well-established by custom. This was the third royal régime inaugurated during Zéspedes' lifetime. Born during the reign of Philip V, first of the Bourbon line in Spain, he had previously celebrated the assumption of the throne by Ferdinand VI in 1746, and the entrance of Charles III into Madrid in 1760. He fervently hoped the new king would be as wise and conscientious as his father. Court gossip had not penetrated the distant frontier province to disillusion the governor. Among Spanish nobles, it was common knowledge that Charles IV spent most of his time hunting, leaving the queen to her own amorous affairs. But these rumors could never diminish the enthusiastic celebrations honoring the new monarchs in Florida or in any other part of the empire. After so many problems regarding succession in past history, the people rejoiced over the crowning of a king who could claim the throne uncontested. Charles IV had been acknowledged as heir apparent at his father's coronation.

The three-day festival in St. Augustine on December 2, 3, and 4, 1789, was a small scale reproduction of events taking place in Madrid when Charles IV made his regal entry in September of the same year. In Madrid, there were private balls, an exhibition of regional dances, and an open air production of a new play written for the occasion by the renowned Spanish dramatist, Ramón de la Cruz. Thousands of foreign visitors flocked to the capital to see royalty parade through streets lined with embroidered tapestries hung from upper balconies. Mild winter weather graced St. Augustine on the afternoon of December 2, 1789 when the stage was set for the local observance of Charles IV's ascent to the Spanish throne. Balconies and doorways on every street were adorned with hangings, flags, or whatever the inhabitants could devise in the way of decoration.

The first event took place in front of the Government House, where wooden balconies were draped with yards of scarlet silks. Outside the residence, against the wall facing the plaza, stood a canopy of crimson damask with plain satin drapes at the side and white taffeta curtains across the front. The canopy rested on a small carpeted platform from which steps descended toward the plaza. Within this throne-like enclosure rested the portraits of Charles IV and his Italian-born queen, Maria Louisa of Parma. The honor of standing guard beside the royal portraits was assigned to the grenadiers, elite crops of the Cuban Regiment's third battalion. Stationed at the four corners of the plaza were pickets of infantrymen. A small artillery squad occupied the side of the plaza toward the Matanzas river, near the buildings serving as guard house and farmers' market. In the center of the plaza, carpenters had erected a large square platform, with thick rugs covering the floor and the steps along one side. The balustrades on the other three sides were decorated with ornamental tapestries.

About the middle of the afternoon, military officers, leading officials of the treasury department, and prominent citizens assembled on horseback before the Government House. At four o'clock,

Governor Zéspedes appeared, sword at his side, mounted on a horse with richly ornamented trappings. The governor was wearing the dress uniform of the Havana Regiment, bright blue coat and yellow vest and cravat, decorated with gold braid and emblems signifying his rank as brigadier of the royal armies of Spain. Accompanied by the waiting escort, the governor first paraded around the tree-bordered plaza, returning in time to meet Lieutenant Zéspedes as he rode through the gates of the Government House on a gaily caparisoned steed. The lieutenant was accompanied by the *reyes de armas*, Colonal Morales and Captain Saavedra, both appearing very impressive in their new white tropical uniforms with violet insignia.

The escorting band formed a double file as the procession marched down the center toward the parish church located on the upper floor of a building on the south side of the plaza. Leading the procession were the first and second adjutants of the military staff, followed by the governor and his son who was bearing the royal standard, and behind them came the *reyes de armas*. At the doors of the church building, the entire group dismounted and accompanied the royal standard into the body of the church where it was consecrated in a brief ceremony. The religious service was in charge of Father Hassett, who was assisted by other priests in the parish.

When the religious ceremony was finished, the men in the procession again mounted their horses for the short ride from the church to the platform at the center of the plaza. By this time the crowd of onlookers had grown to sizeable proportions. The governor and his son and the *reyes de armas* alighted by the steps leading up to the platform. The assembly was called to order by the sonorous intonation of the *reyes de armas* who announced: "Silence, hear, listen, attention!" At this moment, Lieutenant Zéspedes raised the royal standard and led the crowd in three cheers for "Castile!," while the portraits of the new monarchs were unveiled. Simultaneously the air was shaken by the discharge of the field pieces mounted at the end of the plaza, salutes from the government and private ships in the harbor, the roll of drums by the infantrymen, pealing of church bells, and a triple salvo from the artillery in the Castillo San Marcos. In the midst of this joyous din, Governor Zéspedes flung into the crowd the silver medals commemorating the great occasion.

While the wave of excitement continued, the leading officials descended the steps from the platform, mounted their horses and took their places for a grand parade around the town. The procession line lengthened with the addition of a contingent of dragoons and the four infantry pickets previously posted at the corners of the plaza. Marching in time to a military band, the parade headed down St. George street to the barracks located at the southern end of the residential district. Halting at the St. Francis barracks, for a second time they shouted *vivas* for the new monarchs to the accompaniment of artillery fire. From this point, the parade turned toward the river, followed Marine street back toward the plaza, then continued along San Carlos street to the Castillo San Marcos. On the grassy embankments outside, to the sound of cannon in the fortress, the acclamations of the king resounded for the third and final time. Again in motion, the procession passed beside the old line of earthworks extending from the Castillo to the drawbridge and city gates, and returned along Hornabeque street to the Government House. At the conclusion of the parade, the royal standard was placed between the royal portraits under the canopy outside the official residence.

By this time, night was approaching and the general mood of merrymaking prevailed throughout the town. At dusk, bonfires were lighted in the plaza, their flames flickering through the border of orange trees; and candles and lanterns appeared in the windows of the houses. During the evening, talented clerks from Gonzalo Zamorano's staff performed original dances around the bonfires, imitating the rhythmic dances of the Creek and Seminole Indians. The large platform in the center of the plaza became a theatrical stage in the evening, when the Havana Regiment presented the opening night performance of *Amigo, Amante y Leal.*

The title indicates the complicated problem facing the protagonist, Don Félix, caught in the midst of conflicting obligations to his closest friend, his lady love, and his overlord, the Prince of Parma.[5] His initial bold action is to hand over his sweetheart to the unrestrainable desires of the reckless prince, solely in order to serve him with loyalty. The plot becomes increasingly entangled thereafter, requiring a few improbable twists to reach a solution. Emotional tension reaches a climax in the third act when Don Félix appears with a sword, begging his friend to kill him. Almost immediately his sweetheart, Aurora, comes on stage with dagger upraised threatening suicide. In a swift denouement, the prince

---

[5] Modern readers can find the script in a new edition of Calderón's complete works: Pedro Calderón de la Barca, *Obras Completas* (3 vols., Madrid, 1956), II, pp. 345-381.

relinquishes his claims for Aurora, unwilling that Don Félix should suffer for his unreasonable indications of loyalty. Somehow Aurora survives her various encounters with her honor unblemished, and her mind undisillusioned by the wavering behavior of her principal admirer. The play proved to be most enjoyable, with pretty embroidered phrases of the best baroque tradition in the lengthy speeches, as well as rapid interchanges of metrical dialogue. Interest was maintained with a liberal sprinkling of jokes and anecdotes, a servant providing the comic relief. The production was such an outstanding success that repeat performances were scheduled for the two subsequent evenings.

In addition to attending the productions staged in the plaza, the soldiers and townspeople were all gathering in private parties. The most outstanding social event of the evening was the open house at the governor's residence, where Lieutenant Zéspedes acted as host to St. Augustine's leading military officers, government officials, and private families. Shortly after the parade's end, guests assembled for *refresco*, with Spain's famous wines served to the gentlemen, and punch, tea, coffee or chocolate for the ladies. Musicians arrived later to provide enjoyment for listeners and dancers in the form of social entertainment called a *sarao*, a Portuguese term akin to the French *soirée*. Following the general custom, the governor and his wife led the first minuet. A deservedly famous hostess, Doña Concepción brought the aura of opulent Havana society to the provincial ballroom and banquet hall. As the evening grew cooler and spirits gayer, the violin was replaced by the guitar and livelier *contredances* occupied the floor. Forming squares, lines or circles, couples glided and whirled and bowed in a swift succession of figures until the approach of dawn. Late in the evening, an elaborate supper was served, probably featuring ham, turkey, olives, preserved fruits and decorated cakes. The midnight buffet, called by the French word *ambigú*, was adopted by Spanish society in the later eighteenth century when so many French customs became fashionable among the upper classes.[6]

The spirit of revelry was even more animated in St. Augustine's humbler residences, where guests followed the intricate regional dances of southern Spain, Minorca and the Canary islands. But dance partners were not available for all the men in St. Augustine,

---

[6] Charles E. Kany. *Life and Manners in Madrid, 1750-1800* (Berkeley, 1932), pp. 268-273. The terms *refresco, sarao* and *ambigú* are discussed in the same order in which they appear in the official account of the coronation celebration.

a town with a high male population temporarily increased by the lingering Havana Regiment. All the wine shops were overflowing, as well as the convenient tavern opposite the gate to St. Francis barracks. Boisterous groups of soldiers joined in singing popular songs, improvising a few solo lyrics, while their comrades played cards or dice in the background.

Only a brief period of repose was accorded the officialdom of St. Augustine who managed to dance until dawn on the morning of December 3, 1789. At nine o'clock in the morning, the governor and his coterie plus a representation of local residence were present in the parish church for high mass chanted by Father Hassett. At the conclusion of the service, all joined in singing the *Te Deum*, to give solemn thanks to God for the advent of a new and glorious reign. By afternoon, they were ready for a siesta in preparation for a continuation of the festivities. The evenings of December 3 and 4, the plaza again was bright with the light of bonfires providing illumination for the second and third performances of *Amigo, Amante y Leal*. Parties again took place in homes with candle-lit windows, and for two more nights there was wine and punch, supper and dancing till dawn at the governor's residence. Governor Zéspedes, now in his seventieth year, undoubtedly was relieved to have his son assume the responsibilities of host for his social marathon.

The three day fiesta concluded on the evening of December 4, culminating with a triumphal float drawn through town by six horses. This magnificently decorated construction was the work of the local carpenter's guild, a group with a large representation from the Minorcan population. It was large enough to carry all guild members, who sported red cockades in their broad hats and carried flaming torches in their hands. At every street corner they paused to give cheers for the new rulers, echoed by the little groups of observers. By the morning of December 5, participants in these festivities were relieved to lapse into a more ordinary routine. The following week, Governor Zéspedes sent notarized reports of the celebration to the king and colonial secretary, enclosing with each letter three of the commemorative medals.

The streets of St. Augustine were dark for only two evenings following the celebration honoring Charles IV. On Monday morning, December 7, the free Negro serving as town crier was heard in the streets announcing that windows should be illumined on the evenings of December 7 and 8, since December 8 was the day dedicated to the Immaculate Conception of Holy Mary. With drums beating, a small detachment under the leadership of First Adjutant Manual de Aldana marched around to post formal proclamations concerning observance of the Holy Day. On December 9, the governor issued another proclamation with similar ritual ordering a general illumination for two evenings, December 12 and 13, in honor of the baby infanta, Maria Isabel, born on July 16, 1789. News of the royal birth did not reach St. Augustine until the large quantity of mail and passengers arrived in late November, and this was about the first opportunity to render homage to a new member of the royal family. A special mass chanted by Father Hassett took place at nine o'clock on the morning of December 13, attended by all the usual officers, staff members, and loyal citizens of the community.

And so, for a brief interval during December of 1789, the little frontier capital in Florida was engrossed in solemn rituals and exhuberant merry-making, following a pattern characteristic of Old and New World Hispanic communities that otherwise displayed such markedly independent and dissimilar qualities.

XIV

The End of Zespedes' Regime

GOVERNOR Zéspedes could scarcely hope to ride out the concluding months of his governorship calmly presiding over a remote garrison town, surrounded by ocean, thinly populated farm land and the vast wilderness of scattered Indian villages. This isolation in no way provided insulation against the tumultuous developments of the eighteenth century which seemed to accelerate during the final decade. In the recent American Revolution, the basic principle of monarchy was successfully challenged. Since then, liberty rather than loyalty had become the patriotic appeal of increasing numbers of Frenchmen, threatening the Bourbon ruler of France and alarming the Bourbon king of Spain. In July, 1789, a Parisian mob stormed the Bastille and soon held the royal family as virtual prisoners in the Tuileries Palace.

Late in 1789, the first indications of the approaching French Revolution reached the new world. The tottering French throne held frightening implications for the Spanish monarchy, closely allied to France by blood relationship and diplomatic agreements. Furthermore, signs of similar restiveness already were appearing in the Spanish Indies. In Zéspedes' opinion, any threat to the Spanish monarchy, or any sign of weakening in Spain's imperial position would encourage the Georgians to seize land along the Georgia border and further encroach on the coveted Indian hunting grounds. To the end of his régime, Governor Zéspedes had to

remain alert to developments in Europe and America, and sensitive
to any changes of equilibrium in the Indian country.

A warning for redoubled vigilance reached St. Augustine in
the packet of mail arriving from Havana on December 28, 1789.
The secretary of state, in a special communication, advised all
colonial governors to watch out for signs of uprisings in their
provinces. News had reached Madrid by way of France that rebellion was brewing in the Spanish colonies. Zéspedes knew that
local demonstrations had occurred in protest against specified taxes
and individual officials in Central and South America, but he was
skeptical about any general mood of rebellion. Certainly no such
plot could develop in St. Augustine, but he knew it was possible
for agents to stir up trouble in the St. Mary's region. He suspected
that many of the north Florida residents shared the anti-royalist
sentiments of their American neighbors.

Zéspedes already had the St. Mary's area under close observation
because it was an important artery to the Creek country. The
Bowles incident called the attention to the possibility of British
agents reaching the Indians through this channel. The governor
had a second reason for concern over activities in the St. Mary's
region in the fall of 1789. Brawls along the border brought to
light the intermittent traffic in horses and peltry of a few Georgians. Neither the governor nor the Panton, Leslie firm could
afford to let Georgians or Providence Islanders use this avenue to
enter the Indian country and divert trade or diminsh Spanish influence within the Indian towns.

Following the arrival of the secretary of state's letter on December 28, 1789, Governor Zéspedes increased his surveillance of
the American border area. In January of 1790, he adopted four
additional security measures: The inspection of mail and printed
matter, a new investigation of the situation on the south bank of
the St. Mary's river, a new census of inhabitants of the northern
section of the province, and a more careful examination of stran-
gers crossing the border. He put the program into action quietly,
to give no signs of apprehension and create no additional border
tension. These measures to prevent defection or local disturbance
were the best that the governor could devise until the home government could send families from Spain to populate the frontier
and dilute the predominant Anglo-American element.

The inspection of mail was carried out under the pretext of
improving postal service in East Florida. Zéspedes instructed the
chief officer at San Vicente Ferrer to intercept all letters and printed

matter directed to persons living further up the St. John's river or to residents of St. Augustine, paying particular attention to St. Mary's correspondents. From San Vicente Ferrer, the letters went directly to Governor Zéspedes, who saw that they were forwarded promptly and with maximum safety to the addressees. Couriers took the mail on horseback from the St. John's river to the capital, changing horses at the intermediate post twenty miles north of St. Augustine. At the same time this procedure was instituted in East Florida, the postal inspector in Spain began a similar mail inspection to seize all letters containing news of the French revolution.[1]

Zéspedes decided that the investigation of border conditions, and the people crossing the border, was a job for Captain Carlos Howard. Ostensibly, the only change in border procedure was an inspection of trunks, luggage and persons, if feasible, to guard against smuggling of contraband items. Secretly, Captain Howard was instructed to report any evidence of defection, so that the governor and garrison commandant could decide on a suitable penalty. Although he had been lenient and tolerant in past years, Zéspedes was determined to hand out swift punishment to prevent the development of any plots within his jurisdiction.

He hoped that there would be no need for clamping down on the St. Mary's residents. In the long run, he doubted the efficacy of harsh regulations and stern punishment, preferring if possible to win the allegiance of the border population. He planned to achieve this objective under the guise of taking a new census of the St. Mary's river community. In conversation with each family, the census taker might convince these people that the Spanish administration was genuinely interested in their welfare, and that the benevolent king in Madrid knew of their existence, including them among his subjects for whom he felt a paternal affection. By preaching the basic gospel of monarchy, Zéspedes aspired to gain the faith of a group he regarded as essentially untutored in both politics and religion.

It was Father Hassett who finally came to the governor's aid in this delicate assignment. Actually, the governor's political objectives fused with the priest's spiritual concern for the St. Mary's residents. Father Hassett felt that missionary work among the St. Mary's population had been neglected too long. No one had visited the families to administer sacraments since Father

---

[1] Jean Sarrailh, *La España Ilustrada, de la Segunda Mitad del Siglo XVIII* (Mexico, D. F., 1957), pp. 602-603.

O'Reilly accompanied the governor on his tour in February, 1787. The arrival of Spanish Franciscan priests rather than Irish Capuchins was a blow to Father Hassett's plans to establish new churches at Amelia island and San Vicente Ferrer. Thus, with political as well as religious conversion in mind, Father Hassett and four soldiers set out on a six hundred mile journey late in April. Father Hassett felt obligated to remain in St. Augustine throughout the Lenten season and the important Holy Week services, concluding with Easter celebration on April 4.

The most important equipment that Father Hassett took on his trip was a box of English catechisms, printed in New York through arrangements made by Diego Gardoqui. Before returning to St. Augustine on May 31, Father Hassett administered Christian baptism to seventy-eight children and fifty-one slaves, a harvest of souls well worth his exhausting trip.[2] The Irish priest's vigorous and enthusiastic manner usually overcame the prejudice against the "popish faith" ingrained in so many frontier people of the American revolutionary era.

Father Hassett returned to St. Augustine to find the governor considerably perturbed by news that Alexander McGillivray was going to New York to make a treaty with the United States government. The previous day, May 30, a courier had brought word of this unexpected development in a letter from McGillivray to John Leslie, who always shared his correspondence with Captain Howard and Governor Zéspedes. McGillivray's sudden decision seemed partially motivated by fear that federal troops would join the Creek-Georgia warfare. Governor Zéspedes immediately perceived a dangerous correlation between the startling letter from the Creek country and new signs of military activity north of the Georgia border. He already knew that three companies of American troops were arriving in Georgia, one destined for the St. Mary's river border. Observers had also reported the construction of a new stockaded fort on the American shore of the river, a few miles from the harbor. In view of another potential border crisis, the governor submitted a request on May 26, 1790 for additional powder, balls, flints and assorted Indian presents.

Governor Zéspedes, as well as Governor Miró, had urged McGillivray to make peace with the Americans, but only if Spain's preponderant position in the Creek nation was unaffected. Zéspedes

<hr />

[2] Michael J. Curley, *Church and State in the Spanish Floridas, 1783-1821* (Washington, 1940), p. 179.

repeatedly advised the Creek leader that a treaty of peace did not necessitate a trade agreement. The governor realized that since the adoption of the new constitution, President George Washington also was determined to make peace with the southern Indians, but he was under the impression that the federal officials were as unsuccessful as the Georgians in finding a basis for settling differences on the frontier. The last news to reach St. Augustine, prior to the arrival of the courier on May 30, concerned the complete inability of federal emmissaries to formulate a treaty during a brief meeting with McGillivray and other chiefs at Rock Landing in November of 1789. Zéspedes and Leslie knew that Alexander McGillivray had been insulted by the terms proposed by the federal commissioners on that occasion. At Rock Landing, McGillivray explained that his nation would not cede land in treaty with the Federal government that they had refused to cede to the Georgians. Furthermore, McGillivray was particularly incensed by the arrogant attitude of one of the commissioners, David Humphreys, a former aide-de-camp and protégé of President Washington.

Governor Zéspedes was anxious to learn what new element had entered the picture to give Alexander McGillivray such a change of heart. Most of the answer was found in the letter that John Leslie received on May 30. The new element was Senator Benjamin Hawkins of Georgia, a gentleman well-informed and sympathetic toward the southern Indians, who was singularly disappointed to learn that the President's three commissioners had made an unsuccessful trip to Rock Landing. On returning to New York, the commissioners stated simply that McGillivray refused to discuss a treaty with them and abruptly left the site selected for a meeting place. Hawkins immediately decided that McGillivray's case was so misrepresented that federal troops might be called out against the Creeks. He took the initiative in reopening the negotiations with McGillivray after the federal commissioners had failed.

Since the senate was in session, Hawkins could not leave the national capital for a trip to the Indian country, but he selected Colonel Marinus Willett, Revolutionary War veteran from New York, as a man suitably qualified to carry an urgent letter to Alexander McGillivray. Writing forcefully, Hawkins made the Creek leader understand the danger to his nation if he appeared to refuse negotiations with the United States government. McGillivray's attitude was interpreted in New York as one of contempt, and the newly formed nation could not brook such effron-

tery. Hawkins pointed out that individual bands of Creeks were
bound to commit depredations along the Georgia frontier, and
in the future these acts would surely bring retaliation from the
United States army rather than a local militia. To avoid disaster,
Hawkins urged McGillivray to come to New York and state his
case to the president of the United States and form a bond of
friendship with the new government. His immediate personal
appearance was needed to counterbalance the bad reports of the
federal commissioners and the biased propaganda of the Georgians.

Colonel Marinus Willett, bearing Hawkins' emergency message,
sailed for Charleston in March, 1790, then traveled overland to
reach McGillivray's plantation at Little Tallassie early in May.
McGillivray found him an honest and admirable man, and decided
almost immediately to follow his suggestions. From conversation
with Colonel Willett, McGillivray deduced that the national government also desired a treaty with the southern Indians as a
means of thwarting state claims to western lands. Federal officials
were aware of the private land companies being formed with the
connivance of state officials to mark out areas for settlement in the
Creek and Cherokee hunting territory. McGillivray had been approached by several of these promoters who desired his acquiescence
to taking over Indian lands. He dealt with none of the land company representatives, except to keep himself informed of their
activities and report his discoveries to Panton and the Spanish officials. Talking with Colonel Willett, McGillivray understood that
the national congress would not concede to the states the right to
extend their boundaries. Therefore, a boundary treaty between
the federal government and the Creeks would be a blow to ex-
pansionist interests in Georgia and other southern states. The
revelations concerning the land companies convinced the astute
Indian leader that there was more than "justice and humanity" in
the President's desire for an Indian treaty. At the same time,
his heart warmed to the thought that a treaty signed by George
Washington and Alexander McGillivray would be a milestone
in peaceful relations between the nations for years to come.

After discussing Alexander McGillivray's disclosures, John Leslie and Governor Zéspedes decided that the Indian leader should
not enter discussions with the federal government without cautious
advice from his business partners and the Spanish government.
McGillivray had made his momentous decision alone. William
Panton, who usually supplied him with counsel, was three hundred miles distant in the Chickasaw country at the time of Will-

ett's visit. The courier told Leslie that McGillivray had written near the end of his annual spring visit to the Lower Creeks. Representative chiefs were assembling at Coweta to join McGillivray on the trip to New York. Unfortunately, it appeared impossible to communicate with McGillivray, who was returning to his plantation and would depart from the nation before a courier could reach him.

John Leslie was frankly apprehensive about the nature of the treaty which would be proposed to McGillivray in New York. He knew McGillivray might be susceptible to the flattery of diplomatic Americans, particularly after a long journey with Colonel Willett, who evidently commanded his sincere esteem. Governor Zéspedes was more inclined to be confident in McGillivray's steadiness of purpose, but was unwilling to be outmaneuvered by clever Americans at the conclusion of his régime after combating their real and phantom designs for almost six years. Up to the present moment, Zéspedes had carried on a carefully manipulated defensive program, but now he decided on a move that was agressive, but still subtle. Within forty-eight hours after McGillivray's letter reached St. Augustine, Carlos Howard left to intercept McGillivray before he reached New York.

Convenient for the governor's purpose, a ship lay at anchor in St. Augustine's shallow harbor, ready for a return trip to New York. Captain Howard often had considered taking a sea voyage for his health, and now the opportunity and necessity were both present. Captain Howard sailed north on June 1, armed with practical advice from Governor Zéspedes and a long letter of introduction from John Leslie.

Soon after Howard reached New York on June 14, he gave the Spanish legation a translation of McGillivray's letter revealing the reasons behind his visit to New York City. Baron Josef Ignacio de Viar, who had charge of the legation following Gardoqui's departure, was greatly relieved to have available Howard's vast fund of information about southern Indian affairs. Captain Howard remained only briefly in New York, then went to Philadelphia to await the Creek delegation en route in three large wagons. Alexander McGillivray and Colonel Willett, accompanied by twenty-seven Indian chiefs and warriors, traveled overland the entire distance from Alabama to New York. After six years of correspondence, the Scotch Indian and Irish Spaniard finally met in Philadelphia in the middle of July, 1790.

McGillivray's Spanish connection was apparent throughout his visit in the American capital. Howard arranged for McGillivray to make representations direct to the court in Madrid, through Viar, during the period of treaty negotiations. For a greater part of the time in New York, illness confined McGillivray to his lodgings at the home of Henry Knox, secretary of war. Out in public, he was surrounded by attentive American officials. His host and Thomas Jefferson, secretary of state, both accompanied him on his call at the Spanish legation, a diplomatic formality shortly returned by Viar. Captain Howard's unanticipated presence constantly disconcerted American diplomatic efforts. At social functions, the Spanish officer always attended McGillivray, so that their mutual regard was evident during large gatherings at the homes of President Washington and General Knox.

The presence of Captain Howard was only one of the unforeseen elements complicating the transactions in New York City during August, 1790. The British also had an observer, Major George Beckwith, sent to discover why the Americans were treating Alexander McGillivray as head of the Creeks when William Augustus Bowles, with his Indian followers, was in Quebec claiming to represent the nation. Bowles made his story so plausible that he was granted a trip to London at government expense to confer with British ministers. Both Captain Howard and Major Beckwith were shadowed by American agents who tried to prevent them from contacting McGillivray. In fact, a faint "cloak and dagger" atmosphere surrounded parleys preceding the Treaty of New York concluded on August 7, 1790.

For McGillivray, there were two surprise elements affecting his behavior at the treaty conferences. In the first place, he had expected to see Gardoqui in New York, and did not know in advance that the minister had left America the previous summer. Furthermore, he did not learn until he heard from Carlos Howard in Philadelphia that England and Spain were on the brink of war. The crisis arose because a Spanish warship had seized a British ship near an English fur trading settlement on Nootka Sound, an inlet of Vancouver island, area regarded by Spain as part of her Pacific coastal possessions. On May 5, 1790, the king of England had announced the prospect of war, and the Spanish fleet currently was gathering at Cadiz. The problem was resolved by fall, ending a period of tension similar to the Falkland islands affair in 1770. But in August of 1790, McGillivray suddenly realized that he needed alternate trade connections in case war between Spain and England curtailed Panton's supplies.

The possibiilty of war also was in the minds of Washington and Jefferson, who believed that the situation might be exploited so that the United States could acquire the Floridas in the event of hostilities. Yet Americans could not give any overt indication of unfriendliness to Spanish officials in New York, because they wanted to reopen negotiations with Spain concerning a commercial agreement, the boundary of West Florida, and navigation of the Mississippi river.[3] McGillivray was certain that the ubiquitous Captain Howard prevented American representatives from making any forceful demands for territory or Indian trading concessions. He regarded Zéspedes' decision to send Howard to New York as a masterful stroke, and derived private enjoyment from observing American discomfiture. In contemplating his trip to New York, McGillivray had Machiavelli in mind. With later historical perspective, Albert J. Pickett dubbed the Creek chief the "Talleyrand of Alabama."[4]

Considering all the pressures exerted during the conferences preceding the Treaty of New York, the final terms are of interest, but of no great significance since it was impossible to enforce any commitments upon the chiefs of the independent Creek towns. McGillivray accepted future American sovereignty over any portion of the Creek lands included in American territory after the United States settled its boundary dispute with Spain. He relinquished claim to a section of Indian land already settled by Georgians, but the boundary was not as far west as the state desired. Washington guaranteed the integrity of the Creek hunting grounds and agreed to pay for the area ceded in the treaty. McGillivray refused to authorize American trade except in the event of war between England and Spain. According to American records, a secret clause made McGillivray a brigadier general in the American army, but McGillivray said that he refused to accept this commission. The Treaty of New York did not alter the attitude or objectives of either the Creeks or the Georgians, and the provisions were never carried out. The compromise nature of the treaty brought criticism from all interested parties: Spaniards, Georgia traders, and land company promoters. The Creeks refused to permit surveying of the boundary line.

Governor Zéspedes did not get a report of Carlos Howard's suc-

---

[3] Worthington Chauncey Ford. *The United States and Spain in 1790* (Brooklyn, 1890), pp. 16-19, 23.

[4] Albert James Pickett, *History of Alabama and Incidentally of Georgia and Mississippi from the Earliest Period* (Sheffield, Alabama, 1896), p. 432.

cessful mission until late fall, after his own return to Havana. He missed Captain Howard's efficient help during the final weeks of his governorship, but he believed Howard's journey was vital to the royal service. Concluding his term of office required considerable paper work. Fortunately, in March the final budget had been completed, including recommendations for administering the provincial government. Zéspedes requested salary increases for all important officials in East Florida, and an additional assistant for Gonzalo Zamorano. He pointed out that money for the raises could come from cutting superfluous personnel from the hospital staff and the gun boat crews. The budget called for a situado of 154,000 pesos, plus the 50,000 pesos fund for population development. At the end of his régime, Governor Zéspedes faced the usual discrepancy between his financial demands for East Florida and his actual monetary receipts. In April of 1790, the Cuban intendancy sent a stop-gap sum of 6000 pesos enabling Zéspedes to settle some extremely urgent financial demands, but the salaries of officials were paid only through December of 1788.

Governor Zéspedes' final tasks were those of any member of the Spanish colonial administration on preparing to relinquish his office to a successor. In June, he completed indices of his correspondence with officials in Havana and Madrid. In Carlos Howard's absence, he personally went over the files of the secretariat, giving particular attention to recent intelligence coming from outsiders.

Checking the records, he noted his letter of March 12, 1790 reporting to the captain general in Cuba the renewed activities of William Augustus Bowles along the Florida coast. Zéspedes had heard earlier that the adventurer returned to New Providence during the winter, leaving Florida from the Indian river inlet with two Cherokee and three Creek Indians among his companions. The additional news which Zéspedes forwarded so promptly in March, 1790 came from a sea captain who landed at St. Augustine en route north from Havana. According to the Yankee captain, Bowles was established on an island off Cape Florida where he was terrorizing fishermen from Providence. Rumors indicated that Bowles had salvaged from a shipwrecked Spanish vessel, a supply of goods including four brass cannon which were mounted in positions to defend the island. Sailing through the keys in a black sloop, Bowles and his renegades were living by piracy, threatening death to any Spaniards they could capture or to any fishermen who interfered with their activities.

Of course, Zéspedes could not possibly keep up with William Augustus Bowles' rapid travels about the Atlantic ocean in 1790. He was unaware that by the time his letter of March 12 reached Cuba, Bowles was already on a voyage to Canada and thence to England. Although British prime minister William Pitt contemplated making use of the Florida adventurer, as well as the future Venezuelan revolutionist, Francisco Miranda, in the summer of 1790, their services could not be employed after the Anglo-Spanish crisis was resolved in September. By February, 1791, Bowles was back in the Indian country. In the spring of 1790, Zéspedes was convinced that Bowles would make further attempts to establish illicit Indian trade, a suspicion borne out by Bowles attack on Panton's Apalache store in 1792.

Among Zéspedes' last pieces of interesting correspondence was a secret communication, dated April 24, 1790, to Esteban Miró, governor of Louisiana. In this important letter, Zéspedes warned Miró of two questionable characters, Dr. James O'Fallon and Major Tom Washington, who had set out toward the Mississippi river and might possibly turn up in New Orleans. O'Fallon's first contact with Zéspedes had been arranged through Thomas Powell, the Charleston resident who journeyed to St. Augustine in December, 1787 to give evidence about American plots involving the Spanish possessions. Zéspedes' letter described O'Fallon as a man mysterious in his method of operation, independent in spirit, and seditious. For Miró's further information, Zéspedes explained that in the course of three years' correspondence with Carlos Howard, O'Fallon had persistently proposed colonization projects as a cover for insidious personal schemes.

As Zéspedes anticipated, O'Fallon did approach Miró with assorted propositions, boasts and threats. After moving westward from Charleston, O'Fallon participated briefly in the Mississippi valley intrigues which form such a colorful feature of Spanish-American frontier history. On February 21 ,1791, when he was past fifty, O'Fallon married the fifteen year old sister of George Rogers Clark, another Revolutionary War veteran intermittently involved in anti-Spanish conspiracies centered in Kentucky. O'Fallon's career was halted suddenly by his early death, in 1793.[5] In his confidential message to Miró on April 24, 1790, Zéspedes

[5] R. C. [Rogers Clark] Ballard Thruston. "Notes" in the Filson Club Library. Louisville. Kentucky. "O'Fallon died in 1793 according to the statement of his granddaughter, Miss Emily O'Fallon of San José, Calif., made to me (RCBT) in 1910."

termed O'Fallon's companion, Major Washington, a Georiga speculator of depraved intentions. This character assessment was fairly close to the mark. Major Washington later was arrested for counterfeiting and hanged for his crime.

Zéspedes' correspondence in the spring of 1790 also included several letters from Americans waiting on the St. Mary's border, eager to receive land grants which they anticipated would be handed out by the Spanish government very soon. These people were told that their expectations were at least premature, but they continued offering information in order to get on good terms with the Spanish administration in East Florida. The last report gave an account of a proposal by a religious sect called the Quakers, who advocated the prohibition of slavery. His informant predicted that such a movement eventually would break up the newly-formed union of states.

On June 24, Zéspedes completed the last important message of his governorship, the special letter of advice for his successor always supplied by conscientious officials in the Spanish colonial administration. In his letter for Quesada, Zéspedes stressed the two vital concerns for a governor in East Florida: guarding the St. Mary's border and maintaining peace with the Indians. Zéspedes still was worried because no genuine Spaniards lived along the Georgia frontier, an area he feared would be taken over by a wild sort of folk whom he identified as "Crackers." Relations with the Seminole Indians were amicable, but a separate Creek band settled at Spring Garden, east of Lake Gorge, had committed depredations along the St. John's river in October, 1789. This group would bear watching.

As he prepared to leave St. Augustine, Zéspedes recalled with pleasure the colonial secretary's letter informing him that the king approved the skill and devotion with which he had served as governor of East Florida. Zéspedes realized that the temporal end of his regime was not significant. His term of office had been just an extended period of transition and readjustment in the province, but he was satisfied that he had laid the foundations of government. He had secured a permanent garrison for St. Augustine assuring the infant colony adequate military protection, a primary consideration. He was proud of the local school, with masters for both elementary letters and advanced reading and mathematics. Construction soon would begin on the new church, whose location already was marked out on the north side of the plaza. According to advance reports, his successor would institute a program of land distribution, a process which would reassure and increase the stability of the civilian population. He hoped the court would send new commercial regulations, permitting the residents to trade directly with Spain. And he still awaited adequate instructions for handling the troublesome fugitive slaves from the American States.

The governor contemplated a rather quiet trip back to Cuba. His children already had gone from the province. Dominga and Josepha left when their husbands' regiments were transferred in 1788 and 1789. Vicente and Antonio had sailed for Cuba earlier in the spring of 1790 with the last detachments of the Havana Regiment. He had reason to be proud of these young officers. Antonio had acquitted himself well when he served for three months as officer in charge of the post at Amelia island, and Vicente made a notable appearance at the coronation celebration. He was also pleased with his son Thomas, whose personal memorial to the king had brought instructions for him to return to Havana, pending another appointment worth of his rank. He was not as strong as he had been on arriving in East Florida, and would enjoy a peaceful interval in Havana. Doña Concepción was truly eager to see her many friends and relations, and join in the more brilliant society of the island metropolis. Havana would be hot, but they could escape the heat of the city after attending the theatre or a late dinner, and enjoy the ride in a *guadaño* boat across the harbor to a summer place in the hills of Regla. It would be pleasant to cross the Havana bay at night again, and watch the phosphorescent glow in the rippling wake of the slender craft.

Aside from his wife, Governor Zéspedes would have few fellow passengers during his return voyage to Havana. The only official planning to accompany him was Bernardo de Madrid. The old doctor had been granted permission to retire in Guanabacoa, a country village on Havana harbor where his sister was living. His government pension carried the responsibility of administering to charity patients at the village hospital. The new doctor was an Irishman, Thomas Travers, whose ability to speak English and Spanish met Zéspedes' requirements for a provincial staff physician.

In taking over the governorship, Queseda would have the assistance of Zéspedes' experienced staff. The three officers who preceded Zéspedes to St. Augustine were all remaining in Florida: Captain Carlos Howard who would return from New York in September, Mariano LaRocque the chief engineer, and second treasury official Dimas Cortes. Thirty-five year old Dimas Cortes was fast becoming a *Floridano* since marrying Agueda Segui, a local Minorcan belle half his age, in April of 1790. Gonzalo Zamorano was still director of the royal treasury, although he would have preferred a transfer to Cuba or Mexico.

Governor Zéspedes had several days of relative inactivity following the completion of his official corresponding indices, and the composition of his message to his successor. He took care of last minute details of his personal and official business in the early summer of 1790, during the same season of the year he had arrived in 1784. To complete his daily tasks while it was tolerably cool, Zéspedes usually began early in the morning. On such days, the sun, resembling a fiery globe hanging in the pale sky, soon rose high enough above Anastasia island to strike a coral ribbon across the dark waters of Matanzas bay. Along the shore, white cranes on spindly legs poked for snails in the succulent ooze slowly submerged by the incoming tide. The air was silent until about ten o'clock when a little breeze arose, insufficient to temper the scorching heat of the relentless summer sun.

On July 7, flags flashing from the Anastasia island watchtower indicated the approach of a vessel from the south. Zéspedes could see the signals from his quarters on the second floor of the Government House. The ship was "The Terrible" bringing Juan Nepomuceno Quesada and his family to East Florida. The ship crossed the bar at high tide and anchored in Matanzas bay. Governor Zéspedes and his wife warmly welcomed the newcomers to the province. The Quesadas had survived a long and tedious journey from Comayagua, a provincial capital situated far inland in the present-day Republic of Honduras. Señora Quesada was exhausted after the ocean voyage supervising two active youngsters, eight and five years old. Zéspedes immediately turned over the government to his successor.

A week's time usually was required to make a ship ready for the return trip to Havana. During that interval, the crew unloaded the Quesada's belongings and other cargo, then stowed away Zéspedes' possessions in the vessel's hold. Ships bread was prepared by the bakers, working at the huge outdoor ovens which stood near the river edge within the enclosure surrounding St. Francis barracks. At the very last, provisions for the voyage were placed on board. Finally all was in order, and with wind and tide in proper coordination, "The Terrible" hoisted sail on July 15, 1790 to take Governor Zéspedes from East Florida.

St. George Street from City Gates

EPILOGUE

Chronicles of the eighteenth century seldom remained within the confines of a time interval as limited as Zéspedes' governorship in East Florida, from 1784 to 1790. In the tradition of that era of rambling discourse, it seems appropriate to add assorted fragments of biographical information about the subsequent careers of persons who have been mentioned in previous chapters. It may also be well to include a few comments about later events on the Florida peninsula up to the end of the Spanish colonial regimé in 1821, when the United States acquired Florida by treaty with Spain.

After returning to Havana in July, 1790, Zéspedes continued to offer his counsel on Florida affairs until his death on January 21, 1794. His daughter Dominga, whose marriage to Lieutenant O'Donovan created such a flurry in 1785, was already a widow. The considerate attention she received from royal officials justified her father's faith in the king's paternal affection for loyal subjects. In October of 1795, the king's secretary notified Diego Gardoqui, then minister of finance, that Maria Dominga de Zéspedes deserved a pension in recognition of her father's distinguished services as governor of East Florida. Gardoqui doubtless recalled Zéspedes' strenuous efforts to secure provisions for the Florida garrison and his informative communications about American frontier intrigues. As Spanish representative in Philadelphia from 1785 to 1789, Gardoqui grew to appreciate Zéspedes' administrative talent. Although officers' widows normally received pensions, special arrangements had to be made for Dominga, who was barred from that automatic privilege because of her clandestine marriage. When she remarried in 1797, the royal secretary authorized transfer of the pension to her only son, nine year old Juan Vicente O'Donovan.

Gonzalo Zamorano, director of the royal treasury throughout Zéspedes' governorship, remained in St. Augustine until 1809. In that year, he was promoted to a treasury post in Acapulco, the most important port on the Pacific coast of Mexico. Arriving in Mexico on the eve of the Wars of Independence beginning in September, 1810, Zamorano lived through the first phases of the military campaigns. In 1812, he moved into war-damaged Guanajuato, a provincial capital seized by Indian mobs in 1810 but soon retaken by royalist forces. He served there as provincial treasurer with an annual salary of 3000 pesos until 1820, when he either died or retired at the age of eighty. In Guanajuato, his circle of friends included Anastasio Bustamente, who joined Iturbide's independence movement in 1821 and later became president of Mexico in 1830. Of incidental interest is the fact that Gonzalo Zamorano's sixth child, Augustin, born in St. Augustine in 1798, was executive secretary to the first governor of California under independent Mexico, and served as acting-governor briefly in the early 1830's.[1]

Zéspedes' capable administrative assistant, Captain Carlos Howard, was pressed into service along the Spanish-American frontier on several occasions following his return to St. Augustine in September, 1790. As Zéspedes had feared, the subversive influence of the French Revolution eventually spread to the Florida border. In South Carolina and Georgia, agents of Republican France tried to instigate an attack on East and West Florida as one phase of a massive undertaking against both Spanish and English possessions in North America. Between 1793 and 1795, when France and Spain were officially at war, Captain Howard constantly patrolled the border with rural militia and regular infantry under his command. Several clashes occurred, but Howard's clever strategy successfully repelled the sporadic incursions.

The military exploits promoted by French agents were not as dangerous as those of American opportunists who took advantage of the state of war existing between France and Spain. Richard Lang, whom Zéspedes had reluctantly appointed Commissioner of

---

[1] George L. Harding. *Don Agustin V. Zamorano, Statesman, Soldier, Craftsman and California's First Printer.* (Los Angeles, 1934) p. 14-19, 90.

the St. Mary's area in 1788, was drawn into one rebellion involving other Anglo-American residents of the northern section of Spanish East Florida as well as a few Georgians. Another character who appeared on the St. Mary's border in this interval was Elijah Clarke, revolutionary war hero and former Indian trader whom Alexander MacGillivray forced out of the Creek country in 1785 when William Panton took over the Indian trade of West Florida. In 1795, Clarke and a group of personal followers planned to attack East Florida by way of the Indian country.

At this juncture, federal troops arrived in Georgia to end the free lance military activity in the border region. On the north bank of the St. Mary's river, an American officer coordinated his attack with Carlos Howard's overland march along the south shore, so that together they forced Elijah Clarke to make a hasty retreat to the interior. Among the prisoners apprehended by American troops during this action was Daniel McGirt, who had been evicted from Florida thrice during Zéspedes' administration. In 1795, McGirt was wanted both by Governor George Matthews of Georgia and Governor Quesada of Florida. As ususal, however, the rogue was released and this time he vanished into the Indian country.[2]

Carlos Howard's skillful handling of the Georgia-Florida border incursions in 1794 and 1795 brought recommendations for a promotion. In 1796, he became lieutenant colonel of the Louisiana Regiment and military director of Upper Louisiana. He was given the task of secretly evacuating a Spanish post on the Mississipp river which was within the territory given to the United States in the Treaty of San Lorenzo signed in October, 1795. In this treaty, the United States secured the long-disputed Natchez District, as well as the right to free navigation of the Mississippi river. But Howard's most dramatic assignment was to squelch republican enthusiasm among the French inhabitants of St. Louis who had made a noisy demonstration on September 23, 1796 when they celebrated the New Year, according to the new French calendar. In the winter of 1796, Colonel Howard took a squadron of keelboats and galleys up the Mississippi river to suppress French inhabitants of St. Louis, an incident which has been called the greatest military event in the history of Upper Louisiana.[3] As

[2] See Richard K. Murdoch, *The Georgia-Florida Frontier, 1793-1796* (Berkeley, 1951).

[3] Louis Houck, *History of Missouri* (Chicago, 1908), I, p. 322; II, p. 60.

usual, all Carlos Howard's operations were remarkably adroit and successful.

Several characters appearing separately on the scene during Zéspedes' governorship pursued inter-related careers during the later history of the Spainsh-American border. Benjamin Hawkins was already interested in Creek-Spanish relations in March of 1785, when he visited Zéspedes in St. Augustine. When he was senator from Georgia he was responsible for securing Alexander MacGillivray's presence in New York for the negotiation of the Creek treaty in August, 1790. The Florida boundary line established by treaty with Spain in 1795 placed many of the Creek villages within the area of American sovereignty. In 1796, Hawkins became American superintendent for the southern Indians and spent the remaining ten years of his public career trying to guide the Creeks, who had lacked real leadership since the death of Alexander MacGillivray in 1793. William Panton, who lived in Pensacola until his death in 1801, commended Hawkins for his unselfish interest in the welfare of the Creek nation. Hawkins was also instrumental in the final apprehension of William Augustus Bowles, and cooperated with Spanish officials to achieve this objective.

James Seagrove was another contemporary figure long connected with the border scene. Seagrove first came to East Florida as a personal emissary of Governor George Matthews in 1787 when Indian hostilities provoked one of the periodic crises. Seagrove and his wife were among the first settlers of the new Georgia town established near the mouth of the St. Mary's river in 1790. Originally it was called St. Patrick's, but in 1792 the name was changed permanently to St. Mary's. Prior to Hawkins' appointment, Seagrove served briefly as southern Indian commissioner and unsuccessfully tried to diminish Spanish influence among the Creek tribes.

One of the figures in American public life most continuously interested in East Florida was George Matthews, governor of Georgia on two occasions, the first during the Creek crisis of 1787. His second term of office was during the period when French agents were the most active, in 1794 and 1795. Matthews had hoped that the final treaty of peace ending the American Revolution might grant East Florida to the new independent republic. Also, he was somewhat sympathetic to the activities of such men as Elijah Clarke. In 1811, George Matthews became an American secret agent instructed to foment rebellion among the East Florida in-

habitants who would then ask the United States to annex the
peninsula. Concurrently, Madison's proposal to occupy Spanish
East Florida by force was defeated in the Senate by only two
votes. Financed by a secret congressional appropriation, Matthews
even tried to bribe the Spanish commandant at St. Augustine to
cooperate in his unpraiseworthy project. When Matthews' activities, which could not be kept entirely secret, were criticized in the
American press, he was officially disowned by the national administration, a disgrace which broke the old patriot's spirit. He died
in 1812 on his way to Washington to vindicate his honor.[4]

Throughout East Florida's Second Spanish Period, the peninsula was involved in European as well as American affairs. Each
international fracas brought repercussions to the sensitive Florida
border. Activities during the war between France and Spain, 1793
to 1795, have already been mentioned. After England declared
war on Spain in 1796, a new crop of British agents entered the
Florida scene. Piracy and privateering, often indistinguishable, increased along the south Atlantic coast and prize ships were brought
into the harbors of Charleston, Savannah and St. Augustine. Jefferson's Embargo Act in 1807 made a boom town out of Fernandina, a new trading community on Amelia island only seven
miles by boat from the Georgia port of St. Mary's. During the
final stages of the War of 1812 between the United States and
England, British troops in 1816 landed on Cumberland island
and tried to sail up the St. Mary's river, but were bombarded from
both sides of the border.

After the collapse of George Matthews' border mission in 1816,
American diplomats turned their attention to the purchase of Florida, which was arranged in 1819. In the meantime, a pirate controlled Amelia island for several months in 1817 and an offshoot
of Bolivar's South American army planned to attack East Florida
from Tampa bay. In 1818, Andrew Jackson invaded Florida
to fight the Indians, continuing the destruction of crops and villages
begun during the Creek War carried on by Americans in 1811 and
1812 in the Alachua district. By 1819, Spain was defenseless.
Armies for independence which had been suppressed in 1816 now
marched toward victory from Mexico to Argentina. In the same
year, the monarchy faced a republican revolt in regiments stationed
within Spain.

At the end of the Second Spanish Period, East Florida's effec-

---

[4] Rembert W. Patrick, *Florida Fiasco*, (Athens, 1954). This volume portrays
Matthews' career in detail.

tive territory was practically limited to the well-guarded capital, and the northern port city of Fernandina on Amelia island. In spite of their many vicissitudes, the inhabitants of St. Augustine never wavered in their loyalty to Spain, enthusiastically displayed on such occasions as the coronation celebration in 1789. Genuine sorrow existed in the little town when the Spanish flag ceased to fly above the Castillo de San Marcos on July 10, 1821.

St. George Street—East Side

BIBLIOGRAPHY

The majority of original documents concerning Zéspedes' governorship are concentrated in two repositories, the Archivo General de Indias in Seville, where copies of all Spanish colonial correspondence came to rest, and the Library of Congress in Washington, guardian of the East Florida Papers, the provincial files for the Second Spanish Period at St. Augustine which became American property when the United States purchased Florida from Spain. Principal research for this historical study was carried out at the P. K. Yonge Library of Florida History in Gainesville using copies of documents, for the most part from the above two sources, gathered in two large collections, the Stetson Papers and the Lockey Collection.

The Stetson Papers are photostats of documents in the Archivo General de Indias made for the Florida State Historical Society, founded by John B. Stetson, Jr. in 1921. After the society ceased to function in 1933 as a result of the depression, the collection of photostats was placed on sealed loan at the Library of Congress. In 1954, the Stetson Papers were transferred to P. K. Yonge Library of Florida History and for the first time became available for general research. The Stetson Papers include reproductions of more than seven thousand documents, or about 130,000 sheets, dating from 1518 to 1820.

The Lockey Collection represents two decades of work by Joseph B. Lockey, a native of Florida who for many years was professor of Latin American History at the University of California at Los Angeles. In the 1920's, Dr. Lockey began to collect original documents with the idea of publishing a series of volumes covering the Second Spanish Period in Florida history. At the time of his death in 1946, only the first volume spanning the years 1783 through 1785 was ready for publication. Many of the documents for this period of transition from British to Spanish rule came from the Public Records Office in London. The Lockey Collection consists of transcripts from several archives. These typewritten copes of documents have been available at the University of Florida and the University of California since 1949. The collection is more complete for the early years of the Second Spanish Period. Additional research for this study was conducted at the Library of Congress and the William L. Clements Library in Ann Arbor.

Citations to original documents have been omitted from this publication because they seem both pedantic and superfluous. The footnotes refer to various works consulted during the investigation of Zéspedes' governorship. Extensive use was made of the following printed sources: Charles L. Mowat's analysis of East Florida during the British period; John Walton Caughey's volume of McGillivray's correspondence describing Indian affairs; Arthur P. Whitaker's documentary collection relating to Spain's commercial policy in the Floridas; and Joseph B. Lockey's selection of documents pertaining to the years 1783 to 1785 in Spanish East Florida. The records of the Roman Catholic Church are a necessary source of biographical data.

In printed form, this study varies only slightly from the doctoral dissertation submitted to the Horace H. Rackham School of Graduate Studies of the University of Michigan in 1961. Anyone interested in more complete documentation can consult the original dissertation entitled "Vicente Manuel de Zéspedes and the Restoration of Spanish Rule in East Florida, 1784-1790." It is available on microfilm and in the libraries of the University of Michigan, University of Miami, the University of Florida, and the St. Augustine Historical Society. Exhaustive documentation would fill more pages than the printed text.

MANUSCRIPTS

Charles W. Arnade. "Architectural Information of Early St. Augustine." Private manuscript, loaned by author, 1960.

—————————————. "Cattle in Early Spanish Florida." Copy in possession of the author, 1960.

H. M. Corse, collector. "Florida-South Carolina Newspapers," P. K. Yonge Library of Florida History, Gainesville, n.d.

T. Frederick Davis. "Florida Events of History." P. K. Yonge Library of Florida History, Gainesville, n.d.

Charles H. Fairbanks. "Ethnological Report of the Florida Indians." P. K. Yonge Library of Florida History, Gainesville, 1958.

John W. Griffin. "Comments on the Plants of Spanish St. Augustine." The St. Augustine Historical Society, 1956.

—————————————, and Albert C. Manucy. "The Development of Housing in St. Augustine 1565-1764." The St. Augustine Historical Society, 1960.

Lyle N. McAlister. "The Army of New Spain, 1760-1800." Unpublished Ph.D. dissertation, University of California, Berkeley, 1950.

Helen Hornbeck Tanner. "The Transition from British to Spanish Rule in East Florida, 1783-1785." Unpublished Master's Thesis, Department of History, University of Florida, Gainesville, 1949.

GUIDES TO ARCHIVES

Herbert E. Bolton. *Guides to Materials for the History of the United States in the Principal Archives of Mexico.* Washington, 1913.

Archivo Nacional de Cuba. *Documents Pertaining to the Floridas which are Kept in Different Archives of Cuba.* Havana, 1945.

Roscoe R. Hill. *Descriptive Catalogue of Documents Relating to the History of the United States in the Papeles Procedentes de Cuba Deposited in the Archivo General de Indias at Seville.* Washington, 1916.

—————————————. *Los Archivos Nacionales de la América Latina.* (Publicaciones del Archivo Nacional de Cuba XIX.) La Habana, 1948.

North Carolina Historical Commission. *Guide to the Manuscript Collections in the Archives of North Carolina Historical Commission.* Raleigh, 1952.

Luis M. Pérez. *Guide to Materials for American History in Cuban Archives.* Washington, 1907.

James Alexander Robertson. *List of Documents in Spanish Archives Relating to the History of the United States which have been printed or of which Transcripts are Preserved in American Libraries.* Washington, 1910.

William R. Shepherd. *Guide to Materials for the History of the United States in Spanish Archives.* Washington, 1907.

BOOKS

John Richard Alden. *The South in the Revolution, 1763-1789*. Baton Rouge, 1957.

Rafael Altamira. *A History of Spain*. New York, 1949.

Charles W. Arnade. *Florida on Trial*. Coral Gables, 1959.

——————————————. *The Siege of St. Augustine in 1702*. Gainesville, 1959.

Cayetano Alberto de la Berrera y Leirado. *Catálogo Bibliográfico y Biográfico de Teatro Antiguo Español desde sus Origines hasta Mediados del Siglo XVIII*. Madrid, 1860.

John Bartram. Diary of a Journey through the Carolinas, Georgia, and Florida. Annotated by Francis Harper. (Transactions of the American Philosophical Society. n.s. vol. 33, pt. 1, pp. 1-120.) Philadelphia, 1942.

William Bartram. *Travels in Georgia and Florida, 1773-1774. A Report to Dr. John Fothergill*. Annotated by Francis Harper. (Transactions of the American Philosophical Society, n.s. vol. 33, pt. 2, pp. 121-142.) Philadelphia, 1943.

——————————————. *Travels through North Carolina, South Carolina, Georgia, East and West Florida*. Philadelphia, 1791.

Harry Bernstein. *Origins of Inter-American Interest, 1700-1812*. Philadelphia, 1945.

Herbert E. Bolton, and Mary Ross. *The Debatable Land*. Berkeley, 1925.

Mark F. Boyd. *Here They Once Stood; the Tragic End of the Apalache Missions*. Gainesville, 1951.

Caroline Mays Brevard. *A History of Florida from the Treaty of 1763 to Our Own Times*. 2 vols. Deland, 1924.

Daniel G. Brinton. *Notes on the Floridian Peninsula*. Philadelphia, 1859.

A. M. Brooks (ed.). *The Unwritten History of Old St. Augustine*. Translated by Annie Averette. St. Augustine, 1909.

Pedro Calderón de la Barca. *Obras Completas*. 3 vols. Madrid, 1956.

Richard L. Campbell. *Historical Sketches of Colonial Florida.* Cleveland, 1892.

B. R. Carroll. *Historical Collections of South Carolina.* New York, 1836.

John Walton Caughey. *Bernardo de Gálvez in Louisiana, 1776-1783.* Berkeley, 1934.

————————. *McGillivray of the Creeks.* Norman, 1938.

Charlestown Directory for 1782, and a Charleston Directory for 1785. With a foreword by Mary A. Sparkman. Charleston. S. C., 1951.

Verne E. Chatelain. *The Defenses of Spanish Florida, 1505-1763.* Washington, 1941.

Serafín María de Soto y Abbach, Conde de Clonard. *Historia Orgáncia de las Armas de Infantería y Caballería Española desde la Creación del Ejercito Permenente hasta el Día.* 14 vols. Madrid, 1851-1859.

Kenneth Coleman. *The American Revolution in Georgia, 1763-1789.* Athens, 1958.

Verner W. Crane. *The Southern Frontier, 1670-1732.* Ann Arbor, 1929 and 1956.

Michael J. Curley. *Church and State in Spanish Florida. 1783-1822.* Washington, 1940.

William W. Dewhurst. *History of Saint Augustine, Florida.* New York, 1881.

Jonathan Dickinson. *Jonathan Dickinson's Journal; or God's Protecting Providence. Being a narrative of a journey from Port Royal in Jamaica to Philadelphia between August 23, 1696 and April 1, 1697.* New Haven, 1945.

Carita Doggett. *Dr. Andrew Turnbull and the New Smyrna Colony of Florida.* Jacksonville, 1919.

George R. Fairbanks. *History of Florida from its discovery by Ponce de Leon, in 1512, to the close of the Florida War, in 1842.* Philadelphia, 1871.

————————. *History and Antiquities of the City of St.*

Augustine, Florida. 3rd. ed. Jacksonville, 1881. 1st ed. New York, 1858.

James Grant Forbes. *Sketches, Historical and Topographical, of the Floridas; more particularly of East Florida.* New York, 1821.

Worthington Chauncey Ford. *The United States and Spain in 1790.* Brooklyn, 1890.

Charles Gayarré. *History of Louisiana.* 4 vols. New Orleans, 1854-1866.

Pleasant Daniel Gold. *History of Duval County.* St. Augustine, 1929.

Ramiro Guerra y Sánchez, José M. Pérez Cabrera, Juan J. Remos, Emeterio S. Santovenia. *Historia de la Nación Cubana.* 10 vols. Havana, 1952.

George L. Harding. *Don Agustin V. Zamorano, Statesman, Soldier, Craftsman and California's First Printer.* Los Angeles, 1934.

Francis Harper (ed.). *The Travels of William Bartram.* Naturalist's Edition. New Haven, 1958.

Francis Russell Hart. *The Siege of Havana.* Boston and New York, 1931.

Harry Warren Hilborn. *A Chronology of the Plays of D. Pedro Calderón de la Barca.* Toronto, 1938.

Louis Houck. *A History of Missouri.* 3 vols. Chicago, 1908.

———————————— (ed.). *The Spanish Regime in Missouri.* 2 vols. Chicago, 1909.

Ales Hrdlicka. *The Anthropology of Florida.* Deland, 1922.

Alexander von Humboldt. *The Island of Cuba.* With a preliminary essay by J. S. Thrasher. New York, 1856.

————————————, and Aimé Bonpland. *Personal Narrative of Travels to the Equinoctial Regions of the New Continent during the years 1799-1804.* London, 1821.

Charles E. Kany. *Life and Manners in Madrid, 1750-1800.* Berkeley, 1932.

Anthony Kerrigan (ed.). *Barcia's Chronological History of the*

Continent of Florida. Gainesville, 1951. Original edition, Andrés Gonzáles Barcia. *Esayo Cronologico para la Historia General de la Florida.* Madrid, 1732.

Edward W. Lawson. *The Discovery of Florida and its Discoverer, Juan Ponce de Leon.* St. Augustine, 1946.

Hans Leip. *The Gulf Stream Story.* London, 1957.

Irving A. Leonard. *Baroque Times in Old Mexico.* Ann Arbor, 1959.

—————————————————. *The Spanish Approach to Pensacola.* Albuquerque, 1939.

Suson L'Engle. *Notes on My Family.* New York, 1888.

Joseph Byrne Lockey. *East Florida,1783-1785.* With a foreword by John Walton Caughey. Berkeley, 1949.

Woodbury Lowry. *The Spanish Settlements within the Present Limits of the United States.* 2 vols. New York, 1905.

Albert C. Manucy (ed.). *The History of Castillo de San Marcos & Fort Matanzas from Contemporary Narratives and Letters.* Washington, 1945.

Sir Clements Robert Markham. *The Story of Majorca and Minorca.* London, 1908.

Leonardo Martín Echeverría. *España, el Pais y los Habitantes.* Mexico, D. F., 1940.

Eduardo Martínez Dalmau. *La Politica Colonial y Extranjera de los Reyes Españoles de la Casa Austria y de Borbon y la Toma de la Habana por los Ingleses.* La Habana, 1943.

Lyle N. McAlister. *The "Fuero Militar" in New Spain, 1764-1800.* Gainesville, 1957.

Thomas McKenny and James Hall. *The History of the Indian Tribes of North America with Biographical Sketches and Anecdotes of the Principal Chiefs Embellished with Portraits from the Indian Gallery in the Department of War at Washington.* 3 vols. Philadelphia, 1842.

John McQueen. *The Letters of Don Juan McQueen to his Family, Written from Spanish East Florida 1791-1807.* Edited by Walter C. Hartridge. Columbia, S. C., 1943.

Louis Milfort. *Mémoire ou coup d'oeil rapide sur mes différens voyages et mon séjour dans la nation Crёck.* Paris, 1802.

Jedediah Morse. *The American Geography.* Boston, 1789.

William Spence Robertson (ed.). *The Diary of Francisco Miranda, 1783-1784.* New York, 1928.

——————————. *The Life of Miranda.* 2 vols. Chapel Hill, 1929.

Charles Loch Mowat. *East Florida as a British Province, 1763-1784.* (University of California Publications in History, vol. 32.) Berkeley, 1943.

Richard K. Murdoch. *The Georgia-Florida Frontier, 1793-1796.* Berkeley, 1951.

Ceferino Palencia. *España Vista por los Españoles.* Mexico, D. F., 1947.

Rembert W. Patrick. *Florida Under Five Flags.* Gainesville, 1945.

Howard H. Peckham. *The War for Independence: A Military History.* Chicago, 1958.

Jacobo de la Pezuela y Lobo. *Diccionario Geográfico, estadístico, histórico de la isla de Cuba.* 4 vols. Madrid, 1863-1866.

——————————. *Historia de la Isla de Cuba.* 4 vols. Madrid, 1868-1878.

P. Lee Phillips. *Notes on the Life and Works of Bernard Romans.* Deland, 1924.

Albert James Pickett. *History of Alabama and Incidentally of Georgia, Mississippi, from the Earliest Period.* Sheffield, Alabama, 1896.

John Pope. *A Tour Through the Southern and Western Territories of the North America; the Spanish Dominions on the River Mississippi, and the Floridas; and Countries of the Creek Nation; and Many Uninhabited Parts.* Richmond, 1792.

F. Pratt Puig. *El Pre Barroco en Cuba; una Escuela Criolla de Arquetectura Morisca.* Habana, 1947.

Herbert Ingram Priestley. *José de Gálvez, Visitor-General of New Spain, 1765-1771.* Berkeley, 1916.

Claudius Ptolemaeus. *La Geografia de Claudio Tolomeo.* Venice, 1574.

David Ramsey. *The History of South Carolina from its First Settlement in 1670 to the year 1808.* Charleston, 1809.

Rowland H. Rerick. *Memoirs of Florida.* Edited by Francis P. Fleming. 2 vols. Atlanta, 1902.

Charles B. Reynolds. *Old St. Augustine.* St. Augustine, 1885.

Roman Catholic Records. *White Baptisms, 1784-1792.* Records of the St. Augustine Parish. Jacksonville, 1937.

——————————————. *White Marriages, 1784-1801.* From the Cathedral Records of St. Augustine. Jacksonville, 1937.

Bernard Romans. *A Concise Natural History of East and West Florida.* New York, 1775.

Ricardo Rousset. *Historical de Cuba.* Habana, 1918.

Jean Sarrailh. *La España Ilustrada dela Segunda Mitad del Siglo XVIII.* Mexico, 1957.

Johann David Schoepf. *Reise durch einige der mittlern und sudlichen Nordamericanischen Vereinigten Staaten.* Erlangen, 1788. Translated and edited by A. J. Morrison as *Travels in the Confederation, 1783-1784.* Philadelphia, 1911.

John Gilmary Shea. *Life and Times of the Most Rev. John Carroll, Embracing the History of the Catholic Church in the United States, 1763-1815.* New York, 1888.

Wilbur Henry Siebert. *Loyalists in East Florida, 1774-1785.* 2 vols. Deland, 1929.

John Ferdinand Dalziel Smyth. *A Tour in the United States of America.* 2 vols. London, 1784.

William Stork. *A Description of East Florida.* 3rd. ed. London, 1769.

John R. Swanton. *Early History of the Creek Indians and Their Neighbors.* (Bureau of American Ethnology, Bulletin 73.) Washington, 1922.

——————————————. *The Indians of the Southeastern United States.* (Bureau of American Ethnology, Bulletin 137.) Washington, 1946.

John T. Van Campen. *St. Augustine, Capital of La Florida.* St. Augustine, 1959.

Arthur Preston Whitaker. *Documents Relating to the Commercial Policy of Spain in the Floridas.* Deland, 1931.

—————————————. *The Spanish American Frontier.* Boston and New York, 1927.

John Lee Williams. *The Territory of Florida.* New York, 1837.

Thomas S. Woodward. *Woodward's Reminiscences of the Creek or Muscogee Indians.* Montgomery, 1859. Reprinted with Introduction by Peter Brannon, Tuscaloosa, 1939.

ARTICLES

Charles W. Arnade. "Florida History in Spanish Archives. Reproductions at the University of Florida," *Florida Historical Quarterly*, XXXIV (1955), pp. 36-50.

——————————. "Florida Keys, English or Spanish in 1763?" *Tequesta*, XV (1955), pp. 41-53.

Jane M. Berry. "The Indian Policy of Spain in the Southwest, 1783-1795," *Mississippi Valley Historical Review*, III (1916-1917), pp. 462-477.

Mark F. Boyd. "The Fortifications at San Marcos de Apalache," *Florida Historical Quarterly*, XV (1936), pp. 3-34.

——————————. "From a Remote Frontier," *Florida Historical Quarterly*, XIX (1941), pp. 189-201.

Peter A. Brannon. "The Pensacola Indian Trade," *Florida Historical Quarterly*, XXXI (1952), pp. 1-15.

Jack A. Brown. "Panton, Leslie and Company, Indian Traders of Pensacola and St. Augustine," *Florida Historical Quarterly*, XXXVIII (1959), pp. 328-336.

Duvon Clough Corbitt. "The Administrative System in the Floridas, 1781-1821," *Tequesta*, II (1942-1943), pp. 40-67.

Carita Doggett Corse. "DeBrahms' Report on East Florida, 1773," *Florida Historical Quarterly*, XVII (1939), pp. 219-226.

——————————. "Denys Rolle of Rollestown, A Pioneer for Utopia," *Florida Historical Quarterly*, VII (1928), pp. 115-134.

James W. Covington. "Trade Relations Between Southwestern Florida and Cuba, 1600-1840," *Florida Historical Quarterly*, XXXVIII (1959), pp. 114-128.

Isaac Joslin Cox. "Florida. Outpost of New Spain," in A. Curtis Wilgus (ed.) *Hispanic American Essays*. Chapel Hill, 1942, pp. 151-165.

Marie Taylor Greenslade. "William Panton," *Florida Historical Quarterly*, XIV (1935), pp. 107-129.

William B. Griffen. "Spanish Pensacola, 1700-1763," *Florida Historical Quarterly*, XXXVIII (1959), pp. 242-262.

J. C. Harrington, Albert Manucy, and John M. Goggin. "Archeological Excavations in the Courtyard of Castillo de San Marcos, St. Augustine, Florida," *Florida Historical Quarterly*, XXXIV (1955), pp. 100-141.

Walter C. Hartridge. "The Fatio Family—A Book Review," *Florida Historical Quarterly*, XXXI (1952), pp. 140-146.

Louise Biles Hill. "George J. F. Clarke, 1774-1836," *Florida Historical Quarterly*, XXI (1943), pp. 199-253.

Louis C. Karpinski. "Manuscript Maps relating to American History in French, Spanish and Portuguese Archives," *The American Historical Review*, XXXIII (1928), pp. 328-330.

Joseph B. Lockey. "The Florida Banditti, 1783," *Florida Historical Quarterly*, XXIV (1945), pp. 87-107.

——————————————. "Public Education in Spanish St. Augustine," *Florida Historical Quarterly*, XV (1937), pp. 147-169.

——————————————. "The St. Augustine Census of 1786," *Florida Historical Quarterly*, XVIII (1939), pp. 11-31.

Mabel M. Manning. "The East Florida Papers in the Library of Congress," *The Hispanic American Historical Review*, X (1930), pp. 392-398.

Lyle N. McAlister. "Pensacola during the Second Spanish Period," *Florida Historical Quarterly*, XXXVII (1959), pp. 281-327.

——————————————. "The Reorganization of the Army of New Spain, 1763-1767," *The Hispanic American Historical Review*, XXXIII (1953), pp. 1-32.

Minnie Moore-Wilson. "Music of the Seminoles," *Florida Historical Quarterly*, VII (1928), pp. 155-158.

Charles L. Mowat. "The St. Francis Barracks, St. Augustine," *Florida Historical Quarterly*, XXI (1943), pp. 266-280.

W. S. Murphy, "The Irish Brigade of Spain at the Capture of Pensacola, 1781," *Florida Historical Quarterly*, XXXVIII (1960), pp. 216-225.

José del Rio Cossa. "Descripción de la Florida Oriental Hecha en 1787 por Teniente de Navio D. José del Rio Cossa, publicada ahora por vez primera con algunas notas por le P. Agustin Barreiro," Madrid: *Sociedad Geografica Nacional*, Serie B, Numero 61 (1935).

James Robertson. "The Archival Distribution of Florida Manuscripts," *Florida Historical Quarterly*, X (1931), pp. 35-40.

Wilbur Henry Siebert. "Slavery in East Florida, 1776-1785," *Florida Historical Quarterly*, X (1931), pp. 3-23.

Charles W. Spellman. "The Agriculture of Early North Florida Indians," *The Florida Anthropologist*, I (1948), pp. 32-49.

Helen Hornbeck Tanner. "The 1789 St. Augustine Celebration," *Florida Historical Quarterly*, XXXVIII (1960), pp. 280-293.

—————————. "Zéspedes and the Southern Conspiracies," *Florida Historical Quarterly*, XXXVIII (1959), pp. 15-28.

David O. True. "Some Early Maps Relating to Florida." *Imago Mundi*, XI (1954).

Arthur Preston Whitaker. "Alexander McGillivray, 1783-1789," *North Carolina Historical Review*, V (1928), pp. 181-203, 289-309.

—————————. "Commerce of Louisiana and the Floridas at the End of the Eighteenth Century," *The Hispanic American Historical Review*, VIII (1928), pp. 190-203.

—————————. "The Spanish Contribution to American Agriculture," *Agricultural History*, III (1929), pp. 1-14.

Donald E. Worcester. "Miranda's Diary of the Siege of Pensacola," *Florida Historical Quarterly*, XXIX (1951), pp. 163-196.

Irene A. Wright. "The Odyssey of the Spanish Archives of Florida," in A. Curtis Wilgus, ed. *Hispanic American Essays*. Chapel Hill, 1942, pp. 169-207.

MAPS

The most important source of information about maps of Spanish Florida is Woodbury Lowry, *Descriptive List of Maps of the Spanish Possessions within the Present Limits of the United States, 1502-1920,* edited by P. L. Phillips, (Washington, 1912). Valuable eighteenth century atlases are: T. Jeffreys, *American Atlas* (1775), and Sayer and Bennet's *American Pocket Military Atlas* (1776). The famous cartographers of colonial Florida were Bernard Romans and William Gerard DeBrahms, who surveyed the coastline and northeast interior region between 1765 and 1776, during the British occupation.

At the beginning of the Second Spanish Period, East Florida's chief map maker was the engineer, Mariano LaRocque. His "Plano de la Cíudad de San Agustin, 1788" is the only city map of St. Augustine drafted during Zéspedes' governorship. On the La-Rocque map of St. Augustine, each building is assigned a number. The accompanying "Descripción del Plano Particular de la Cíudad de San Agustin de la Florida Oriental: Año de 1788," is a twenty page manuscript describing the construction and condition of the individual buildings, in some cases providing information about ownership. Mariano LaRocque's map of 1788 has been used as the basis for the project directed toward the restoration and preservation of St. Augustine.

In the preparation of this manuscript, four groups of maps were used: (1) Manuscript maps from the Karpinski Collection, William L. Clements Library, Ann Arbor; (2) copies of Crown Collection maps from the British Museum and other manuscript maps in the William L. Clements Library; (3) photostats of British maps loaned by the Map Division, Library of Congress; (4) Quadrangle Maps from the United States Geological Survey, Department of Interior, Washington D. C. Individual maps of unusual interest are listed below:

Louis C. Karpinski. Manuscript Maps Prior to 1700 relating to America: photographic facsimiles made from originals in various libraries and archives in Paris, Spain, and Portugal. 14 vols. William L. Clements Library, Ann Arbor.

No. 27. Pedro Ruiz de Olano. Plano del Sitio de la Florida. 1740.

No. 144. Pablo Castello. Plano del Castillo del Presidio de San Agustin de la Florida visto interior y exteriormente en el estado en que se hallaba en 21 de julio de 1763.

No. 162. Manuel Joseph de Ayala. Mapa de la Costa de la Florida desde el Cabo Cañaberal. 1728 (?).

No. 187. Juan Joseph Elixio de la Puente. Plano del Presidio de San Agustin de la Florida. 1769.

Of the maps loaned by the Map Division, Library of Congress, the most detailed is the DeBrahms map of northeastern Florida, four feet by ten feet in size, published by John and Samuel Lewis in 1769. Other informative DeBrahms maps are:

No. 181. Plan of St. Mary's, 1770.

No. 184. Plan of Nassau Inlet, 1770.

No. 187. Plan of Amelia Island, 1770.

No. 190. Plan of St. Juan's Inlet, 1768 and 1770.

No. 225. Plan of St. Augustine Inlet with its Environs, 1765 and 1766.

No. 229. Plan of Muskito Inlet & Environs, 1765 and 1767.

The United States Geological Survey Quadrangle Maps are approximately the same scale as the large DeBrahms map printed by John and Samuel Lewis in 1769, both being about one inch to a mile. Unfortunately, there is a slight discrepancy in both longitude and latitude, making comparisons difficult. The following Quadrangle Maps cover the St. Augustine and lower St. John's and St. Mary's river area: Boulogne, Kingsland, Hilliard, St. Mary's, Fernandina, Cambon, Jacksonville, Mayport, Orange Park, Palm Valley, Bostwick, St. Augustine, Palatka, Dinner Island and Matanzas.

INDEX

Santo Domingo, 4, 151
San Vicente Ferrer, 101, 127, 160, 183, 210
sarao, evening party, 206
Savannah, Georgia, 20, 60
school, at St. Augustine, 171; regulations for, 172; Father Hasset's school at Philadelphia, 173; first primary school in Cuba, 13; José de Gálvez donates school in Spain. 173. For St. Augustine school, see no. 16 on city map
Seagrove, James, 101, 155, 226
Secoffee, or Cowkeeper, Seminole chief, 83
Segui, Agueda, 222
Selorte, Antonia, see Antonia Garriga
Seminoles, 56, 82, 97
Seven Year's War (1756-1763), 7, 20
Shipwrecks: Spanish troop ship, 53, 54; Spanish frigate in Keys, 56; British evacués, 66; supply ship, 109; troop ship, 111; supply ship aground on Cape Canaveral, 111; Canary Island families, 125; schooner with troops lost, 160
Shivers, Isabel, 70, 71
Sierre Leone, Africa, 193
situado, budget appropriation, 112, 117
Sivelly, Sergeant Juan, 70, 73, 167
slaves, number counted in census of St. Augustine, 126; in East Florida in 1788, 135; fugitives, 221, 81. See also, Negroes
social life in St. Augustine; incoming Spaniards feted, 35; ball honoring Zéspedes, 36, 37; farewell celebration for British, 74; State dinner for American officials, 61; celebrate coronation of Charles IV, 203, 207; theatrical production, 205
social problems: Antonio Garriga, 164, 166; Juan Sivelly, 70, 73; homosexuality, 167 Delany's murder, 72; case of the notary, 168; Rumford, 169; vandalism, 185; in jails, 186; illegitimacy, 167
Solano, Manuel, 51
South Carolina Loyalists, 16
South Carolina Navy, 16
Spalding, James, 87
Spain: war for succession to throne, 3, 5, 19; in War of Jenkin's Ear,

6, 19, 82; in Seven Years' War, 7, 20; in American Revolution, 12, 15; war with France, 227; Nootka Sound crisis, 216; war with England, 227
Spaniards in St. Augustine, 124, 126
Spanish Armada, 4
Spring Garden, Florida, 220
surveyor, 139

"tabby," construction material, 30
"taffy," rum, 90
Talbot island, 128
Tallapoosa river, Alabama, 85
Tampa, 84
tasajo, dried meat, 23
teniente del rey, Zéspedes serves as. 16; Domingo Cabello serves as, 197
Tensaw, Alabama, 194
Terrible, Spanish vessel, 222
Thomas, John, British bailiff, 51
Tonyn, General Patrick, last British governor of East Florida, 30, 33. 40, 44, 65, 66, 83, 122, 165
Traconis, Father Francisco, hospital chaplain, 171, 179; see no. 42 on city map of St. Augustine
trade: Spanish restrictions, 13, 107, 144, 150, 151; with Philadelphia. 63; with American ports, 108. 146; contracts for commissary supplies, 105, 106; with Havana. 115; exports from Florida, 140. 141; emergency trade with Georgia, 111; with Spain, 146
trade, contraband: at Santiago de Cuba, 14; facilitated by asiento, 5; factor in War of Jenkin's Ear, 6; on St. Mary's river, 210
Travers, Thomas, new doctor, 221
Treaty of New York (1790), 217
Treaty of Paris (1763), 1, 9
Treaty of Paris (1783), 1, 16, 20, 143, 150
Treaty of Pensacola (1784), 95
Treaty of Picolata (1765), 83, 84
Treaty of San Lorenzo (1795), 162. 163, 225
Treaty of Utrecht (1713), 5
Tunno, Adam, Charleston merchant. 118
Tunno, Thomas, British merchant in St. Augustine, 118, 189, see no. 21 on city map of St. Augustine